Five Hundred Years to Auschwitz

Five Hundred Years to Auschwitz

A Family Odyssey from the Inquisition to the Present

Irene Lawford-Hinrichsen

For Tony

With All Good Wishes

Irene Lawford-Hinrichsen

10th Nov. 2008

EDITION PRESS

British Library Cataloguing in Publication Data. A catalogue record for this book is
available from the British Library.

ISBN 978-0-9536112-1-8

This book production has been managed by Neil de Cort. www.self-publisher.co.uk
Typeset in 11/12.5pt New Baskerville by Servis Filmsetting Ltd, Stockport, Cheshire
Printed and bound in Great Britain by MPG Books Ltd, Bodmin, Cornwall

This book is dedicated to my children,
Julie Anne and Trevor Michael Lawford,
and to my grandsons,
Oliver Max and Elliot Jack Lawford

THE HENRIQUES/HINRICHSEN
(Condensed to those relevant to this book;

Previous generations include:
Da Veiga, De Andrade, D'Evora, Rodriques, Gomes,
Dias, Lopes, De Palacios, Barbosa, Furtado,
De Nis/Dinis

Guiomar Gomes De Milão m
(1549-1613)

Manuel Cardoso	**Beatriz Henriques De Milão**	Gomes Rodrigues
(Alias Manuel Teixeira)	(Alias Abigail)	(Alias Daniel Abensur/
(1571-1644)	**(1573-1632)**	De Hollande/De La Piedra,
m ?	**m Alvaro Dinis**	Abraham Israel De Sequiera)
	(Alias Alberto Dionis, Albert	(1574-1678)
	Denis/De Nis, Samuel Yachia)	m Beatriz Rodriques Cohen
Gabriel Milan	**(1565-after 1650)**	(cousin)
m ? Musaphia (cousin)		

Reubin bar Jachia-El Henriques
Registered **Ruben Henrichs** 1646, also **Hinrichs**
(1607-1690)
m 2) Sara Mussaphia

Michel Ruben Henriques/Hinrichs	Esther	Lazararus	Mordechai	Reuben Hinrichsen
(c.1649-1710)	(m cousin)	(m cousin)		
m 1) Simcha Henriques (cousin) div. 1674.		**m 2) Selche (Cäcilie) Chasan (?-1745)**		

Jonathan	Mose	**Ruben Michel Henrichs (Hinrichsen)**
(d. young)	(1668-1692)	**(1682-1757)**
		m Hindche Poppert (d.1795)

Berend	Wolf	Judith	Selche	Leser	**Michel Ruben Heinrichs**	Martha	Samson-	Ruben
					(Hinrichsen) (1735-1812)			
					m 1) Elkele Abraham Cohn	**m 2) Gitel Poppert**		
					(d.1792) div.	**(d.1787) div.**		

Ruben Michel Hinrichsen	Behrend-Michel Hinrichsen
(1760-1825)	(1771-1855)
m 1) Hanna Meyer div. (1769-1821)	

Schönchen	Mever-Michel	Hannchen	Benni	Jette	**Abraham Hinrichsen**	Selly
(1791-1833)	(1792-1842)	(1799-1834)	(1804-67)	(1806-?)	**(Adolph) (1808-1887)**	(1809-57)
					m Bertha Gumprecht (1811-77)	

Robert Hinrichsen	Caesar	Eduard	Carl
(1835-1917)	(1837-1915)	(1839-76)	(1845-95)

FAMILY TREE
bold type indicates line of descent)

Previous generations include:
De Caceres, Lopes, Gomes

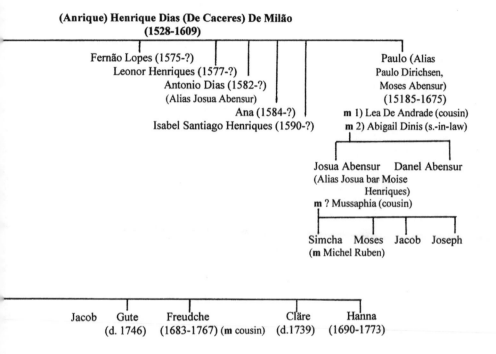

(Anrique) Henrique Dias (De Caceres) De Milão
(1528-1609)

Fernão Lopes (1575-?)
Leonor Henriques (1577-?)
Antonio Dias (1582-?)
(Alias Josua Abensur)
Ana (1584-?)
Isabel Santiago Henriques (1590-?)

Paulo (Alias
Paulo Dirichsen,
Moses Abensur)
(15185-1675)
m 1) Lea De Andrade (cousin)
m 2) Abigail Dinis (s.-in-law)

Josua Abensur   Danel Abensur
(Alias Josua bar Moise
Henriques)
m ? Mussaphia (cousin)

Simcha   Moses   Jacob   Joseph
(**m** Michel Ruben)

Jacob   Gute   Freudche   Cläre   Hanna
         (d. 1746)   (1683-1767) (**m** cousin)   (d.1739)   (1690-1773)

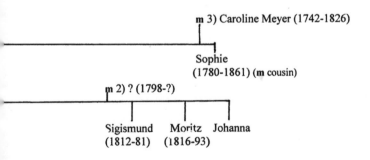

m 3) Caroline Meyer (1742-1826)

Sophie
(1780-1861) (**m** cousin)

m 2) ? (1798-?)

Sigismund   Moritz   Johanna
(1812-81)   (1816-93)

THE FAMILIES OF MARTHA (NÉE BENDIX) AND HENRI HINRICHSEN

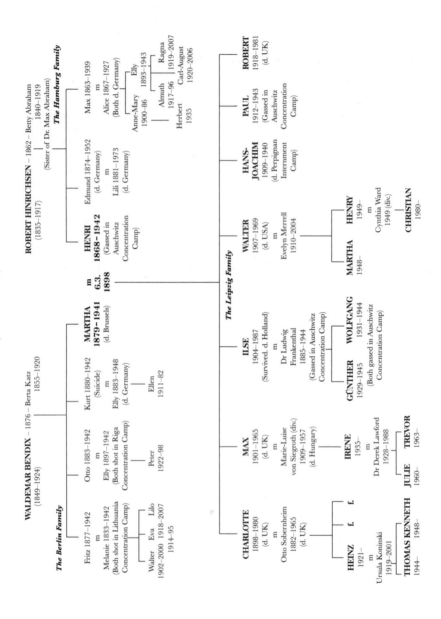

Contents

List of Illustrations

All illustrations are from the author's collection.

About The Author

Irene was born into the music publishing business of C. F. Peters, Leipzig. Her parents brought her to England as a baby. After leaving school, she spent time abroad, learning the business before joining her father as his 'eldest son' in his music publishing business, Hinrichsen Edition Ltd. and Peters Edition, London. She opted out in 1960 for marriage to a scientist and motherhood.

In 1969, she was co-founder of an international society, The Philatelic Music Circle, of which she became president. In 1985, she gained her Open University BA with Honours. She is a linguist and an experienced journalist, author and lecturer.

Irene was editor for 27 years, then consultant editor, of the magazine *The Baton*. She has written articles for magazines, has broadcast and has also contributed to several books including *The Grove Dictionary of Opera*.

Irene likes to say that she was reborn in Leipzig – in the former GDR – in November 1991. Becoming involved with her half-Jewish background, and working to promote Jewish memory there, has motivated her life since. It led to her researching and writing her highly acclaimed book: *Music Publishing and Patronage – C. F. Peters: 1800 to the Holocaust*. She feels honoured that the late Yehudi Menuhin wrote the foreword. The book received many excellent reviews.

Five Hundred Years to Auschwitz – A Family Odyssey from the Inquisition to the Present is Irene Lawford-Hinrichsen's second major book.

Acknowledgements

Going back a long way, I am grateful to my grandfather Henri Hinrichsen for writing the *Chronik* in 1933 and to my father, who died in 1965, for bequeathing it to me. I am also grateful to my Aunt Lotte Sobernheim, my Uncle Walter Hinrichsen and my Uncle Robert Harris, all deceased who during my youth kindled my interest in the past. They gave me photos, documents, books and family trees – all of which went into a box, untouched for about forty years. Thanks go to second cousins Walter Bendix, Eva Maass and their sister Lilo Bendix-Stern, all recently deceased, for eyewitness accounts of my grandparents and of their own grandparents; to my second cousin the late Dr Carl-August Pauly of Hamburg. My cousin Martha Hinrichsen of Connecticut deserves a special vote of thanks for finding many documents for me and being so enthusiastic about this project. Thanks also to my cousin Henry Stanton in California. More distant relatives who have provided information are the late Dr Klaus Hinrichsen of London and his brother Jürgen in Argentina. I am indebted to a very distant relative, Joseph Ben Brith of Israel, for the benefits of his researches into our mutual Portuguese ancestry and to another distant relative Dr Peter Clemens of Schwerin.

I am very grateful to Carol Rankin, whom I met as a tour guide/lecturer in Portugal, who was immensely helpful with historical information on Portugal; also to Michael Studemund-Halévy for information about Hamburg. My dear friends Annerose and Horst Kemp of Leipzig have been most helpful and Norbert Molkenbur of Leipzig is a mine of information, which he was happy to share with me. Thanks also to Fred K. Prieberg, Monika Groening-Gombart, the Handelskammer of Hamburg, Jürgen Sielemann of the Staatsarchiv Hamburg and the ladies of the Staatsarchiv Leipzig. I would also like to express my appreciation to the authors of the many books which I consulted for historical background for the benefit of their researches; and I am indebted to the anonymous contributors of information on the Internet for useful pointers. I thank Mark Gerson for permission to use his photograph of my father and Neil de Cort for his assistance in publishing this book.

The encouragement and thoughtful comments of my daughter Julie have been immeasurably helpful. Her and my son Trevor's patience with my technophobia as regards the computer have been invaluable.

Irene Lawford-Hinrichsen.

Preface

Without ancestors
is to be a brook
without a source
a tree without leaves

Old Yiddish proverb

My saga begins at a time of unspeakable horror, 500 years before the Holocaust which shattered my family and so many others. It begins in the thirteenth century with the Spanish Inquisition which led to the banishment of the Jews from Spain in 1492. It is a tale of survival, ingenuity and trade and the determination to triumph against bigotry, discrimination, persecution and murder. It is the story of how my ancestors, knowing themselves to be always a minority, adapted their lives to being Jews, first secretly in Portugal; then openly in various centres in Germany that had regarded them as inferior for many centuries; and finally in England and the USA. It is a story of hope, perseverance and triumph against considerable adversity.

This history recounts the progress of one dynasty through 500 years of European turmoil. It tells of how their actions were influenced by history and politics and of how members of succeeding generations influenced events in the places to which they migrated. The Henriques/Hinrichsens were not passive observers; they were active protagonists, always in the forefront of enterprise, creating something new and leaving their mark on society.

The story is seen from an objective historical and social perspective, not from a Jewish viewpoint. I am not Jewish. Whilst it is the history of my Jewish paternal family, this is told within the political and social events of the time which led to the successes, failures and emigrations of the generations. I present the facts in human terms, within their historical and legal context, and tell the fascinating, continuous story of one family throughout 500 turbulent years of achievement, emigration, persecution, horror and survival. It is an exciting saga of enterprise and endurance, beginning with the era of political duplicity and discrimination that marked my ancestor Henrique de Milão's grandfather's expulsion from Spain in 1492; through Henrique's own execution by being burnt at the stake in Portugal; through the political reasons for his descendants to settle first in Hamburg, then Glückstadt, Schwerin, and their return to Hamburg over the course of 400 years. The story continues with the move to Leipzig of Henrique's namesake and descendant, my grandfather Henri Hinrichsen – his achievement in the field of music publishing and his terrible death, echoing that of his Portuguese ancestor, in the gas chambers of Auschwitz. But the story does not end there. My father's survival as a British citizen and my uncle's survival as a US citizen revitalize the family's progress and achievement.

But how did I come to write my story?

When I was a child during and after World War II, I used to spend my holidays in Shropshire with my aunt Lotte and uncle Otto. Christmas was the time for a family gathering with their daughters – my elder cousins – as well as my parents, Max and Marie-Luise, and my uncle Robert, my father's and Lotte's youngest brother. They would often talk about *früher*. '*Früher* we used to do this' or '*früher* we used to go there', or '*früher* we had that', or '*früher* so-and-so would visit'. The German word *früher* has a subtle variety of meanings such as 'earlier', 'previously', 'in the past', 'formerly' 'before', 'in the old days'. The adults used to talk about Mama and Papa and about their other brothers and sisters. They talked a little about their home in Leipzig and about the music publishing company which the family had owned; but they talked very little about what they had left behind, what they had lost. I never heard them talk about what had happened to Mama and Papa, Paul and Hans-Joachim, to Ilse and Ludwig and their children, or about their aunts and uncles and cousins – these were all just shadowy names to me, without substance. But the names stuck in my mind, even though at the time I couldn't work out who they all were.

As I got older, my aunt gave me a set of photos of portraits of many of the ancestors before the time of *früher*. Later, my uncle Walter, who had gone to America, sent me a printout about the Court Jews of Schwerin in the seventeenth and eighteenth centuries – our ancestors – as well as a massive academic book about them (both in German) and some family trees. From my uncle Robert, I got pages of family names and dates. I acquired other books and documents. All this went into my cupboard – largely unread – where it stayed for 30 or so years. Stuff was accumulating but I had no plans for its use. By the time I was ready to research all this material properly, my parents and all the aunts and uncles were dead.

I wanted to retrace my family's steps and find out about those times. My voyage to *früher*, after the collapse of the German Democratic Republic when Leipzig no longer found itself on the wrong side of the Iron Curtain, sent me on a new path. Starting in 1991, finding out about those times, those places and those events became the fascination of my life. It became the motivation for historical research and for my commitment to commemorate those who had gone before, especially those who had contributed so much to Leipzig and whose memory had been so horrendously obliterated. Our family had kept in contact throughout the years and my father's younger, by then somewhat aged, cousins – my second cousins, since also sadly all deceased – were able to give me much family information. As children and teenagers they had often visited my grandparents and could tell me about the family household in Leipzig before the war. My uncle Walter had taken many family documents with him to the USA and his daughter, Martha, kindly sent me these and many letters written between family members during the war. And I acquired many books on history.

Whilst I had a mass of information going back to 1646 when the first of my ancestors was registered as a German citizen, this only told me that his antecedents had come from Portugal and, prior to that, from Spain. Searching for more information, I contacted a very distant cousin in Argentina who I knew was interested in genealogy. He sent me a book, published in Germany, written by an Israeli descendant of my 1646 ancestor. He had traced our mutual ancestors back to their roots in Spain.

I like to say that I was reborn in Leipzig in November 1991. How my rebirth came about is recounted the penultimate chapter of this book. The final chapter is the story of how I was able to revitalize and to commemorate the past in Leipzig, the city that owed so much to my grandfather, Henri Hinrichsen.

London, April 2008

CHAPTER ONE

1492–1602: Lisbon – Immigration, Shipping and Trade

The condemned wound their way painfully down the narrow, twisting Rua Augusta on a cold, overcast day. The crowds on either side poked and jeered, cursing and spitting on the damned souls, some of whom were taking their last walk on this earth. They carried unlit green candles in their hands. All the condemned were made to parade around the Praça do Ribeiro in hair shirts with flames painted on them; flames pointing upwards indicated that the wearer was due to die, flames pointing downwards that the wearers were spared to do years of penance.

The prisoners were then compelled to shuffle back to the Rossio where they could see the faggots of timber piled high in front of the Offices of the Inquisition in the Estaus Palace. The crowd bayed for blood, flames and vengeance against the heretics. A ghoulish roar of triumph rose as the seven unfortunate prisoners, on whose hair shirts the flames were pointing up, were tied to the stake and the faggots were lit. When the flames began to lick at their feet, their screams of anguish only served to augment the excitement of the crowds. By the time their agony was eased by unconsciousness and the air was filled with smoke and the acrid stench of burning flesh, the crowd had grown bored and moved away.

I strolled up the Rua Augusta on a sunny day in July. This wide pedestrian boulevard had replaced the medieval alleyway of old, after the great tidal wave and earthquake had devastated Lisbon in 1755. I was part of the crowd of happy holidaymakers sporting brightly coloured T-shirts and baseball caps, straw sunhats and skimpy dresses. But as I reached the National Theatre I could not help picturing the scene, which had taken place almost 400 years earlier when this had been the site of the Estaus Palace.

Henrique de Milão was number 71 in the penitential procession of some 75 tortured bodies shuffling its way slowly from the Dungeons of the Inquisition on the Rossio to the Praça Ribeiro – now the Praça Comercio in Lisbon – on 5 April 1609. The old man's face as he dragged his tortured legs showed the agony of the recent years. His smartly trimmed beard was now grown ragged and his once sleek hair was long and matted. This previously tall, proud man, his skeletal frame shrouded in the penitential hair shirt, knew that his last hour had come.

Along with Henrique de Milão, one other man and five 'guilty' women were burnt to death at the stake during a *grand auto da fé* in Lisbon on that fateful day in 1609. A victim of the infamous Inquisition, Henrique had been questioned repeatedly and tortured for two and a half years. During all of this time, this refined gentleman had been incarcerated in the dank, rat-infested dungeons of the notorious prison on the Rossio.

The wealthy 81-year-old, his body broken but his spirit unbowed in spite of his terrible agony, had refused to recant. A *converso*, or New Christian as they were called in Portugal (so-called because his family had been forced to convert to Christianity), he had been found guilty of secretly practising his allegedly heretical religion, Judaism, all his life. Now, as an old man, deprived of everything and with life nearing its close, he felt that he had nothing more to lose by remaining true to his beliefs. The time for living a public lie had come to an end for him and he refused to renounce the faith that had given him strength and courage throughout his long life; he would die proudly – a martyr and a Jew.

The flames of religious bigotry and state-ordained terror that consumed Henrique in Catholic Portugal were a cruel foretaste of the terrible end that was to be inflicted upon his descendant and namesake, my grandfather Henri Hinrichsen, 333 years later in Nazi Germany, in the gas chambers of Auschwitz concentration camp.

The background

Henrique's family had lived in Portugal for well over a hundred years since his grandfather, Antonio Lopes, had been forced to flee from Spain with his wife Beatriz Dias in 1492. Jews and Muslims had been assimilated into Spanish society for centuries. Spain had benefited tremendously from the integration of these two large minority groups who were allowed to follow their own faiths alongside the Christians. It was the Jews who were responsible for the promotion of the Spanish language; they had translated the laws from Latin into Spanish. However, around 1391 when the Catholics were trying to exile the

Muslims in Spain, they also began their pogroms against the Jews. Thousands of Jews were slaughtered when they refused to convert whilst nearly a third of Spanish Jews accepted baptism.

It is alleged that over the following hundred years or so, 200,000 Spanish Jews were killed as enemies of Spanish Christianity. Apparently a further 200,000 were baptized and converted to Christianity when they became 'New Christians' or *conversos* but were known derisively as *marranos* (pigs). They acquired this epithet as a result of deliberately being seen to eat pork in public in an effort to show that they were no longer Jews, who are not permitted to eat pork, and that they fully accepted their baptism into the Catholic Church. Ironically, Jews have been equated with pigs at different times throughout history and in various places – not least in Nazi Germany. The *conversos* became universally reviled and hated. In 1476, a law was enacted which forced Jews to wear an insignia denoting their religion, preceding by some 450 years the Nazi laws that compelled Jews to sew a yellow star on their clothes.

Towards the end of the fifteenth century the Spanish Inquisition, under the infamous Dominican monk Tomás de Torquemada, the first Inquisitor General, began its murderous and cruel reign. Torquemada, though himself descended from Jews, determined ruthlessly to remove Jews and Muslims as alleged obstacles to Spain's national security and the Roman Catholic religion. A similar doctrine would be pronounced by Adolf Hitler in Germany. The first major expulsion of Jews took place in 1486. Under Torquemada's authority, the Inquisition was empowered to try people accused of heresy, apostasy, bigamy, witchcraft, usury, etc. He authorized the use of torture to extract confessions and he organized tribunals and their procedures. The authorities sought out those *conversos* who were still secretly practising Judaism and thus were guilty of heresy. Many Jews were persecuted and, by 1490, some 3,000 had been burnt at the stake because of their beliefs.

1492: The Jews expelled from Spain

After King Ferdinand of Aragon and Queen Isabella of Castile united their kingdoms through marriage, they decreed that only the Holy Catholic Church should be recognized as the true religion throughout their realm. Their devout stance is hard to understand as, like Torquemada, they both had Jewish forebears. They proclaimed the Edict of 1492, which ordered the expulsion of the Jews. On 31 March 1492, Jews were told they either had to be baptized by 31 July or to leave the country with nothing – sacrificing all their wealth and possessions. They were obliged to sell all their goods, their possessions, their houses and their estates, just as my parents were forced to do when they fled Germany in 1937, receiving paltry compensation because of the urgency. What little they did receive was confiscated along with their jewellery, gold and silver and other valuables, so that when they left Spain they would be penniless. The wealth thus confiscated from the Jews enabled Ferdinand and Isabella to hire an army to rout the Moors and to finance Christopher Columbus on his epic voyage of 1492 to discover the New World. In expelling the Jews, Spain lost its financiers, doctors, intellectuals, educators, poets, philosophers, astronomers and business men. Mirroring their stance, Hitler was able to finance his war against the allies in the same way and with the same after-effects.

Figures have been suggested of between 800,000 and 2 million Jews who chose to emigrate. A more reliable figure may be 250,000. These Jews who originated in Spain were henceforth to be known as 'Sephardim', Sepharad being the ancient Hebrew name for Spain. (By contrast, Jews practising the French and German-Polish Jewish culture are called 'Ashkenazim'.)

Thousands of Sephardim went to Italy, the Balkans, Germany, North-west Europe, Morocco and other Middle Eastern countries. However, the largest number of those forced to emigrate were Castilian Jews who had relatives or business contacts in the neighbouring country. Approximately 120,000 refugees – asylum seekers as we would call them today – went west overland to Portugal which at the time was the most progressive, affluent country in Europe. Amongst these was Henrique de Milão's grandfather, Antonio Lopes. Rather than pretend to something that they could not accept, Antonio Lopes and his family abandoned everything they owned for what they anticipated would be a more tolerant life in Portugal. On payment of a head tax of eight *cruzados*, the refugees were given permission to remain for eight months. Then they either had to move on or, if they had become successfully established in business, they were permitted to purchase Portuguese citizenship. Henrique's grandfather, an entrepreneur, quickly established himself in business and acquired citizenship.

Portugal had offered a welcome to the refugees as Jews had been contributing towards the commercial success of the country for over 200 years. They had been an integral part of the educated and professional classes in medicine, education, finance, government, astronomy, philosophy and as advisers on shipping, designers of maps and nautical instruments as well as being amongst the first typographers and printers. The rulers had even permitted them to build a synagogue in Lisbon. With the new influx from Spain in 1492, Jews made up approximately one fifth of the population and by the end of the fifteenth century totalled some 200,000 souls. Antonio Lopes chose to settle in Portugal as he already had family and business connections there. (In fact, there is some evidence to show that his ancestor, Ibn Yahya, was the first chief rabbi of Portugal in 1150.)

However, only four years after the Lopes family had settled in Portugal, their security was once again threatened. Ferdinand and Isabella promised the hand of their only daughter, Isabella, to the Portuguese heir to the throne, King Manuel I 'the Fortunate'. The condition attached to the match was that Portugal should follow the same anti-Semitic policy as Spain; so an order of banishment against Jews was issued in Portugal on 5 December 1496. Manuel knew that on his marriage – to the first of his three wives – he would become the sole heir to the Spanish throne; however, he realized that if he forced all the Jews out of Portugal, the economy would suffer severely. Hence a proclamation was issued obliging all Jews to convert to Christianity. The date set for this obligatory baptism was 19 March 1497. All children between the ages of four and fourteen were to be baptized on this one day; it was hoped that this would encourage the parents to want to remain in Portugal. Later, 20,000 Jews were forced to be baptized and become *conversos*. Many did not want to convert which led to thousands of Jews making for Lisbon or the nearest harbour in the hope of escaping by ship. The ports were sealed and there was a massive slaughter of those Jews who refused baptism; their property was confiscated and distributed to churches and monasteries. Many Jews agreed to be baptized and were allowed 20 years to stop practising their traditional Jewish customs.

Antonio Lopes was an honourable man who did not wish to renounce his faith but expediency and a sense of preservation cautioned him to accept compromise. Having resettled in a new country where he had established a business, he decided he would have to acquiesce, at least nominally, and allowed himself and his family to be converted and baptized. However, like many of the *conversos*, they continued to follow Jewish beliefs and to say Hebrew prayers and to keep the Jewish holidays in secret, teaching their faith to their children who in turn taught it to their children. At first the family felt secure but in due course each individual member was to suffer mounting harassment. Anti-Semitic activity was rife and the New Christians were to find themselves constantly persecuted.

Manuel I reigned from 1495 to 1521 and his era, marred only by his persecution of the Jews, became known as Portugal's 'First Golden Age'. He was responsible for a code of laws named after him and made his court a centre for chivalry, art and science. Under his sponsorship Portugal became the finest naval power of Europe. With his support Vasco da Gama opened up the sea routes to India. With Spanish funding, Magellan led the first circumnavigation of the globe. Cabral discovered Brazil in 1500, which was later to become one source of Henrique's wealth – and of his downfall. Portugal gained control of the Indian Ocean and of the lucrative spice trade to become the mercantile centre of Europe with its huge shipping trade. It was in this sphere that the family of Henrique de Milão made their contribution to Portugal's wealth.

However, having given the converted Jews the right to Portuguese citizenship, King Manuel issued a decree on 20 April 1499 closing all the borders for New Christians. Lengthy negotiations had to be conducted in order to obtain an exit permit. In a foretaste of what was to happen in Germany later, Manuel turned a blind eye when the rabble inflicted the most terrible pogroms against the Jews, smashing their homes, stealing their property and murdering them by sword and fire. The Lisbon massacre took place during the three days of Passover in April 1506. Provoked by the Dominican monks, around two thousand New Christians were killed by a rapacious mob, many being burnt to death in the Rossio, the main square of Lisbon. When the riot had subsided, Manuel ordered the troops in to restore order. New Christians were still forbidden to leave Portugal but this law was rescinded two years later. It might have been wiser if Henrique's grandfather had, like so many other *conversos*, chosen to leave Portugal in 1507.

King Manuel positively encouraged the burning and destruction of Hebrew books and it was a criminal offence to own or to sell such books. Printing was then in its infancy and, as most of the Hebrew books would have been hand-illuminated, they were very valuable indeed. Henrique's grandfather, like many converted Jews, chose to risk his life by hiding his few precious religious books and studying them secretly, in a hidden chamber in his house – the nearest equivalent to a synagogue at a time when synagogues were forbidden.

1528: Birth of Henrique de Milão

Annrique-Henrique de Caceres (to give Henrique his full original name) was born into this gruesome and intolerant era in Santa Comba Dão, Portugal, in 1528. When his grandfather originally sought asylum in Portugal, surnames often indicated where a person came from so that when Henrique's father Manuel Lopes married Leanor de Caceres, who had come from Caceres in Spain, this became the family surname.

Henrique was still a toddler when King João III personally invited the Inquisition into Portugal in 1531. This terrible institution, which was ultimately to lead to Henrique's shocking death and to the persecution of his children and his children's children, was established with papal permission in 1536, though it took until 1547 to become properly organized. It flourished for 300 years until the Marqués de Pombal endeavoured to force it to cease its operations in 1821, though it resurfaced spasmodically until 1834. Those Jews who fled Portugal during those years established Sephardic communities in Hamburg, London, Amsterdam, Venice and Bordeaux amongst other places in Europe. Many also settled farther afield, in Brazil and Suriname in South America, the West Indies, the New World – America – and other countries. Henrique's father would have been wise to join the exodus but he had a family of eight young children and his business was flourishing; he did not want to start all over again somewhere else. Moreover, there was no suspicion against him that he was practising his Judaism, as taught him by his father, in secret.

Henrique's induction into the commercial world started when he was thirteen. His father sent him to Lisbon to undertake an apprenticeship in business. There he experienced for the first time the excitement of the new maritime discoveries, the world of shipping and trade with faraway places, exotic smells and flavours of the East. He loved to wander the streets where he found himself surrounded by examples of the Manueline concept of adorning buildings with maritime embellishments. He was fascinated by the way churches and public buildings were decorated with carved motifs associated with the sea; these were ropes, seashells and the popular armillary sphere, showing the motions of the celestial bodies and used as an aid to navigation in early voyages of discovery. Henrique was enraptured by all of this and was fired by an understanding of the sea as a route to riches. The boy was inquisitive and eager to learn all he could about the shipping trade.

His father brought Henrique's nine-year-old brother Antonio Diaz Caceres, his junior by thirteen years, to Lisbon in 1550. This was a dangerous time, as the Inquisition had been fully established in Portugal for some years and the king and the Church sanctioned the arrest and torture of those New Christians who were discovered to be still practising their Jewish faith in secret. The situation forced many *marranos* to leave Lisbon by 1550 in fear of their lives. However, at this time the family was still living in relative obscurity and Antonio Diaz was able to complete his education as a court page in the home of aristocrats before joining the navy, where he served on Spanish warships. He married in Lisbon but after his wife's death he emigrated to Mexico, which had been a Spanish colony since 1532, where he became a ship owner and seafarer and where he remarried.

As was customary, Annrique-Henrique de Caceres, own marriage, to Guiomar Gomes de Milão in 1569, was arranged by his father. His wife's grandfather, Dr Thomas de la Vega (Thomé de Veiga) had also

come from Spain in 1492. Guiomar, born in 1549 in Covilhã in the
Serra da Estrela, was 21 years younger than Henrique who had, by the
age of 41, become a successful businessman. Henrique adopted his
wife's family name, becoming Henrique de Milão. (The spelling varies
and the pronunciation, being Portuguese, sounded more like Milan.)
This was a noble name as the family had been elevated to the aristocracy for their services to their country. Guiomar's father and her three
brothers had been officers in the Portuguese army and had been
killed fighting for their fatherland. As the three de Milão sons produced no male heirs and the name would have died out, it was logical
that Henrique should follow the custom of the time and adopt his
wife's surname. Subsequent generations of the family, in order to
honour their illustrious and martyred forefather, took on the name
Henriques as their surname, meaning 'son of Henrique'. Later the
name was to be further adapted until it reached its definitive form,
Hinrichsen, in the eighteenth century.

Fortunately, it turned out to be a happy marriage though the couple
lived in increasingly cramped circumstances in the Rua de Barão, one
of the steeply winding streets, running from the harbour to the Sé
Cathedral in the Alfama district of Lisbon. Henrique and Guiomar
had both been born in Portugal into *converso* families and had therefore been baptized Christian, as had each of their several brothers and
sisters.

1571: Birth of Henrique de Milão's first son

They were seen to be practising Catholics and belonged to the Sé
Cathedral. This was where all their nine children, born over the
course of nineteen years, were baptized. The first five children, born
in fairly rapid succession between 1571 and 1577 and carrying various
family names relating to both their parents' forebears in addition to
their own first names, were: Manuel, Beatriz, Gomes, Fernão and
Leanor.[1] Life for the de Milão family, already very difficult, became
even more stressful. Henrique de Milão insisted that his children
should study the religion of their forefathers and adhere to a Jewish
lifestyle, which had to be done in secret and which placed them all in
great danger. Following the death of the then king, Sebastião 'the
Regretted' in 1578 in a doomed attempt to invade Morocco, Portugal
was without an effective leader. The country was briefly ruled by the
Cardinal King Henrique (1578–80) and, as he had previously been
Inquisitor General, this did not bode well for anyone with Jewish

---

1 For full names and dates, see the Henriques family tree. p. xii.

connections. Being a cardinal without heirs created a problem of succession and left the way open for Spain to occupy Portugal in 1580. Henrique de Milão was prominent in his opposition to the new regime, as a result of which the family suffered severe anti-Semitic persecution.

Five years after the birth of Leanor, three further children were born to Henrique and Guiomar between 1582 and 1585: Antonio, Ana and Paulo. Their youngest child – their little treasure – a daughter Isabel was born in 1590, five years after Paulo, when Guiomar was already 41 and Henrique was 62.

The worsening situation for Jews in Portugal drove several close relatives to emigrate to Hamburg, Amsterdam, Antwerp, London, India, Brazil, Mexico and other countries. The European destinations proved to be safer than those distant countries occupied by Spain, which in due course also inaugurated their own Offices of the Inquisition. This enforced emigration served a twofold purpose as it also created the basis for the establishment of a successful worldwide family import–export shipping trade; Henrique assiduously maintained his far-flung family connections, which family trait was maintained throughout the following centuries. As the owner of a successful business empire, he chose to remain in Lisbon with his family. We will see how his descendant Henri Hinrichsen was to reach a similarly misguided decision when he chose to remain in Leipzig, in Nazi Germany with his music publishing business.

Lisbon was one of the main ports in the world, a gathering point for many different cultures. Henrique, as the proprietor of a shipping company, importing and exporting timber, spice and other goods, had contacts in Brazil, Hamburg, Amsterdam, London and other ports. The spice trade was particularly important as spices were needed for the preservation of food. In general, it was the Muslims who controlled the spice trade which was centred on Genoa and Venice. However, after Henry the Navigator rounded the Cape of Good Hope in 1488 and made it possible to go to Africa following the route taken by Vasco da Gama, spices could be imported directly to Lisbon.

In 1590, just as Isabel was born, Henrique sent his eldest son, Manuel, aged 19, to Pernambuco in Brazil to be his business agent. Manuel's younger brother, Gomes, joined him in 1592, when he was only 18. When Cabral had discovered the route to Brazil in 1500, he sailed in a very small square-rigged caravel. By the time Manuel and Gomes sailed, the style had been adapted though the ship was still very small. The sail carried a large red cross as a tribute to the monks whose learning had contributed to the improved design. The crossing would have taken six weeks to three months during which time the tiny ship would have been at the mercy of the huge, storm-ridden Atlantic Ocean.

Manuel and Gomes de Milão were responsible for choosing the exotic woods which Henrique imported from Brazil for the carved furniture, then so fashionable. Whilst the French aristocracy preferred their elaborately carved furniture to be gilded, the Portuguese wanted to enjoy the beautiful wood, carved, polished and left in its natural state. So Manuel and Gomes would make perilous journeys into the interior to bargain with the natives, carefully selecting only the finest timbers. Brazilian timber was of such a high quality that even that used for making the boxes holding sugar was made into furniture when it reached Madeira; this became known as sugar box-style furniture and it survives to this day.

The timber was so highly valued that importers even undertook the perilous journey to Brazil themselves to select their timber. One of these enterprising businessmen was Felipe Dinis, who was accompanied by his son Alvaro whom he was training in business. The three younger men immediately took a liking to each other. This first meeting was to have far-reaching consequences. When Manuel and Gomes wrote and told their father about the visit, he was most impressed by the character reference they gave Alvaro.

In Portugal, the Inquisition was unleashing its full force against the 'Secret Jews'. They were regarded as heretics and were arrested, imprisoned and encouraged to confess. If they did not confess, they were tortured, when they usually confessed their 'guilt'. Punishment could be spiritual penance, public humiliation, confiscation of property, whipping, forced slavery (most often as oarsmen in the barges) or death. Those who adamantly refused to confess or repent were subjected to an *auto da fé* ('act of faith') which consisted of a public procession and execution, usually by fire. It is estimated that between 1481 and 1808 more than 300,000 people were charged by the Spanish Inquisition, at least 30,000 of whom were publicly executed, though the figures are far from certain. Amongst these were Muslims, Protestants and other so-called deviants from the Catholic norm, but most were Jewish *conversos*, the New Christians.

CHAPTER TWO

1602–1611: Lisbon – The Inquisition, Persecution, Torture and Death

An insistent pounding at the front door roused Guiomar de Milão's terrified sister, Ana d'Andrade, from her sleep on the morning of 5 February 1602. The officers of the Inquisition had come to arrest her, as the first unfortunate member of the extended de Milão family, rightly thinking that she would easily be persuaded to betray her relatives. As anticipated, under torture Ana offered her testimony 'of her own free will'.[1] She was forced to give the names of all the family members and their friends and contacts. The record-keepers of the Inquisition were as assiduous in their work as were the Nazi record-keepers later. The victims' personal details, the method of their torture, their 'confessions' and their subsequent sentences were all faithfully recorded.

With the testimony of Ana's 'confession', the Portuguese authorities now decided to use the offices of the Inquisition to wreak their revenge on the de Milão family for their many transgressions in business as well as in their family life. From 1603 on, their house in the Rua do Barão in the business area of Lisbon was under constant observation. In order to avoid this intrusion on their privacy, Henrique decided, in 1605, to sell the house and to move to the suburb of Alcantara; in spite of his thriving business, which he would have to abandon, he was planning to flee Portugal with his family. Not only did he hope for some privacy in the new house but, as it was nearer the River Tagus, it should also serve to ease their flight. However, in their haste to move somewhere safer, they did not realize that the

---

1 Quoted in Salomon, H. P., *Portrait of a New Christian Fernão Alvares Melo (1569–1632)*, Paris, 1982, pp. 41–6 (Ana d'Andrade de Milão: ANNT 16420 and 141409); pp. 46–65 (Henrique de Milão: ANNT 6677).

house they had purchased was directly opposite a convent of Flemish nuns. The nuns were ordered by the Inquisition to spy on the de Milão household from the windows of their cells from which they could observe all the comings and goings at the house. They faithfully reported every visit to the Inquisition, often exaggerating the details to make the 'sins' of the de Milãos appear even more heretical.

It was against this background that the de Milão and Caceres families felt that their only option was to emigrate. They had many relatives and business contacts throughout the world and could have chosen from a number of destinations. However, they wisely rejected any thought of emigrating to any country ruled over by the Spanish. Hamburg, a busy shipping port where Henrique had relatives and business contacts, seemed the obvious option.

1606: A marriage is arranged

Henrique needed to consolidate his plans for the family's escape. In 1605 he secretly sent a family friend, Vicente Furtado, to visit his cousin Alvaro Dinis in Hamburg who was a business partner of Henrique's. Furtado's brief on his month-long visit to Hamburg was to arrange a marriage between Henrique's eldest daughter Beatriz, still a spinster at the age of 33, and Alvaro Dinis. To Alvaro, who had met and liked two of the lady's brothers on a business trip to Brazil, this was an advantageous match. Not only would it unite two prominent families, confined to a select social grouping where there was little choice of partners, but it would also unite two successful businesses, thus enabling Alvaro to consolidate his fortune. Having agreed the financial details, Furtado returned to Lisbon with the good news in October. Nobody asked Beatriz whether she was happy with the match; daughters were chattels to be used as pawns in business, in the same way as princes and princesses were used in marriage to unite kingdoms. She spent the winter preparing her trousseau for marriage to a man she may only have met once before – if at all.

In the spring of 1606, Beatriz de Milão, together with her friend Violante Barbosa, was smuggled to Hamburg. Beatriz's youngest brother Paulo and their faithful servant Francisco Barbosa accompanied the two women. Though a Christian, Francisco Barbosa hated the Spanish and felt himself more closely allied to the *marranos*. Obliged to have spent her life as a Catholic, Beatriz knew nothing of Jewish rituals. Beatriz was married soon after her arrival in the unfamiliar full Jewish ceremony. She had no idea what all the Hebrew incantations meant but fortunately Alvaro turned out to be a sympathetic guide. Paulo and Barbosa remained in Hamburg for several months, making all the necessary preparations for the evacuation of the whole of the de Milão family from Lisbon to Hamburg. They returned to Lisbon on 7 October.

Henrique was 78 when he had to liquidate the family's business before their planned flight to Hamburg. His energy having declined over the years, he summoned his son Gomes, now aged 32, to return from Pernambuco to help him. Gomes's younger brother Antonio, now 24, was sent out to Brazil to help his brother Manuel to run the agency. Henrique also had another plan. With a view to keeping the family wealth intact, he wanted to arrange two further marriages: between Gomes and his cousin, Beatriz Rodrigues, and between his daughter Leanor and Beatriz's brother, the well-known physician Henrique Rodrigues (later Samuel Cohen).

New Christians in Lisbon – even third-generation New Christians as were Gomes and his cousins – who wished to marry were subject to discriminatory laws. Henrique Rodrigues had to travel to Rome to ask the Pope for permission. He made full use of the obligatory long journey to Rome also to request permission for the marriage of his sister Beatriz to Gomes. Pope Klemenz only granted such permission to 'New Christians' who were otherwise faithful to Christianity; Henrique Rodrigues was able to lie sufficiently to convince his Excellency of their devotion.

1606: The escape is planned

Meanwhile, Henrique's brother, Antonio de Caceres, who had earlier emigrated to Mexico, became a victim of the Inquisition there where the *conversos* practised their Judaism in secret. He had been forced to witness his wife Catalina da Cueva's death by torture in 1598. He himself suffered terrible torture at the hands of the Inquisition before his release. Horribly deformed, Antonio de Caceres had been able to escape to England in 1601. Despite the fact that 'New Christians' were permitted neither the right of entry to Portugal, nor the right to travel from Portugal, he nevertheless was prepared to risk his life by returning to Portugal secretly from Weymouth in 1606 to visit Henrique. After their discussions, de Caceres left Lisbon as secretly as he had arrived, promising to help to make the arrangements with the captain of a French ship for the evacuation of the entire de Milão family to Hamburg, planned for the autumn of 1606.

However, unbeknown to Henrique, the spies of the Spanish–Portuguese authorities had had the business dealings of the de Milão family under observation since 1603. They had noticed then that, when the de Milão's ships had docked in Lisbon, they had been loaded with Polish bricks, pillars and other Baltic goods. This was blatantly in contravention of the regulations, as de Milão had licensed the ships for the journey to Pernambuco. They should have been bringing Brazilian timber and sugar, which was subject to a high import duty, to Lisbon; and then, without unloading, a further duty was due for payment on exporting the cargo elsewhere. These hefty taxes, inaugurated in 1601, were specifically directed against Marrano businessmen. Henrique wanted to avoid paying them and so his sons in Pernambuco arranged to ship the goods directly to his business associate and future son-in-law, Alvaro Dinis, in Hamburg. The Lisbon customs authority discovered this ruse and Henrique de Milão was arrested and brought in for interrogation on the day that Paulo and Barbosa returned from Hamburg. He was unable to extricate himself from the subsequent lengthy legal action in which he became involved.

A friend of the family, Fernão Alvares Melo, was persuaded against his will to help in the family's escape. He was aware of the de Milãos' huge outstanding tax bill and that they wanted to flee to Hamburg where Alvaro Dinis lived. Melo owned the boat which was to transport the family from the Madeira Wharf in Lisbon to a fishing cutter whose captain had agreed to take them to Hamburg. As he had good connections with the harbour officials, Melo was able to bribe them to let his boat pass. The family with all their transportable possessions embarked upon Melo's boat and were rowed to the cutter. However, their luck ran out at the last moment. The captain of the cutter, having been warned by the Inquisition, was not prepared to take the enormous risk; he regretted his initial willingness to transport the family and refused to take them on board. In deep distress, all their elaborate plans for their escape having to be aborted, the family had to prevail upon the unwilling Melo to take them and their baggage back to Alcantara where they knew they faced certain persecution.

The family had been betrayed. Not only had the Flemish nuns been spying on them but one of their own friends, who had been helping with the escape plans, was actually a spy for the Inquisition and reported all the plans and preparations to his masters. During the night of 28 October 1606, in the small hours of Saturday morning, the house in Alcantara was stormed by the troops of the Inquisition and the whole of the de Milão family, together with six partly armed companions, were awoken and arrested. The companions, two of whom were close relatives of the de Milãos, were taken to the Jesuit Catechism School, the 'Escolas Gerais'. The members of the de Milão family and their servants were imprisoned in the main prison of the Inquisition in Lisbon.

One companion, Manuel Cardoso de Macedo, a relative of the Inquisitor, was arrested when he was trying to help Henrique's youngest daughter Isabel and her maid to escape Lisbon with the two small sons of her sister Ana, who was in prison. Isabel who, on her arrest on 28 October 1606 was only 16, was imprisoned with the rest of her family and released after spending two years in the Escolas Gerais, being 're-educated' in the Catholic religion.

Returning to Lisbon, having obtained permission for two marriages from the Pope in Rome, Henrique Rodrigues was appalled to learn of the family's incarceration and immediately went into hiding. Evading the officers of the Inquisition, he fled Portugal to find sanctuary with his cousin Beatriz and her husband Alvaro Dinis in Hamburg.

Initially released, all members of the de Milão family and their companions were rearrested towards the end of 1608. The crime that they had committed was listed as the secret discussions that had taken place on 11 October 1606, planning the attempted flight of the de Milão family. Secretly planning to leave Portugal was the crime committed by many other *converso* Jews who were arrested and, under torture, made to confess their sins, recant and pay their penance to the Church. They were then made to spend time in the Jesuit Catechism School in Lisbon and were thus able to save their lives. Those who would not confess were burnt at the stake.

Henrique de Milão was no ordinary 'sinner'. A respected and successful businessman and citizen of Lisbon, the Inquisitors felt that their prestige was at stake if they did not force him to recant. They demanded a great show to prove their power to the population; and so it was of particular importance to them that Henrique should confess his sins and renounce his beliefs. He, however, refused to cooperate fully with the requirements of his torturers, though he did confess to having fasted on the Jewish Day of Atonement, 11 October 1606. He also confessed to having borrowed a Jewish prayer book.

On 12 February 1609, after two and a half years of incarceration, in one final attempt to force Henrique to comply, the Grand Inquisitor himself visited him in his gruesome, dank dungeon. The aged Antonio Dias Cardoso, resplendent in scarlet robes with white lace-frilled overskirt, a heavy gold chain bearing a large bejewelled cross around his neck and his gnarled fingers heavy with precious rings, was desperate to persuade Henrique to ask for pardon. But this brave man replied: 'Even if you tie me to the stake in order to burn me alive, I will not confess to something of which I am not guilty.' As his death sentence was pronounced, his hands were tied behind his back. From now on, the only way in which he could save his own life was by accusing those people who had betrayed him. He was also expected to name his own family members as fellow sinners.

1609: Henrique condemned to death

The 81-year-old Henrique de Milão was listed as number 71, condemned to be paraded before being burnt alive at the stake in the
auto da fé of 5 April 1609. In addition to the crimes of his planned
flight and of attempting to evade paying his debts, he was accused of
having contacts with a small group of foreign Jews who, as registered
Jews, were living quite legally in Lisbon. The Inquisition was no
longer engaged in fighting these Jews, only those who had converted
to Catholicism and were practising their Jewish faith in secret. It was
under torture that Henrique's faithful servant, Antonio Barbosa,
had been made to inform on his master; he ultimately withdrew
this statement but the Inquisition ignored his denial. Though a
Christian, Barbosa confessed himself a Jew, after having suffered two
years in the dungeons of the Inquisition. He had tried to extricate
himself by pretending to be insane and had also gone on hunger
strike. The authorities even brought Henrique's youngest son Paulo
from his filthy dungeon to try and persuade his friend Barbosa to say
he was a Christian; but it was all to no avail. As accused number 72,
he was to burn alive alongside his master and five 'guilty' women
(Fig. 3).

Henrique was one of 75 New Christians condemned to suffer this
terrible death on the same occasion; of these, 68 had confessed under
torture and were spared their lives at the last moment. They all had to
take part in the penitential procession.

For his unwilling part in trying to help the de Milão family in their
attempted escape, Fernão Alvares Melo was arrested for the second
time, two days before Henrique's death sentence was carried out. He
was interrogated under torture for almost two and a half years. He
withstood the torture without ever confessing to any sin, though
he named all those who had been instrumental in the attempted
escape. On payment of a huge fine and on making a sworn statement
to rigorously follow all church prayers and fast days, Melo was released
in 1611 but forbidden from leaving Portugal. However, he managed
to escape to Antwerp. He was a poet who had translated the *Psalms of
David* into Spanish and he brought these with him. In fear of being
caught once again by the Inquisition, Melo adopted the Jewish name
of David Aben-Atar. He settled in Amsterdam where he opened
a Jewish–Spanish book printing works and was appointed Rabbi
of the Portuguese Synagogue Bet Yisrael. He apparently moved to
Glückstadt, then to Hamburg where he printed the 150 *Psalms of
David*.

Fig. 3 1508 woodcut: torture by winch, burning and hand amputation.

1610: Paulo de Milão

Under torture Henrique's youngest son, Paulo de Milão, aged 25, was made to denounce the armed men who were to have accompanied the de Milão family in their bid to escape and who had, in the meantime,

been released by the Inquisition. He was sentenced to a year's deten-
tion in the Escolas Gerais, to be followed by a further year living under
the supervision of the re-educator and jail supervisor in the Santa
Marinha quarter; he was obliged always to wear the penitential shirt.
However, Paulo was a renegade with scant respect for any rules, laws
and conventions. His freedom of spirit was such that he was able to
bribe a guard to let him out, to be seen in other parts of the town
wrapped in a sleeveless black cape and sporting a sword on his hip.
Spies reported his escapades in taverns, where he met women of
dubious repute, to the Inquisition on several occasions; but his persecutors did not apprehend him, possibly in the belief that he would
lead them to further transgressors of their punitive laws.

An attempted escape with help from the inept Manuel Cardoso
de Macedo, the relative of the Inquisitor who had helped in the
misbegotten escape attempt of Isabel de Milão with her sister Ana's two
children, was equally unsuccessful. Then, one day, the jail supervisor on his rounds discovered Paulo's penitential shirt neatly folded on
the chair in his cell. Its wearer had disappeared, having apparently
bribed a warder to give him the key. The brazen Paulo was thus the first
of the de Milão family to flee from Portugal, around 15 January 1610.

Fernão Lopes de Milão and his friends tortured

Henrique's son Fernão, aged 34 and under torture by the Inquisition
for two years, was a penitent in the terrible parade which preceded his
father's death. His sentence was that he should be incarcerated in the
Inquisition dungeons for the rest of his life. In order to try and gain a
pardon and to prevent his further torture, he 'voluntarily' requested
an audience with the Grand Inquisitor. On 7 April 1609, he was forced
to present the judges with a new confession. In this he referred to a
meeting in the apartment of Diogo Lopes Cardoso in October 1606
for the purpose of planning the family's flight; he named the
participants as Fernão Alvares Melo, the owner of the boat used in
the de Milão family's aborted escape, and Gaspar Fernandes Penso, a
relative.

Fernão de Milão attempted to save the life of his fellow prisoner,
Vicente Furtado, who had arranged his sister Beatriz's marriage in
Hamburg. He testified to Furtado's strong Christian beliefs and his
desire to marry a Christian woman. This led to Furtado's release but,
tragically, for only two days. He was rearrested when Fernão was again
tortured and questioned about his meeting with Furtado three years
earlier; he was then forced to make a long statement under duress. His
suffering and his 'confession' barely saved his life and was of no help
to his fellow sufferers.

Furtado and Penso were both accused of practising forbidden religious rites. They suffered two years of torture which only produced confessions of a negligible nature including that, on 11 October 1606, they had taken part in the discussions about the escape. Furtado did not survive the Inquisition; his file was closed in 1615.

Penso, the natural son of a Christian woman and a Marrano man, was accused of his part in the de Milão family's aborted escape. He was terribly tortured. He was stretched on the rack four times and once was thrown from a height with his wrists tied to a gallows, so that his arms were pulled from their sockets, after which he was condemned to death. He was only saved through the confessions of Henrique's wife Guiomar and their daughters Leanor and Isabel, extracted on 16 August 1610. Perjuring themselves, but in the sure knowledge that Paulo was well out of the way by then, they declared that their son and brother Paulo had only testified against Penso because Paulo owed him money and thought he could evade repaying it in this way. This assumption, which Penso had also attested to, led to the withdrawal of the death sentence, which was commuted to one of three years as an oarsman on the barges – a horrendous sentence for someone whose arms had been so cruelly mutilated. A year later, on 29 May 1612 and on payment of a substantial sum, he was pardoned by the High Inquisitor.

In due course Henrique's son Fernão was released into a sentence of 'house arrest' next door to the Escolas Gerais. Under constant observation from the Inquisition, he was sentenced to wear his penitential hair shirt, embellished with flames, for the rest of his life. On forfeiture of a considerable sum of money, he pledged never to leave the city or the country. He was also banned from personal contacts with other citizens. However, Fernão Lopes de Milão did somehow manage to escape and probably reached Amsterdam in 1610.

Gomes Rodrigues de Milão

His brother Gomes Rodrigues de Milão, like all the family and friends of Henrique de Milão, eventually confessed after torture to what appears to have been their main crime: that they had fasted on 11 October 1606, thus proving their secret Jewish practices. He also confessed to having taken part in the meeting at which the plans for their departure had been discussed.

Gomes was paraded as penitent number 23 in the procession which ended in his father's death by burning. His sentence was that he should wear the penitential hair shirt painted with flames for the rest of his life and should serve as an oarsman on the barges for five years. He was assigned to a Spanish captain who chained him to the rowing bench.

Gomes asked for relief from this hard labour as he was too weak for this sort of work owing to his epilepsy and various other illnesses. However, he could not afford to pay the high fine of 500 cruzados for release to lighter duties, so he remained at the oars. Gomes wrote many letters to the Inquisitors asking for clemency and submitted himself to medical examinations by the Church doctors who eventually confirmed his poor physical condition. Finally, on 3 September 1610, after one and a half years of this gruelling labour, his sentence was eased. Eventually, his relatives in Santa Comba Dão paid 300 cruzados for his release from the remainder of his sentence. How Gomes, who was under constant observation from the Inquisition, eventually left Portugal is not known; but his name was listed in Amsterdam on 16 October 1612.

Beatriz Rodrigues, Gomes's cousin and fiancée, was accused number 68 in the penitential procession. She had been condemned to death by being burnt alive at the stake on the grounds of insufficient repentance for her sins. Shortly before her sentence was due to be carried out, she confessed to everything that was expected of her by her torturers. Her sentence was commuted to one of having to wear the penitential hair shirt embellished with painted flames for life. This meant that she could never again be free to mingle with other people and her only option was to enter a convent and become a nun. It is unclear how she escaped to reach freedom but when she did she was able to marry Gomes.

1611: Henrique's two sons travel from Pernambuco to Hamburg

Manuel Cardoso and Antonio Dias, Henrique's two sons in Pernambuco, had somehow been warned of their family's incarceration and never returned to Portugal. They managed to go directly to Hamburg where their sister Beatriz and her husband Alvaro Dinis welcomed them. From there they schemed and contrived to help their mother and their brothers and sisters to escape from Lisbon.

All the women of the family – Henrique's widow, Guiomar Gomes de Milão, together with her daughters Leanor, Isabel, Ana and the children, the maid Victoria and cousin Branca Rodrigues who had cared for the children – were able to flee from Portugal to the safety of Hamburg on 25 February 1611. The happy ending was the prelude to an entirely new life for the participants. However, with a new identity, new country and new trade came renewed persecution at the hands of the Inquisition and its spies.

One of the conspirators who had helped plot the de Milão family's failed escape attempt, Manuel Sanches, who had also been imprisoned was released earlier than the rest of the group. Nobody thought to question this good fortune at the time. Many years later it became apparent that, far from being a friend, he was in fact a spy in the pay of the Inquisition to whom he faithfully reported every plan of the de Milão family. His reports would have been directly responsible for the tragedy of their foiled escape attempt and to their incarceration and terrible torture at the hands of the Inquisition. He later appeared, in disguise, as a prominent Jew in Hamburg and Amsterdam where he called himself Heitor (or Hector) Mendes Bravo. He continued to report faithfully to the Inquisition in Portugal on the activities of the Portuguese Jews who had made their homes in Hamburg and Amsterdam.

So, even long after their escape from the reign of terror in Portugal, Henrique's widow and his sons and daughters were not able to attain the peace and tranquillity in Hamburg which they so desperately sought and for which they had suffered so much.

Henrique de Milão's descendants never returned to live in Portugal. However, during the 1920s there was a brief resurgence of Judaism in Portugal. A Portuguese army officer named Captain Barros Basto, who recalled his Marrano ancestry, built a synagogue in Porto and persuaded those people who had some recollection of their Jewish ancestry and who also wanted to revive their Jewish faith to join him in forming a community. The movement was short-lived and quashed through the efforts of the local Catholic priest in 1935. Barros Basto was arrested; the thousands of *marranos* whom he had inspired to research their Jewish ancestry decided that, even after more than 400 years, the time was not yet right for a revival of their faith. Interestingly, there currently appears to be a renewed interest in Portugal amongst descendants of Portuguese *marranos* who are trying to trace their Jewish roots.

CHAPTER THREE

1611–1618: Hamburg – A Haven?

Portuguese Jews were made welcome when they first settled in Hamburg in the 1580s; they were regarded as desirable citizens because of their trade connections. The Sephardim who settled in Hamburg at that time were wealthy merchants with extensive trading connections overseas. It was their participation that made the foundation of the 'Hamburg Bank' possible. By 1612, some 125 Sephardic Jews had settled in Hamburg and it was with the assistance of their business acumen that their chosen city became an international centre for trade and finance in the seventeenth century.

However, Hamburg was not quite the haven which the Portuguese Jews so desperately craved. The situation in which they found themselves reflected their grandparents' and parents' experiences in Portugal. There was much jealousy of their success. Already by 1603, when Jews were officially recognized, indigenous citizens were airing their resentment. The city council demanded of the Senate that the Jews be expelled and over the next decades the clergy made repeated demands for their expulsion. Public abuse and physical violence directed against the Jews were not uncommon. However, the Senate realized that the financially powerful Jews with their international connections were contributing considerably to the economy of Hamburg. A kind of stability was achieved in 1612 when the Senate confirmed the Jews' right to live in Hamburg; on payment of 1,000 marks they were accorded a five-year permit to reside in the city. But complete religious freedom remained denied to them.

Whilst opportunities were generous, they did not differ much from those available to other foreigners like the Dutch or the British. However, unlike them, the Portuguese Jews were forbidden to own property or to join the associations of Christian businessmen. There was also a restriction on the number of brokers and they were hemmed about by petty regulations.

1606: Beatriz de Milão's new life

When Beatriz de Milão escaped from the terrors of Lisbon to marry Alvaro Dinis in Hamburg in 1606, she was entering not only a new and unfamiliar country, with a strange language, but also a completely new life. Beatriz had grown up as a third-generation baptized Catholic daughter in a family ostensibly living a Catholic life and attending mass regularly. As a girl, she would not have been educated in the Jewish religion, nor would she have been more than fleetingly conversant with any Jewish traditions. Such Jewish rituals as were practised in her parents' home would have been highly secretive and generally confined to the men. As was customary at the time, especially between Jewish merchants, sons entered the family business whilst daughters were used as pawns in the marriage stakes. Love was not at issue; marriages were arranged between family members or close business associates, with the aim of keeping the family wealth intact. When she went to Hamburg to marry Alvaro Dinis, Beatriz had to put her lifelong upbringing as a Catholic behind her and to adopt the totally unfamiliar and devoutly practised Jewish lifestyle of her husband, with all its restrictions. She hated the rule that decreed that she must always have her hair covered when in the presence of any man other than her husband and she was unhappy with the style of clothes which she was obliged to wear. She had to learn to conform to certain dietary requirements and to adopt certain unaccustomed rituals. And above all, she was required to run a household in this new and unfamiliar way, ensuring that her servants, who were not Jewish, were taught the correct way of preparing food. One of the servants, an African woman called Felippa, had originally been a servant to Alvaro's father, Felippe, who had brought her with him from Italy; so she at least was schooled in the Jewish ways and could teach the ignorant new bride.

Beatriz entered a select new and somewhat restricted society. By law, Jews were virtually non-persons and were obliged to wear black clothes for instant identification. This was, however, also their preference as black showed respect to their God and avoided frivolity; they felt that it helped them to distance themselves from others. Because of the intermarriage between relatives or business associates, many members of this group were related to each other. Social life was generally confined among them and the Jews rarely mixed with the indigenous population other than in the way of business. Amongst themselves they continued to speak Portuguese or Ladino – a type of Spanish – and Beatriz, like many of them, never learnt to speak German at all.

After her father Henrique's horrifying death and her brothers' and sisters' terrible experiences at the hands of the Inquisition torturers, Beatriz's husband became the new head of the family. In choosing Alvaro Dinis as husband for his eldest daughter and in entrusting him with the responsibility for his other eight grown-up children, Henrique had made a wise decision. His business partner in Hamburg was a man of strong character and excellent business sense and deeply schooled in Jewish teachings. He was also a relative of Henrique's wife.

Alvaro Dinis's background

Alvaro Dinis[1] was born in northern Portugal in 1565. Like Henrique's, his grandfather had also come from Spain in 1492 to avoid having to convert to Catholicism. His father, Felipe Dinis, who had been born in Portugal had, however, been forced to convert in order to be allowed to remain there. As a *converso* he built up a successful business in northern Portugal. By 1570, when Alvaro was only five years old, as we have seen, the situation in Portugal had become horrendous for *conversos*; so the family, as Catholics, emigrated to Antwerp. This was the first of many moves that Alvaro was to experience throughout his long life. When the Catholics were expelled from Antwerp in 1575, Alvaro and his family moved to the thriving business centre of Cologne in Germany and Alvaro was sent to his great-uncle in Italy, the Rabbi Gedalya Ibn Jahia, to receive instruction in Judaism. Leaving Cologne, they moved once more to settle in Venice where they were able at last to re-convert to Judaism. In 1578 when he was thirteen, Alvaro, unlike his father before him, was able to celebrate his bar mitzvah.

However, life was no more acceptable in Catholic Italy for the Jews, who had to practise their religion in secret, than it had been in Portugal. There were terrible pogroms against them. Alvaro was 20 when his father Felipe was condemned for being a practising Jew. Alvaro fled with his mother and sisters to Salonika, together with Rabbi Gedalya and his family, because amongst the Ottomans they could live openly as Jews. A year later, they returned to Italy to find Felipe; but in order to secure his release, they once again had to convert to Catholicism. Jews could not live openly as Jews until after the unification of Italy in 1866 when they became totally assimilated. They enjoyed their citizenship rights until Mussolini imposed the Nazi-inspired racial laws in 1939.

---

1 The spelling has regional variations: originally in Portugal it was de Nis; in Italy – di Nis; in Hamburg – de Nies or de Nyes, also Dinis or Denis; finally in Glückstadt – Dyonis. Dinis will be used here for consistency.

Rabbi Gedalya Ibn Jahia died in Italy in 1588 and Alvaro and his parents returned to Antwerp where his mother died. Alvaro, now called Alberto in Italian, at the age of 23 fully schooled in all Jewish customs and rituals, was trained by his father to go into business. The widowed Felipe married again and had three further children. It was around 1590 when the 25-year-old Alvaro and his father, now calling himself Samoa Hiae or Samoa Dinis, made their first voyage to Brazil and met Henrique de Milão's sons, Manuel and Gomes, who were working in Pernambuco as his agents. The men's close business connections and firm friendship was the prelude to Alvaro's marriage to the de Milão's sister Beatriz.

Unable to settle permanently in Italy, Alvaro and his family moved to Hamburg towards the end of the sixteenth century where Felipe died on 30 September 1599. Alvaro, known by the German name of Albert de Nies, now became head of the family and took full responsibility for the business. He also became a prominent member of the Jewish community in Hamburg, having installed a secret Jewish prayer chamber in his house as early as 1605. He developed the business to become a major trading company. Shipping Brazilian goods, mainly sugar and timber which he imported for sale, he purchased goods, largely from the Baltic states, such as corn, rope, saltpetre, tar and masts, for shipment to the Iberian peninsula. Alvaro Dinis received the admiration of the Senate for being one of the major importers of sugar and was praised warmly as a 'first-class businessman' for his efforts to expand his business to Danzig.

The surname Henriques is introduced

The birth of a son to Beatriz and Alvaro Dinis in 1607 marked the introduction of a new generation. Also, Reuben (Bar Jachia-El) Henriques was the first member of the family to carry the surname 'Henriques'. Whilst it was already a family name, in naming him they were following the Portuguese-Jewish custom of honouring his grandfather, the martyred Henrique de Milão. The couple created a new family tradition in choosing 'Reuben' as his first name; a son was named Reuben throughout the next seven generations.

The de Milão brothers change their names

The first of Henrique's nine children to arrive in Hamburg after Beatriz were his two sons from Pernambuco, who travelled direct from Brazil without going home to Lisbon to face the Inquisition. In Hamburg they changed the Portuguese spelling of the family name of de Milão, to de Milan. In avoiding Lisbon, Manuel, now aged about 30 and his brother Antonio, his junior by nine years, also thought to evade paying the iniquitous taxes which had been imposed upon the de Milão business. However, the Portuguese authorities continued to persecute them for many years and they were forced to pay considerable fines for their part in their father's practice of evading the payment of extortionate sums of customs duty. Legal proceedings against them for illegally escaping Portugal and for not paying the *marrano* taxes continued until 1608. Two years later, they were again accused of practising the Jewish religion. They realized that the only way in which they could escape the continued persecution by the Portuguese and also by the citizens of Hamburg was to change their identities completely.

Manuel Cordoso de Milão became Manuel Teixeira; building on his experiences in his father's business, he ran a thriving import–export business, travelling to London and Amsterdam and specializing in sugar and diamonds. In Hamburg he also joined his brother-in-law Alvaro Dinis's currency mint, becoming a banker and financial adviser. He married and his son, Gabriel Milan, in due course became governor of the then Danish dependency, the island of St Thomas in the Antilles. His brother Antonio changed his name to Josua Abensur.

Broken in body but resolute in spirit after their terrible experiences in Portugal, the remainder of the de Milão family arrived in Hamburg between 1610 and 1611 and were helped to build a new life by Alvaro and Beatriz. This haven of safety welcomed them and allowed them finally, after three generations, to practise their faith openly.

Ana was reunited with her husband and children and Isabel married a man originally from Lisbon, a relative of Alvaro's. At last the marriages for which permission had had to be obtained from the Pope in Rome four years earlier could be consecrated: Leanor married her cousin, Henrique Rodrigues (alias Samuel Cohen) and Gomes Rodrigues de Milão married Rodrigues's sister, Beatriz Rodrigues Cohen.

Gomes and his wife and family in Amsterdam

The birth of the first of Gomes' and Beatriz's two sons in Hamburg, Abraham do Porto, in 1611 was quickly followed in 1612 by that of Itzhac Cohen Henriques, who later also named himself Itzhac Rodrigues-Cohen. As a consequence of his crippling experiences at the hands of the Inquisition and subsequent eighteen-month sentence as an oarsman on the Portuguese barges, Gomes was terrified of incurring a further brush with his persecutors. He decided to move on to Amsterdam where, in order to evade the spies of the Inquisition, he took the opportunity of his relocation to change his name to Daniel

Abensur or, sometimes, de la Piedra. Gomes's younger brother, Fernão Lopes de Milão, having escaped from the Inquisition's sentence of a life penance, went with him. They jointly managed Alvaro's business interests there. A further son and two daughters were born to Gomes and Beatriz. Amsterdam offered him the freedom to educate his sons in proper Jewish practices, without the many restrictions imposed on Jews in Hamburg.

In Holland, life was easier for the Jews and they had had an officially recognized synagogue since 1598. But by contrast with the restrictions placed upon the Jews in Hamburg, the more liberal authorities of Amsterdam, where the Portuguese-Jewish community had been in existence for 20 years, did not allow the community there to acquire a Jewish cemetery until 1614.

Jews had been safe in Holland since the twelfth century and the first major immigration had been by sea from Spain and Portugal in 1580. The Sephardim, with their trading contacts in the Iberian peninsula, were welcomed for their financial acumen and contributed hugely to Holland's prosperity. They had been granted the freedom to live anywhere in the city in 1601, instead of being confined to Jewish ghettos. With further immigration from the north and east, Ashkenazi Jews eventually outnumbered Sephardim. On 16 May 1616, when the two Jewish communities of Amsterdam – the Ashkenazim and the Sephardim – came to an agreement, Gomes was one of the 170 signatories to the agreement. His signature was number 23, as Daniel Abenzur, alias Gomes Rodrigues de Milão. Always petrified of being caught by the Inquisition, when on board ship sailing close to the Iberian peninsula, he would call himself Daniel de Hollande.

By the middle of the eighteenth century, Amsterdam could boast the largest Jewish community in Europe. The 23,400 Jews living in Holland were granted full civil rights in 1796 and Holland was the first country in Europe to elect Jews to its parliament.

1610: Paulo de Milão

Henrique's youngest son, Paulo de Milão the renegade, was 25 when, through his guile and ability to bribe the right people, he was able to escape from Lisbon to arrive in Hamburg in 1610. He became Mosche Abensur and as a businessman in the northern countries he was Paul (or Pauwel) Dirichsen. Paulo was a consummate liar, having lived openly as a Catholic but secretly as a Jew all his young life in Portugal; he could make anybody believe anything he told them. Paulo, with his radiant eyes and head of dark curls cascading to his shoulders, could have passed equally for an aristocrat or a brigand. His character fell somewhere between, moulded partially by his horrific experiences at the hands of his torturers. He was determined to have his revenge on the world at large and became an adept manipulator of people, both in his personal life and especially in his business dealings. In spite of his arrogance and somewhat volatile temperament, Alvaro employed him as a bookkeeper. In keeping with family tradition, he married first a relative from Antwerp – Lea d'Andrade – and later his brother-in-law Alvaro's younger sister, Abigail Dinis. Their eldest son was Josua Henriques, alias – in the Jewish community – Josua bar Moise Abensur, probably born in 1614 or 1615, who turned out to be a very unpleasant character; their second son was Daniel Henriques-Abensur, who eventually lived in Copenhagen.

Alvaro was very fond of his young brother-in-law, the somewhat wild Paulo, but his forbearance was often sorely tried. Paulo, whose escapades and walkabouts from his imprisonment in Lisbon were legendary, had always been a rebel. As he grew more confident, his way of life became even more outrageous and Alvaro would frequently have to bail him out of trouble. However, Paulo was fiercely loyal and so Alvaro trusted him as his sales representative in the Baltic states and as his secretary in the creation and operation of his mint. In 1613, when opening a new corn trading business in Danzig, it was Paulo whom Alvaro employed as his agent. However, his time there was short-lived. He got into serious trouble through having an affair with a Christian girl; Alvaro was only able to extricate him by paying a heavy fine. But when Paulo was accused of beating a servant to death with a whip in one of his renowned rages, even a huge fine would not placate the judiciary of Danzig and Paulo was forced to leave.

1613: Death of Guiomar de Milão

Henrique de Milão's widow, Guiomar Gomes de Milão, was 64 when she died in Hamburg in 1613. She was one of the first free Jews to be interred in the new Jewish cemetery in the town of Altona. The purchase of this first Jewish cemetery in northern Europe in 1611 was one of the many contributions and concessions that Alvaro Dinis obtained for the Jewish community in Hamburg. He was one of a small group of businessmen from the Portuguese community who negotiated the purchase of the land from Count Ernst III of Schauenburg. The Hamburg City Council regarded the fact that the Jews wanted to bury their dead separately from the Protestants as a transgression. The Council joined the Church authorities in demanding that the Senate, the governing body, should reprimand the Jews who, they said, had obviously shown themselves to be heretics. However, the Senate took into consideration the huge income to the city derived from the taxes paid by the successful Portuguese-Jewish businessmen which it did not wish to lose. After consultation with the theological authorities in Jena, a compromise was reached: the Jews could retain their own burial ground if they strictly observed 17 rules, which included showing no outward sign of leading a Jewish life.

The economic success of the Jews and the creation of a viably Jewish community life laid the foundations for the continuing growth of the Jewish community in Hamburg and enabled the eventual foundation of an Ashkenazi community who arrived there from Eastern Europe. Not only did the kings of Portugal and Spain make use of the Hamburg Portuguese-Jewish businessmen's acumen in the seventeenth century but so too did the dukes of Tuscany and the kings of Denmark, Poland and Sweden, as well as the Kaiser of Vienna. On their visits to Hamburg, the various kings and dukes would often stay with their Portuguese financial advisers in their elegant homes. Foreign visitors remarked on the luxurious lifestyle of the Portuguese in Hamburg.

Meanwhile, things were not going so well for Alvaro Dinis and the de Milão family in Hamburg. When the Inquisition spy, Manuel Sanches, who had ingratiated himself with the family in Lisbon as their friend and fellow conspirator, turned up in Hamburg as a Marrano named Hector Mendes Bravo, nobody recognized him. He returned to Lisbon in 1617 and took great pride in making a full report to the Inquisition authorities on the activities of some 200 former Portuguese Jews living in Hamburg and Amsterdam. Having gained the confidence, incognito, of Alvaro Dinis, he could report on every aspect of the lives of Henrique de Milão's sons and daughters, who were then living in Hamburg and Amsterdam. When Sanches's duplicity was finally discovered, they all feared for their contacts and relatives that were still in Portugal. They also realized that they themselves were in considerable danger of pursuit by the Inquisition, who employed spies in many places. Sanches also informed the authorities that there were synagogues in three houses belonging to Hamburg Jews all, including Alvaro Dinis, members of Henrique de Milão's extended family: this opened up new persecution for the family, causing them to take ever more evasive action.

In fear of having his goods impounded by the Spanish and Portuguese authorities, Alvaro ceased his profitable shipments to the Iberian peninsula. He concentrated instead on doing business with his northern contacts – with Bistum Bremen, the principality of Sachsen-Lauenburg, the Schauburg earldom of Holstein and the realm of Denmark; these states all stood in competition with Hamburg. He became their supplier of silver, spices and other valuable goods. This new tactic was to the disadvantage of the Hamburg exchequer that stood to lose considerable income from the taxes that

Alvaro would have paid. The Hamburg authorities, unconcerned with the reasons behind Alvaro's change of business interests, found the loss of revenues unacceptable. His caution cost him the valuable patronage of the Hamburg Senate which had until then always supported him.

One of Alvaro's many trading interests was diamond dealing with which he was able to redress some of his shipping losses. His eldest brother-in-law, Manuel Cordoso de Teixeira, who had never been in the hands of the Inquisition was able to travel for him and Daniel Abensur between Hamburg and London, dealing in diamonds.

In 1618, the Hamburg Senate issued a warrant to arrest Alvaro Dinis, accusing him of unlawful business dealings with the alien neighbouring states. Warned of the approaching law officers, Alvaro leapt on his horse and managed to flee to nearby Altona. At the time this was a Danish city within Hamburg which itself was a collection of cities, mostly Prussian. His wife Beatriz, together with her unscrupulous brother Paulo, followed in a coach. Now Alvaro, at the age of 53, was forced to make a major life-saving decision. He had to leave his home in Hamburg, where he had been living for some 20 years or more and where he had built up a successful business, to head for a new life in Denmark.

King Christian IV had recently founded a new city at the confluence of the River Rhine and the River Elbe, which he called Glückstadt ('Luck City'); he needed energetic and successful businessmen and investors to create a trading city and had already wooed Alvaro Dinis. Alvaro agreed to accept the king's invitation under certain conditions. He insisted that he and all fellow Jewish believers who might follow him should be guaranteed a tolerant environment in which to lead their lives; and he required of the king special privileges for the founding of a Jewish community in the new Glückstadt.

Alvaro Dinis, now Dionis, made a wise and far-reaching decision in choosing to move his family out of Hamburg to Glückstadt. Paulo and his brothers and sisters, who had only been settled there for seven years, also had no further interest in remaining in the city which for them was becoming almost as uncomfortable as Lisbon had been.

Religious freedom was not sanctioned for the Jews in Hamburg until 1650, when they were permitted to practise their religion in private; however, it was still forbidden to build a synagogue, even though by then there were some 600 Portuguese Jews living in the city. Feeling themselves to be persecuted in Hamburg, many Sephardic Jews followed Alvaro and accepted the concessions granted to them in Glückstadt. By the end of the seventeenth century, many of the influential Hamburg Portuguese Jews had died. In 1697, the town council and the Senate emulated the rulers of Portugal a century earlier, demanding considerable annual payments for permission to remain in Hamburg. When concurrently their right to practise their religion was rescinded, many of the richer families chose to emigrate to the more tolerant Danish-ruled Altona and Ortensen (now suburbs of Hamburg) and to Amsterdam. By the eighteenth century, the Portuguese community was so diminished in Hamburg that they retained very little influence. However, in the early nineteenth century members of the Henriques family – by then renamed 'Hinrichsen' – were to return to join the newly invigorated Jewish community and make their homes in Hamburg.

CHAPTER FOUR

1618–1688: Glückstadt – Business and Continued Persecution

In 1618, when the Thirty Years War began in Europe, King Christian IV ruled Denmark; he was the first Danish king to establish connections with Jews. An enlightened man, he had ordered the creation of Glückstadt in what is now the state of Schleswig-Holstein in Germany but was then Danish territory. Situated on the right bank of the river Elbe, between Hamburg and Cuxhaven, the town had been planned and laid out in three sectors, converging on a town hall and other administrative buildings in the centre. The king assigned the three sectors to immigrants from various parts of Europe. Thus, one third had been reserved for Danes, one third for Germans and Dutchmen and the remaining third went to the Portuguese Jews. All three groups had equal representation on the town council. A remarkable democratic constitution with prerogatives as to taxes, etc., had been drawn up with the intention of attracting men of skill or commercial abilities and connections.

It was this promise of emancipation and toleration, enabling them to follow their own religious beliefs, that attracted Alvaro Dinis, his wife Beatriz and her brother Paulo (now Paul Dirichsen) to settle in Glückstadt. When the Glückstadt Jews received the concession for the 'Portuguese nation' on 3 August 1619, they were the first group of newly confessed *marranos* in northern Europe to acquire this right. Between 1620 and 1625, more relatives of Alvaro and Beatriz, as well as other Portuguese Jews from Hamburg, came to settle in Glückstadt. The close business and family network continued when Henrique's brother's extended family, the de Caceres, settled in Hamburg and Amsterdam.

Alvaro Dinis creates a new community

Alvaro had moved home many times and now, after 20 years of running a successful business in Hamburg, was uprooted and obliged to start from scratch. Only 30 miles from Hamburg, the new location nonetheless presented an entirely new set of challenges. He had made an agreement with King Christian IV which allowed the new settlers to form a real Jewish community. They were permitted to build a synagogue and to inaugurate a Jewish cemetery, to found a Hebrew printing works and to celebrate marriages in the Jewish style, as well as to have their male babies circumcised. Shops were opened and industries were started. Apart from running his shipping business, Alvaro Dinis was commissioned by the king to found a mint to produce mainly low-value coins for everyday use. Alvaro negotiated further privileges for the Portuguese Jews, giving them the right to trade freely in Denmark and to provide luxury goods to the Danish court and arrange large loans for the Danish kings. Alvaro and his family lived well; like other wealthy Portuguese Jews in Glückstadt, he employed black servants from Africa.

But the 'luck' after which the city was named was to elude the new settlers. Tragedy struck only six years after their arrival, in the winter of 1624–5, when a storm flood devastated Glückstadt. Alvaro, along with the other investors, lost a fortune. The following year brought a catastrophic defeat for Christian IV at Lutter am Barenberg, which broke Denmark in military terms. The humiliating peace agreement of 1629 and Gustav Albert II of Sweden's subsequent military triumphs caused Sweden to become the leading power in the Baltic region. There was doubt that Denmark could survive as an independent state. Under these circumstances and anticipating better prospects, albeit subject to greater religious restrictions, most of the investors returned to Hamburg or moved to Amsterdam.

However, Alvaro Dinis remained true to the city that had offered him his first real freedom. He was also one of the few older survivors of a plague epidemic which had taken many lives. At the age of 60 and having spent his life moving from place to place, he decided that, after having made his home in Glückstadt for the past seven years, this was where he wished to remain. In order to make the city a viable trading centre he, as one of the founding fathers, needed to attract more Portuguese Jews to come and settle in the now somewhat depleted Glückstadt. With this aim in mind, he set out on a perilous journey, bearing in mind that the Thirty Years War had been raging for seven or eight years throughout Europe. As a Jew though, this conflict, which was to bring ruin on Germany, was to his advantage. The Jews generally subsidized the war, supporting the various rulers. For this they received certain concessions, a bonus of which was that, for the first time in their history, Jews were treated better than the rest of the population.

Alvaro travelled to Silesia (now part of Poland) and to Prague – a round trip of some 4,000 kilometres – by coach and horses, over unmade roads peopled by highwaymen and vagrant deserters from the various armies. This arduous journey met with scant success, the Portuguese Jews preferring to stay where they had settled. Even though a new sea wall was built in Glückstadt, which saved the city from further floods, the worldwide trade of which the Portuguese settlers dreamt never materialized.

Meanwhile, Alvaro and Beatriz wanted their son, Reuben Henriques, to be properly schooled in Jewish studies, so they sent him as a young child to Amsterdam where the sons of the Portuguese Jews from Glückstadt and Hamburg could study. There he lived with his uncle, Daniel Abensur (Gomes Rodrigues de Milão). Reuben studied together with his three cousins. Jewish studies for the sons of Portuguese businessmen generally ended when they were 12 or 13 years old. Then, after their bar mitzvah, they would become apprenticed in their fathers' trades or on their ships, which was the course taken by the Abensur sons. However, in Reuben's case, the next few years after his bar mitzvah in 1620 remain an undocumented mystery. He was warned by his parents not to let it be known that he was the grandson of Henrique de Milão; this was in order to save him from the persecution which was still being maintained by the Inquisition against all of the de Milão descendants and relatives. Reuben dropped his bracketed middle name and became Ruben Henriques.[1] At this time, the majority of Portuguese Jews, who kept themselves fairly rigidly within their community, spoke almost exclusively Portuguese; they continued to speak Portuguese, eventually alongside German, for several generations to come.

As there was no rabbi in Glückstadt, Alvaro, as a deeply religious man who had studied with a rabbi in Italy during his childhood, took on the responsibilities of religious leader. In 1629, in Hamburg, he published a volume of 30 sabbath sermons in Portuguese for use in Glückstadt and Hamburg – though there, owing to the lack of religious freedom, the sermons had to be preached in the privacy of the home.

As the community leader, in 1630 Alvaro agreed a new set of advantageous concessions for the Jews with the king. He also resumed his

---

1 The secrecy and subsequent deliberate confusion about his name and origins has led to some researchers questioning whether the sparsely chronicled early years were indeed those of the same man. I am convinced that this was one and the same person.

trade with Spain, obtained the salt monopoly and the monopoly for the issue of Spanish escort passes for Friesian ships and founded a sawmill on the Glückstadt docks. He imported Norwegian timber for new building and, as the owner of some building land, he was now permitted to erect a few houses – a rare concession for a Jew in Europe.

Meanwhile, a new generation of the de Milão (Abensur-Milan) and de Caceres families was growing up. The executed Henrique's six de Caceres nephews were involved in the shipping trade in Hamburg with Alvaro Dinis. In the 1630s, like their predecessors, they imported timber, saltpetre and hemp from Poland via Danzig. They crossed the Atlantic via the Canary Islands to Brazil to buy coffee and sugar and they traded with the West Indies and the coastal towns of West Africa, taking part in the profitable spice trade.

1632: Death of Beatriz (de Milão) Dinis

Back in Glückstadt, Alvaro's wife Beatriz died in 1632 at the age of 59. Alvaro was now alone but he was still the entrepreneur he had always been. Around 1640, he was appointed as political business adviser in Hamburg. The Danish crown prince, Christian V, recognized his skills in this respect and made the appointment, contrary to the wishes of his father, King Christian IV. The crown prince knew that Alvaro's recommendation for collaboration and a treaty between the neighbouring powers made sound business sense and he received a salary for his appointment not only from the Danish prince but also from the Hamburg Senate.

Until the early 1640s, Alvaro Dinis was one of the most influential Jews in Glückstadt and Hamburg and a member of the Glückstadt Senate. However, his luck ran out in 1642 when he found himself in terrible trouble. Being in need of further capital for the development of his mint, he had borrowed 20,000 Rth. from Joa da Rocha Pinto. Alvaro had not realized that Pinto was not as solvent as he had implied when he negotiated a good return on his investment. Pinto had overstretched himself financially and was made bankrupt a year later; this led to all of Alvaro's assets being seized to pay off Pinto's creditors. Alvaro was suddenly rendered penniless. In desperation, he borrowed enough to cover his debts from his brother-in-law and partner, the renegade Paul Dirichsen, whom he had helped so much in the past. When the king heard about his trusted settler's shame, Alvaro fell from favour and in 1643 he lost his concession for running the mint. He was ordered to deliver the mint moulds to the chancellery under penalty of a heavy fine if he failed to comply. Alvaro thus lost the generous patronage and trust of Christian IV which he had enjoyed over the course of 25 years. Alvaro was to be hit yet again. Sweden chose this particular time to attack Denmark which proved disastrous for Alvro, as suddenly the ports were blocked. All of his ships were confiscated and he lost his entire life's investment in his shipping business.

If these disasters were not enough to break the entrepreneurial, but now aged, Alvaro Dinis, the worst blow was to hit him the following year. Following some major family disagreements, his nephew and business colleague, Diogo de Lima, cut himself off from the family and returned to Lisbon. Once arrived, he denounced his entire family living in Amsterdam, Emden, Hamburg and Glückstadt as Jewish, giving their names, their addresses and their business affiliations. He himself reconverted to Catholicism. The reason for his betrayal may well have been that, after his uncle's disgrace and bankruptcy in Glückstadt, he thought that he himself could claim the de Milão's assets which had been confiscated in Lisbon some thirty years earlier.

Once again the children and grandchildren of Henrique de Milão, as well as those of his brothers and sisters, felt impelled to disappear from where they had settled and to move on to somewhere new. In their efforts to hide their tracks and in the hope of eluding the Portuguese authorities, several of them changed their names yet again. The resulting deliberate confusion as to who they were and where they had come from, designed to put the authorities off their tracks, has also led to subsequent uncertainties for researchers.

Alvaro became Alberto Dionis and was never again registered in Glückstadt. He escaped his shame and his debts by moving to Amsterdam with his new wife and family where his younger brother Benjamin Musaphia held office in the Rabbinate. Benjamin was a doctor, scholar and kabbalist for whom he had some years previously obtained the appointment as royal physician to the Danish Court in Glückstadt. As the respected founder of the Jewish community in Glückstadt, Alvaro now became a rabbi in Amsterdam. This dynamic entrepreneur and instigator of so many social reforms lived to be over 85, dying after 1650. He had travelled a long way and negotiated many concessions for the betterment of the lives of Jews during his long life. And he had lived to see the Peace of Westphalia which finally ended the Thirty Years War in 1648.

The war had devastated the country; following the Swedish mercenaries' occupation, populations declined, fields lay uncultivated, rampant starvation led to disease and pestilence was followed by an intestinal illness, leading to further deaths. When the young Frederick William, at the age of only 20, became Elector of Brandenburg-Prussia, few in Europe had much faith that he could achieve anything worthwhile with such a devastated realm. But he was to astound them all, eventually rightfully becoming known as the Great Elector. His reign was to be a major turning point, uniting Brandenburg-Prussia into a fearsome state that was to become the leader of a later united Germany, and eventually the strongest state in all Europe.

By this time the extended Henriques family, many members of whom had changed their names several times, were exceedingly numerous. Henrique de Milão's nine children had produced many children themselves who were now in their turn bringing the next generation into the world. Because they belonged to a somewhat restricted society, and also in order to keep the family fortunes intact, there was much intermarriage between cousins. To confuse matters still further, there were favourite family names; many first cousins were often given the same name. In the interests of clarity, this account will only follow through the lives of my direct ancestors and some of their immediate relatives.

1646: Ruben Henriques and his cousin Josua Henriques

Alvaro Dinis's son – Henrique's grandson, Ruben Henriques – returned to Glückstadt in 1646 when he was about forty. He was registered as a citizen two years before the death of the Danish king, Christian IV. His name was entered in the *Bürgerbuch* (Citizens' Register) as Ruben Henrichs, Portuguese national, merchant, on 26 July in the year 1646.[2] Ruben Henrichs was also sometimes called 'Portuguies'. His father's business empire no longer existing, he made a completely new life for himself. His professions were registered as businessman, schoolteacher and butcher. Three years later he was a verger. He appears to have lacked the entrepreneurial talents and single-mindedness of his father and grandfather because later still we find him registered with the Jewish authorities in Glückstadt as barber and Kosher slaughterer, for which he was paid a regular fee. These pursuits led him to run a business sharpening knives, swords, sabres and any cutting implements.

When Alvaro had disappeared from Glückstadt, he was the owner of two houses, one of which was occupied by the impecunious Ruben Henrichs. Alvaro was still in considerable debt to his brother-in-law, Paul Dirichsen, who then considered it his right to take possession of his other house where he remained until he left Glückstadt for Hamburg in 1660, dying there five years later at the age of 80. One of Paul's sons and Ruben's cousin, Josua Henriques, born about 1614 in Hamburg, was as arrogant and devious as his father. Hoping to increase his own meagre resources, Josua made a claim in 1646 for whatever could be traced of Alvaro's one-time wealth in Glückstadt.

---

2 *Glückstädter Bürgerbuch*, Volume I, 1620–1706.

Josua, who acquired citizenship of Glückstadt in 1649, is officially listed as having been a sailor and a post-rider by royal appointment as well as having owned a printing works. More successful commercially than his cousin Ruben, his business interests were multifaceted and included the marketing of building materials. He became the head of the Jewish community in Glückstadt, where he was known as Josua Bar Moise. A difficult man to get along with, Josua was responsible for many of the arguments and disagreements in the small Jewish community; he was often called to the Rabbinate in Hamburg following complaints from other members but he refused to share his leadership of the community with anyone. Josua and another cousin were respected as guarantors responsible for the settlement of new citizens in Glückstadt. For this they added the aristocratic Spanish name 'Bueno' – good – to their names. Good to others they may have been but they seem to have been particularly unkind to their unfortunate cousin Ruben. Eventually, in 1659 Ruben felt compelled to bring complaints against them to the Rabbinate in Hamburg because they were trying to deprive him of his meagre salary as slaughterer to the Jewish community in Glückstadt; he had to complain again in 1667. On both occasions he had the full support of the Rabbinate but the persecution by his cousins did not abate. Eventually Bueno Josua Henriques moved to Amsterdam where he died in 1675.

1649: Michel bar Ruben Hinrichs

Ruben's eldest son, Michel Bar Ruben Hinrichs, was born around 1649 and acquired citizenship rights in Glückstadt on 7 April 1671. An enterprising man, he took after his grandfather Alvaro Dinis and his great-grandfather Henrique de Milão. Following family tradition, he married a relative – the ruthless Josua Henriques's daughter, Simcha – his second cousin, with whom he had two children, only one of whom reached adulthood. Whilst marriage to a cousin seemed expedient and logical to the young Michel Ruben, it proved absolutely disastrous. Simcha turned out to be a shrew who never gave him a moment's peace; divorce became the only option. Simcha instigated an acrimonious and financially ruinous legal action before a settlement, costing the unfortunate Michel Ruben a considerable part of his fortune, was reached. Wanting to get away from the eternal family feuds with his brother-in-law, he moved to Altona. There he married Cecilie Chasan from Hamburg with whom he had a further five children.

Glückstadt's prosperous era was over. At the beginning of the seventeenth century the city was not only a town with a garrison, a fortress and a royal residence, but above all it was an international port and trading centre. Its success in this respect was mainly thanks to two quite different groups of inhabitants that had left their homelands on the grounds of religious persecution – the Portuguese Jews and the reformed Dutch. They were educated people who came to Glückstadt with their capital, their ships and their worldwide trade connections and founded new trading companies. Sadly, King Christian IV's vision of a democratically run, thriving, commercial community of cultured business people failed to last more than 40 years. Towards the end of the seventeenth century, when it became apparent that Glückstadt would never enjoy the commercial success of Hamburg, most of the foreigners left. The town became dominated by the military and only small local trades, of use to the army, remained.

By that time the Sephardic Jewish community of Glückstadt had dwindled to very few members, all of the rich Portuguese Jews having moved to more prosperous areas. However, Ruben's younger sons remained where they had been born and became the leaders of the Jewish community. Poor German and Polish Jews arrived but the king did not accord them the same concessions as the rich and educated Jews from Portugal. When the Sephardic Jews of Glückstadt dispersed, they left little trace of the community's once thriving existence. Amongst the few clues to be found are the weather-beaten incisions, which included names and coats of arms, on the worn tombstones of the Jewish cemetery. It is interesting to note the frequency with which family coats of arms are discernible in Sephardic cemeteries. The Sephardic Jews brought their coats of arms with them from Spain and Portugal and had them engraved on the gravestones of their deceased relatives, regardless of whether their distinction was recognized by their new host country. The outlines of the Henriques family crest are still to be seen on one of the disintegrating tombstones. These remain as a lasting tribute to the enterprising Alvaro Dionis who had achieved such initial success in the founding of the town and in the building of his own business empire.

CHAPTER FIVE

1688–1869: Mecklenburg-Schwerin – Court Financiers

Alvaro Dinis's grandson, Michel Bar Ruben Hinrichs, and his wife Cecilie moved from Altona to Schwerin, the capital of the state of Mecklenburg, where they brought up their six children. At the time, Germany was not the cohesive country we know today. It was a part of the Holy Roman Empire of several hundred states and principalities, 39 of which would form the Confederation of Germany after the Congress of Vienna in 1814–15. Otto von Bismark subsequently united these in 1871 under the autocratic rule of Prussia to become the German *Reich* (Empire) which, following numerous different divisions and designations, is now the Federal Republic of Germany.

Germany being an entity of different states, each state was autonomous and ruled over by a duke or prince. These rulers were not always adept at organizing their own finances and, after the end of the Thirty Years War, when their coffers were depleted and their lands ravaged, they needed financial help. So they turned to the far more commercially orientated Jews to help them finance their continuing wars and their extravagant lifestyles. Thus began the era of the Court Jews which marked the beginning of modern Jewish life in Germany. It was the local ruler who employed a Court Jew. They performed services as bankers, jewellers and purveyors of fine delicacies; they provided military uniforms and fodder for horses. Through their network of relatives and Jewish business colleagues in other courts and other countries, they were able to make advantageous financial transactions and to move currency with ease at a time when the transportation of sacks of gold was always prey to robbery on the highways. Court Jews received tremendous concessions and remuneration for their services and were exempted from many of the restrictions imposed upon other Jews, most of whom were abjectly poor.

Michel Bar Ruben Hinrichs was appointed Court Supervisor to the Duke of Mecklenburg-Schwerin in 1688 when he was 39. Michel and some of his descendants – nine members of the family in all – were to remain there for nearly two hundred years, initially as general Court Supervisors, later as Court Administrators, acquiring many and varied concessions. Titles by which they were known included: *Hoffaktor* (Court Supervisor), *Hofjude* (Court Jew), *Hofprovediteur* (Court Provisioner), *Hofagent* (Court Agent), *Kabinettfaktor* (Cabinet Supervisor), *Kommerzienrat* (a title conferred on a distinguished businessman), *Generalprovediteur* (General Provisioner).

Most of the 300,000 or so Jews living in Germany at the time were forced to inhabit the Jewish ghettos. However, a few were able to improve their lives by securing appointment as Court Jews, protected by a prince or by a royal court. They distanced themselves from those left in the ghettos by whom they were held in contempt rather than envy. Court Jews led a privileged life with ready access to the sovereign whom they financed. They had the right to travel anywhere whenever they wanted, at a time when other Jews had to seek permits. They were exempt from Jewish courts and most local courts as they came under the jurisdiction of the princely court – the *Hofgericht*. Court Jews formed a distinct class, not only amongst the general population but also amongst the Jews. They were employed in many courts throughout Europe but mostly in Germany. Whilst the Court Jews became more emancipated than the poorer Jews and hence were despised by them, they did not withdraw from their origins and frequently used their influence to benefit their less affluent co-religionists. They became the first German-Jewish aristocrats, often leaders of their community and patrons of Jewish culture and learning.

Other members of the extended Henriques family also belonged to this aristocracy – the de Caceres family was attached to the Danish court and the Abensurs worked for the kings of Poland. It was customary for Court Jews to marry other Court Jews – when they were not marrying their cousins. Thus, in due course, many Court Jews were interrelated. Considering themselves to be somewhat above other Jews, the temptation was always present to assimilate completely with the aristocracy. Many were privileged to have their own coats of arms – members of the Hinrichsen family eventually acquired four of these. Uniquely for Jews, Court Jews were allowed to carry pistols and to wear swords. They were allowed to buy a house outside the Jewish quarter and could live where and how they pleased, in elegant surroundings with servants, and they rode in carriages. At a time when there were definite laws, which prescribed what clothes Jews were permitted to wear, the women were not confined to a strict dress code. Court Jews were not constrained to abide by the laws defining which streets Jews could walk on and at what times, how many Jews could attend a wedding party and which foods their state or town would allow them to eat. At that time there were many professions and trades closed to Jews, along with laws designed to prevent Jews from marrying or from studying many subjects at university. It was a long time before these anti-Jewish laws were abolished in Germany, only to be re-enacted in far greater measure by the Nazis after 1933.

Michel Bar Ruben Hinrichs with his wife and family were amongst the first Jews to settle in the state of Mecklenburg for 200 years. Those who had lived there earlier had been banished, murdered or burned to death in 1492 in Sternberg, 30 km east of Schwerin. They had been accused of having disgraced lost icons. When the family arrived in 1688, the state had been in constant turmoil for many years. Though the Thirty Years War had ended in 1648 with the signing of the Peace of Westphalia, conditions throughout the land were no better than they had been during the war. Mecklenburg, as the through-route for troops between Sweden, Denmark and Brandenburg, was one of the states most affected by the war. Only about 300,000, approximately one quarter of the population, survived. The position of the rulers of the states – the local dukes and princes – was considerably strengthened with the signing of the Peace and they collaborated in their claim to absolute rule, successfully establishing their claims in most areas.

On his deathbed in 1658, the then duke of Mecklenburg-Schwerin warned his sons against too severe a domination. Not entirely trusting his eldest son Christian, the Duke had, in his will, divided his kingdom between the three eldest of his six sons. However, Christian managed to suppress his father's will and take over the entire inheritance. War raged throughout the state between Sweden, Brandenburg and Poland from 1655 to 1660 whilst Christian neglected his duties in favour of foreign travel, especially to France. There were constant disagreements between his deputies and himself and Christian built himself a second home in France. He divorced his first wife, a cousin, and married the French Duchess Isabelle Angelique de Chatillon with whom he returned to Schwerin in 1671; he went again to France three months later, leaving his wife to rule. The marriage failed.

There was constant war throughout the land as well as between Christian's brothers, who fought for supremacy. A brief peace prevailed from 1679 until 1684 when war returned between the Mecklenburgers, the Brandenburgers, the Lüneburgers and the Danes. This was soon brought to a conclusion through the mediation of Duke Friedrich Wilhelm. Mecklenburg was in turmoil as a result of the constant absence of its ruler, Duke Christian; he died in Holland in 1692. After a period of family infighting, it was Duke Friedrich

Wilhelm, Christian's nephew, who triumphed to become the new ruler in 1692; he was just 17 years old and became ruthless in his determination to achieve absolute power. However, Michel Ruben Hinrichs initially had good reason to be pleased about Friedrich Wilhelm's accession.

1690: Michel Ruben Hinrichs

The duke leased the tobacco monopoly to Michel in 1690 when he became known as Meister Michel and as Michel Tabakspinner (Master Tobacco Twister). He was also referred to as Michel Portuguies, as his family had originated in Portugal, and Michel Glückstadt, after the town from which he had come. Under Michel, the tobacco industry reached a new high of development. The tobacco monopoly was renewed until 1708, when it was taken from the Court Jews after pressure from envious members of the aristocracy and court officials. The Duke announced the decision to rescind the monopoly with the words: 'As, Pursuant to an agreement with the cities, all monopolies in the State are now being terminated . . .' Michel's concessions as official Court Jeweller, after his appointment by Duke Friedrich Wilhelm in 1692, continued in partnership with his brother-in-law, Benedix Goldschmidt. His duties included supplying the court household with the required jewellery and silver tableware and to 'carry out all kinds of appraisals and purchases as directed by higher authority'. He later became official Court Administrator. This concession entitled him to move freely around the country, selling his and his partner's jewellery and silverware without paying duty. Other jewellers were forbidden to do so under penalty of having their valuables confiscated. As court jewellers, they also supplied the court household with candles and torches.

Michel was a man of deep religious convictions and established a synagogue in his house, which was called the 'Grand House'. He was, in fact, the founder of the Jewish community in Schwerin, together with the rabbi, whom he supported financially. An interesting sidelight on his activities on behalf of the Jewish community shows that he had strong feelings about the injustices meted out to the Jews. In Mecklenburg at the time, there was a poll tax on Jews and on all livestock. He and Benedix Goldschmidt managed to obtain the consent of the duke for the abolition of the humiliating poll tax for all Jews and Jewish travellers in Mecklenburg-Schwerin, as long as either of the two lived. (In Berlin, Jews continued to be discriminated against in this iniquitous way for many decades after. There were city gates for citizens and travellers which remained barred to Jews. The Jews had had to pay a commodity tax, equating them with merchandise at the same rate as imported Polish oxen and they were only permitted entry at the gate reserved for cattle.)

Michel was accepted as a member of court society. However, as a Jew he could still not do everything he wanted and he sometimes went too far and aroused the duke's anger. To celebrate the circumcision of one of his sons, he gave a solemn circumcision reception to which he invited several Christian men and women who witnessed the cere-monies and stayed for the banquet. The duke took a dim view of this outrageous effrontery and directed the clergy to explain in their sermons the difference between Christians and Jews and to ask that Christians in future abstain from attending Jewish rituals.

However, this did not detract from the influence that Michel Hinrichs and his partner Benedix Goldschmidt had with the duke. In 1691 they received a lifetime dispensation from the payment of the Jewish poll tax. This is one of the earliest examples of poll tax repeal in any German kingdom and represented a personal favour from Duke Friedrich Wilhelm to his court factors. Benedix and his brother Ruben Goldschmidt were among the Duke's moneylenders, although both resided in Hamburg and only occasionally spent time at the Schwerin court.

Sometimes the duke intervened on Michel's behalf in family litiga-tion. An acrimonious case was held between Michel and his cousin, Moses Josua Henriques in Glückstadt, the brother of his first wife Simcha whom he had divorced. As no property reconciliation could be reached, Michel Hinrichs was threatened with excommunication, a step that would have been economically catastrophic for the Court Administrator. Michel appealed to his duke, pleading for intervention with the Danish king so as to avert this ostracism. Moses Josua Henriques, who was also a Court Administrator, countered by asking the Danish king to force Michel, under this threat, into an amicable settlement with his divorced wife.

1692: Conversion of Michel Ruben's sons

Michel had two sons from his first marriage to his cousin Simcha Henriques: Jonathan, who died young, and Moses. Both brothers, whose surname in the meantime had become Hinrichsen in an attempt to gain entry into gentile society, were in 1692 amongst the first of the Court Jews to convert to Christianity in the seventeenth century. In so doing Moses took on the names of the duke, becoming Friedrich Wilhelm Hinrichsen in the hope of being granted the tobacco monopoly for other districts – but the duke was not impressed. He also hoped to open a tavern serving beer and liquor and a hostel in Rehna but nothing came of these ambitions. In direct competition with his father, he did manage to acquire the tobacco monopoly for the annual trade fairs from the duke. This conversion to Christianity of two Court Administrators, as early as the seventeenth century, represents one of the earliest endeavours of rich Jews to gain entry into society.

Such freedoms as the privileged Jews in Mecklenburg-Schwerin enjoyed were not shared by the Jews in Prussia where the Jew-hating King Frederick William I demanded a payment of eight thousand thalers each from Jews for the concession of not having to wear the mandatory yellow patch. Ironically, the Jews in Nazi Germany, some two centuries later, were to be obliged to wear the mandatory yellow star on their clothes as well as to forfeit their fortunes.

1710: Michel Ruben's widow, Cecilie Hinrichs, takes over

On Michel Hinrichs's death in 1710, his widow, Cecilie, inherited her husband's business affairs and became a 'Privileged Court Jewess'. She carried out his functions with great aplomb and vigour – and considerable ruthlessness – until her death in 1745. Over time, she acquired various other commercial concessions and reached a position in business and society quite unusual at that time for a woman, and a Jewish woman at that. Cecilie still shared the business concessions with her late husband's partner. In due course her eldest son, Ruben Michel, born in 1682, who would assume the surname Hinrichsen, joined the family firm.

With the naming of their eldest son Ruben Michel, Michel and Cecilie Hinrichs had established a confusing family tradition. Generations of the family were to name their sons alternately Ruben Michel and Michel Ruben. To add to the confusion, in this expanding extended family several cousins and second cousins were also given these names.

Duke Friedrich Wilhelm von Mecklenburg-Schwerin needed some income. Having failed as an alchemist to produce gold he had, as a nature lover, realized that local prosperity had to take into consideration the sandy nature of the soil. Sheep breeding seemed to be the ideal basis for an export industry in wool and cloth and, in conjunction with this, the duke created dyeing factories. He traded his products via Hamburg, Lübeck and Rostock. Tobacco, timber, grain and glass were also exported. The Court Jews were naturally involved in all of these enterprises, using their family and business connections in other cities to facilitate trade. It was to their advantage when the duke decided to move the duchy mint from Dömitz to Schwerin.

Cecilie and her son Michel ran their various businesses and concessions together. After Duke Friedrich Wilhelm's death at the age of

38 in 1713, things became slightly more difficult when his brother, Duke Karl Leopold, followed his benign but womanizing predecessor. The new duke was ruthless and somewhat similar to his late uncle, Duke Christian, in personality. Cecilie and her son suffered considerable setbacks, even though Karl Leopold extended their concessions and rights for 30 years. In 1715, Ruben Michel Hinrichsen officially became a Court Jew and jeweller. He managed to obtain his father's concession from the duke of a dispensation from the Jewish poll tax for thirty years. Ruben and his partner Goldschmidt also obtained the right for all itinerant Jews to have their taxable goods treated like those of other merchants rather than taxed more severely because they were Jewish. This was an extraordinary concession for the Jews and can only be explained by the two court agents' great influence with the duke. It was all the more remarkable when one considers that war raged once again in the state of Mecklenburg from 1700 to 1721. Sweden wanted expansion and this war united the Russians, the Prussians, the Saxons and the Danes against the Swedes.

Throughout her long tenure of office, there was a great deal of jealousy from other traders on account of Cecilie's success in business, resulting from her various concessions and monopolies. Other, non-Jewish, traders constantly tried to undermine her authority and the favourable conditions of her employ with the duke. As a result, she fought many legal battles in and out of court to maintain her privileged position and monopolies. Through her strong will and sheer determination, she was nearly always triumphant, to the great chagrin of the many merchants whom she deprived of business opportunities. Cecilie was delighted that her son had married Hindche Popperz from Hamburg who was to bear him eight children. Two of these would continue the business of finance, timber and tobacco with great success.

The crisis which engulfed the European economy for several years from 1719 affected the Hinrichsens and Benedix Goldschmidt, along with the duke. They suffered serious financial setbacks which placed them in huge debt; it was some years before Ruben could extricate himself. When in 1722 Ruben Michel held a bill of exchange for 16,000 Guilders owed him by "his Majesty the Czar", it was the Duke who assisted him in redeeming the funds. Again, when he had to file a suit against members of the Court for outstanding debts, the Duke came to his assistance.

The future looked bleak until in 1724, by pure chance, a secret cache was discovered by a member of the household. He was sitting meditating, mourning the death of a relative, when he caught sight of an object glittering in a niche in the wall. It turned out to be a considerable fortune in gold, hidden there by Ruben's father, Michel, for some emergency. This was Ruben's lifeline, that enabled him to pay off his debts and revive his business.

The duke had always valued the business acumen of Ruben Michel Hinrichsen and, when in a fit of pique he expelled all Jews from Mecklenburg in 1741, he made an exception for the Hinrichsen family, so Cecilie was able to die in her own bed in 1745. The Jews did not stay away long and by 1752 there were again 40 Jews in Schwerin.

1749: Ruben Michel Hinrichsen appointed Court Agent

Ruben Michel was involved in major financial problems and negotiations with regard to his concessions; these included some very unpleasant business arguments with his cousins and his mother-in-law with whom he finally severed all business dealings. His affairs were so complex that they involved the intervention of the Duke, as well as of King Frederick the Great of Prussia who was anti-Semitic and always unwilling to make any concessions to Jews. Ultimately the Duke lost patience and on 11 September 1744 the case was considered closed. However, the duke did not feel inclined to honour his debts to Ruben. This resulted in Ruben getting into difficulties with his creditors and proceedings being instigated against him for bankruptcy. Once again, Ruben extricated himself and the relationship between the Court Administrator Ruben Michel Hinrichsen and his sovereign remained good. After Karl Leopold's death in 1747, Christian Ludwig II became ruler of Mecklenburg-Schwerin and relations continued in the same manner so that, in February 1749, Ruben was appointed Court Agent, with an annual remuneration of 200 German thalers. He was the first Hinrichsen to be awarded the highest title of Court Agent.

One of his achievements was to obtain the sole right for the sale of passes to the itinerant Jewish traders. Though the court advisers were opposed to the granting of such a power of attorney, Ruben managed to persuade his duke to his way of thinking. Like his mother before him, Ruben pursued business advantages aggressively throughout the country. However, his petition to acquire the tobacco monopoly was unsuccessful. He made up for this loss in revenue by lending money to the courtiers in exchange for a good rate of interest. Hence the Court Agent was also the court banker and a privileged dealer in goods who guarded his rights with the same zeal as his mother had done. He shared his business with three of his brothers-in-law. Another brother-in-law became the senior rabbi of Mecklenburg-Schwerin in 1763, whilst Ruben himself was the leader of the Jewish community.

The Seven Years War raged from 1756 to 1763. This major European conflict was rooted in rivalry between Austria and Prussia and the imminent colonial struggle between Britain and France in the

New World and the Far East. The first invasion of the Prussians into Mecklenburg-Schwerin lasted from December 1757 to June 1758. The reaction of the Schwerin duke and his military force was to be repeated several times during the conflict: Friedrich fled to Lübeck from where he continued to reign and his troops were ordered to stay clear of the war and to go to Schwerin. War raged between the Prussians and other nations around Mecklenburg. The second wave of fighting started in December 1758 when recruitment amongst the peasantry depleted the land of its workers. This time the duke fled to Altona. The entire military troop of 800 from Mecklenburg fled. The Prussians invaded Mecklenburg for the third time in 1759 when Sweden came to the aid of the beleaguered state. The last years of the war were the worst and almost the entire male population of Mecklenburg was recruited; this proved disastrous for the economy. War was finally ended with a treaty between Russia and Prussia and the Hamburg treaty between Prussia and Sweden. Mecklenburg suffered huge financial losses and many farms and houses were destroyed by fire. The after-effects of the war lasted many years. All this military activity, whilst devastating to the population as a whole and ruinous to the rulers, served to increase the revenues brought in by various businesses conducted by Court Jews attached to the various principalities involved.

1757: Death of Ruben Michel

Early in the war, in 1757, Ruben Michel died, having outlived his mother by only twelve years. His monopolies passed to Nathan Aaron, not a member of the family, who had been called to Schwerin from Frankfurt/Oder, by the then current duke, Christian Ludwig. He and Ruben's widow, Hindche, ran the business together; she was the second Court Jewess in the family and pursued the interests of her firm and her children as aggressively as her mother-in-law, Cecilie, had done. The only Jews to be allowed to hold property and houses were Nathan Aaron, the widow of Ruben Michel Hinrichsen and two others. Ruben's house, his father's 'Grand House', is standing to this day. It now houses the city museum in the charming town of Schwerin which still retains many of its medieval streets and houses.

Whilst Nathan Aaron was not a member of the family, his offspring through the next five generations time and again intermarried with the Hinrichsens, just as the Hinrichsens kept marrying their cousins, thus appreciably reducing the number of ancestors. There might have been little choice, as they had a tendency towards extremely large families – as many as 13 children in some cases. The name was of such social standing that, on several occasions, men marrying into the family would adopt the name of Hinrichsen rather than retain their own surname. Members of this very extended family started new dynasties in several cities – amongst them Lübeck, Emden and Güstrow – all within a range of only 30 miles from Schwerin, and of Hamburg, just 60 miles away.

1782: Michel Ruben Hinrichsen appointed Court Agent

The third generation of the Hinrichsen family to function as Court Agents to the ruler of Mecklenburg-Schwerin was Ruben Michel and Hindche's eldest son, Michel Ruben, born in 1735. He eventually rose to an even higher rank than his father and was confirmed as Court Agent in 1782 under Duke Friedrich the Pious (1756–86), receiving Letters of Patent as Chief Court Agent in 1802. The duke entrusted him with handling all bills of exchange for a yearly remuneration of 400 thalers. As Chief Court Agent, Michel Ruben Hinrichsen acted as court banker on a larger scale than his father had done. The Chief Court Agent also became the founder of the public loan bank in Schwerin. He managed to negotiate exemption from various taxes for himself and his family and to arrange for his concessions to be passed on to his son after his death. Michel Ruben was even more unfortunate than his grandfather in his choice of wife. He was divorced twice and was outlived by his third wife.

A glimpse into the Chief Court Agent's financial position can be gleaned from the marriage in 1795 of his daughter, who was to live in Detmold. The dowry was to be 1,000 German Louis d'Or thalers. As the 'duke's servant', Michel Ruben Hinrichsen petitioned the duke for an exemption of the emigration tax incumbent on him. He argued that the marriage of his sons to women from Berlin and Hamburg had brought in much capital to the country. His request was granted. A subsequent regulation passed after the Court Agent's death specified that the tax waiver was applicable to the total inheritance, which included a further 5,000 German thalers given to his daughter. With an eye to the continued family position, Michel had arranged that his privileges be passed on to his son. When he died in 1812, he left three children, one by each wife.

Whilst many members of the Hinrichs family were already using the name Hinrichsen, it was only in 1814 that the name was finally officially changed to the form that it has retained to the present day.

1797: Ruben Michel Hinrichsen appointed Court Agent

Michel Ruben's eldest son, Ruben Michel Hinrichsen, born in 1760 and brought up by Michel's third wife, Caroline Meyer, represents the fourth generation of Court Agents. His claim to his father's position as Court Agent was already confirmed in 1797, though he didn't accede to all the rights and concessions until 1815. Whilst his petition for the timber monopoly was rejected, he was, however, successful in his quest to handle all the financial transactions of the court. He carried out his varied duties with aplomb until his death in 1825. Ruben married twice; it is through his first wife, Hanna Meyer, with whom he had seven children, that the succession continued.

1828: Meyer-Michel Hinrichsen – Court Agent and Government Inspector

Ruben and Hanna's eldest son, Meyer-Michel (1792–1842) inherited the business as the fifth generation of Court Jews and was to climb even higher as Court Agent. In 1828, he was appointed Government Inspector and two years later asked permission of the sovereign, Grand Duke Friedrich Franz I (1785–1837), to take up residence in Hamburg, an important banking centre, where he could serve his own and the duke's interests better. Hence the Hinrichsen family returned to Hamburg which they had left for Glückstadt more than two hundred years earlier. A cousin, the lottery inspector Aaron Hinrichsen, was invited to take Meyer-Michel's position in Schwerin. The two men worked in close collaboration, each helping the other to achieve ever greater success and promotion.

In due course, Meyer-Michel Hinrichsen joined the diplomatic service, becoming a consul in Hamburg and chargé d'affaires, receiving a good commission on all his financial transactions, both on behalf of the duke and of the government. Ultimately, by 1858, he had become inspector accredited to the legation; the Court Agent and Inspector Aaron Hinrichsen had become financial councillor and later privy financial councillor.

Meyer-Michel was able to take an important place in wider German society because by this time some of the barriers against Jews were crumbling and the more affluent Jews were able to assimilate to a certain extent with the broader German population. Those Jews confined to the Jewish ghettos generally spoke either a version of Ladino, the language of the Sephardic Jews, or Yiddish, the language of the East European Jews. But wealthier parents had seen to it that their children were brought up with an understanding of German culture and were able to communicate in the German language. In Berlin, Dessau, Hamburg and Frankfurt, Jewish free schools were set up for the purpose of educating the sons and daughters of the privileged in the German cult of *Bildung* and *Kultur*. *Bildung* was a concept of the Enlightenment and denoted the refinement of the individual and character in keeping with the ideals of the Enlightenment. Whilst born into devout Jewish families, these young people were able to assimilate into German society within twenty or thirty years, something that would take the Jews from Eastern European many decades longer.

1830: Adolph Hinrichsen moves to Hamburg

When Meyer-Michel Hinrichsen moved to Hamburg in 1830, his younger brother, the second son of Ruben Michel Hinrichsen, Abraham (known as Adolph), born in 1808 in Schwerin, went too. It is through Adolph that the story continues. As his elder brother had taken over the family financial business on their father's death, he decided to branch out into a completely different field where he would make his own mark on the world.

CHAPTER SIX

1823–1887: Hamburg – Corsets and Culture

Adolph Hinrichsen, born in 1808, was the youngest of the seven children of the court financier of Schwerin, Ruben Michel Hinrichsen. He had received a good all-round education and had completed his military service in the 3rd Schwerin Battalion, earning his release on 1 May 1829. After the excitement of his military service, he found life in provincial Schwerin rather boring and felt there were no opportunities to interest him in his home town. His elder brother, Meyer-Michel, persuaded him to move, like himself, to Hamburg where there were greater prospects for a young man wishing to make his way in the world.

Hamburg, which Adolph Hinrichsen's illustrious forebear Alvaro Dinis had left in 1618 to become a founder of the Jewish community in Glückstadt, once again offered a guarded welcome to the Jews. The ghetto had been abolished in 1671 and the independent Hanseatic port city of Hamburg had the largest Jewish population of any city in Germany, approximately eight thousand Jews, representing about 6 per cent of the population. Throughout Germany, the Jews represented only about 0.5 per cent of the German population.[1] However, the Jews did not enjoy equal citizenship rights and there was an ongoing struggle for equality. Since Alvaro Dinis's departure over two hundred years earlier, several of his descendants, members of the extended Hinrichsen family not connected with the court of Schwerin, had over the generations been returning to Hamburg and had established themselves in prominent governing positions in the city. The *Hamburgische Wappenrolle* (the Hamburg Heraldic Directory)

---

1 This was ultimately to rise to less than 1 per cent by the time the Nazis took control a little over one hundred years later.

of 1912 illustrates separate coats of arms for four Hinrichs and four Hinrichsen families. However, becoming established had not been easy for them.

The Enlightenment brought many improvements in attitudes towards Jews who became more – though not entirely – accepted in Germany; but the period of general unrest which followed the French Revolution contributed towards the ostracism and vulnerability of the Jewish community. Working people in many states in Germany were demonstrating for more human rights, something which should also have been extended to Jews, but the riots throughout Germany in 1819 saw mobs running wild through the streets yelling *Hep! Hep! Jude verreck!* ('Death to all Jews').[2] In Hamburg, hundreds fled the city to seek refuge in nearby Denmark. The riots were apparently spontaneous and their cause was unclear but the Jews were held responsible for the economic crisis of 1819, just as they were to become the scapegoats for the economic crisis following World War I a hundred years later. Echoing what happened in Portugal in the sixteenth century and in a foretaste of what was to happen in 1933, the police and militia arrived at the scene late and stood by, withholding intervention, whilst the mob savaged Jews and vandalized their property.

Prince William of Prussia used the continuing unrest to thwart the full integration of Jews into German life. In this, Germany lagged far behind England, France, the Netherlands and America, each of which had introduced constitutional government and allowed respectable Jewish integration.

Success in the Hamburg Jewish community came through hard work. The Jews' main achievements were in banking and business. Eschewing a luxurious lifestyle, they created businesses and supported younger members of their extended families in new enterprises. It was into this atmosphere of encouragement and support that Adolph Hinrichsen settled, in a city where there already existed an extended family network of businessmen. Hamburg was a city whose prosperity was founded on trade.

1830: Adolph Hinrichsen founds a corset factory

As a man with generations of entrepreneurial endeavour behind him, Adolph looked for a gap in the market to provide him with a respectable income – and his instinct guided him towards ladies'

---

2 In using the verb *verrecken*, the mobs were equating Jews with animals, as had been customary in many parts of Europe for centuries and would continue with a vengeance in the Nazi years.

Fig. 4 Adolph Hinrichsen 1808–1887. Founder of a corset factory.

fashions, specifically towards corsets. Corsets in one form or another had been supporting ladies for centuries but they had been accorded a very low priority during the eighteenth century. It was as a mark of the greater morality of the middle classes that they were introduced as a major fashion item early in the 1820s. This led to the founding of the first corset factories. Not only women but men, whose degree of vanity was akin to that of women and exceeded their desire for comfort, avidly took to wearing this figure-shaping garment to enhance their bearing. Even though corsets were undergarments, they were subject to huge changes in fashion. Each change in the fashion of outer garments necessitated a reshaping of the undergarment. The length, which affected the number of eyelet holes and the length of the laces, went up and down with the seasons' fashions, as did the décolleté. The type of lace, decorative detail, ribbons and quality of the whalebone stays indicated the financial resources of the wearer. The basic fabric was usually cotton denim but could also be leather, covered in muslin or satin. With fashions in a constant state of flux, women's requirements for new corsets were ongoing in order to keep pace with the changes.

This was a business that could prove very lucrative and Adolph was determined to be an early participant in the industry and to establish a good reputation before there arose too much competition in the field. His brother and his banker cousins were only too happy to provide financial support and to become the backers for his new venture which they anticipated would represent a sound investment. With this encouragement, the 22-year-old budding entrepreneur founded Adolph Hinrichsen & Co. Korsett Fabrik at 40, Glasshüttenstrasse, in 1830. Once again, a young Hinrichsen took control of his own destiny in establishing a completely new business enterprise for himself.

Fig. 5 Bertha Gumprecht 1811–1877.

With Adolph, the whole strategy of family business changed. His forefathers had been middlemen – buying from one person to sell to another and loaning the profits to finance local rulers. Now Adolph and his descendants became creators – manufacturers, buying raw materials to create new products. The industrial era of manufacturing, which was to change the face of Europe, attracted enterprising Jews for whom the easing of restrictions meant that they could broaden their base of enterprise. The younger son of a successful court financier became a merchant in Hamburg in a novel way. With his upright posture, fashionably dressed and proudly sporting the latest style in side whiskers, Adolph Hinrichsen was an excellent advertisement for his own product (Fig. 4).

Adolph needed courage and energy to build up his business in an atmosphere hostile to himself and to his background. Whilst he had the financial backing of his relatives, he needed to fight against a tide of bigotry, jealousy and racial intolerance in society. But he was confident that, as a descendant of a dynasty of entrepreneurs whose every generation had endured similar strictures, he had the necessary drive to succeed. With the optimism of his youth, he felt himself to be well up to the challenge. Hence, corsets became his livelihood.

After sleepy Schwerin, the new disturbances, which arose in Hamburg in 1830–1, came as something of a shock to Adolph. They once again offered the stimuli for anti-Jewish excesses and Jew-hatred, now that Jews in Germany were better educated, more secular and, at least nominally, citizens and in the public eye. But Adolph didn't take fright and remained firmly confident. In Hamburg, the persecution took the form of handbills entitled 'Down with Jews, the Police and Taxes'. Added to this was a petty new public complaint that: 'Jew-boys who peddle during the week' threw their weight around and monopolized newspapers in the coffee-houses on their Sabbath, a complaint which could have been levelled against Adolph who found the coffee houses to be congenial places for meeting business colleagues and, of course, for reading the newspapers. Yet the world was modernizing and the Jews were changing faster than anybody in their desire for equal citizenship, rights and acceptability. Whilst he welcomed all the changes, Adolph chose to remain true to his background and beliefs and was not amongst the Jews who were converting to Christianity in unprecedented numbers.

Once established in business, Adolph Hinrichsen was ready to establish himself socially and to set up his own household. In 1834, at the age of 26, he married the 22-year-old Bertha Gumprecht (Fig. 5) who was descended from a family whose ancestors, like his own, were associated with money as far back as the thirteenth century. Bertha had suffered an isolated childhood as the only child of a child bride. Her mother Betty Schwabe, born in Hamburg in 1793, was an immature 18 when she married Dr Joseph Jakob Gumprecht, a medical practitioner, in 1811. The marriage was a failure and the couple were divorced a year later, in 1812, after the birth of their daughter. Bertha grew up in the care of her young mother. With memories of her somewhat lonely childhood, she was looking forward to having a large family of her own. She would dearly have loved to give birth to some daughters but over the course of the next ten years she and Adolph were to bring four sons into the world.

Even the better educated and wealthy Jews were very much a part of their own community and had relatively little social contact with the wider gentile community; those who did try to integrate felt themselves to be outsiders. At that time Jews were still only permitted to live in certain streets but in due course those who could afford it moved to the smarter areas. Capital and property formed the foundation of political influence and, in order to be considered as a member of the bourgeoisie, Adolph had to demonstrate that he was in possession of both. Through his business acumen, Adolph purchased an elegant house in a desirable area and maintained a modest, though cultured, standard of living. The family was in fact assimilating, superficially at least, into Hamburg society. The old, Portuguese Sephardic community to which the Hinrichsens belonged was dwindling rapidly and now numbered only about 100, whilst the Ashkenazi, or East European community, had grown to some 9,000. (The two communities were in due course to amalgamate.) However, as previous generations had experienced, anti-Semitism was always rife and Adolph encountered much jealousy from the gentile German businessmen who saw the success of Jewish entrepreneurs as a threat to their own undertakings.

1835: Birth of Robert Hinrichsen

This then was the atmosphere into which Adolph and Bertha gave birth to a new generation of Hinrichsen sons. Robert, Caesar and Eduard were born in Hamburg in 1835, 1837 and 1839 respectively and Carl was born some years later, in 1845. In naming his eldest son Robert, the German form of Ruben, Adolph continued the family tradition that had prevailed over the past six generations of naming a son Ruben. Grandmother Betty Gumprecht revelled in being a part of this enterprising and boisterous family until her death at the age of 66 in 1877.

Learning had always been a priority for the Jews and, alongside their schooling in the Jewish traditions, Adolph saw to it that his sons received an excellent all-round education. He wanted them to be able to take their place in German society and to excel in business, to be accepted as equals with the Germans, not to be derided and reviled as second-class citizens. In spite of the various riots and anti-Semitic attacks over the years, Hamburg was a more tolerant city than many in Germany and a few Jews had been elected to seats on the city council since as early as 1808. In fact, one of Adolph's cousins, the banker Siegmund Hinrichsen, born in 1841, was to become president of the Hamburg city parliament in 1892, a post which he held until his death in 1902. A marble bust of him is still to be seen in the town hall and a street in Hamburg, Hinrichsenstrasse, is named after him.

The boys were born into an age of rapidly growing tolerance. The Revolution of 1848 was a crucial turning point for Jews; it brought about a greater emancipation of the Jews of Hamburg and many other states in the German Confederation. Their fight for equal citizenship rights in the town had been partially rewarded by 1849; however, their struggle for total equal citizenship rights, in which Adolph was a staunch participant, was to continue for a further 30 years.

By 1849, it was obligatory to acquire Hamburg citizenship, which in turn entitled citizens to certain rights – the most important being the right to get married or to buy a house. Adolph had been proud to acquire his Hamburg citizenship (*Bürgerrecht*) on 28 March 1847. Citizenship did not come cheap and as a businessman he had to pay a substantial sum. The basic cost was between 50 and 80 marks with various obligatory supplements, which could amount to as much as 200 marks. However, this only covered the 'small citizenship right'. The 'large citizenship right', by contrast, for those like Adolph Hinrichsen wishing to run a business, cost considerably more, around 750 marks. (By way of comparison, a local council official earned about 1,000 marks per year.) Democracy was an unknown concept, as membership of the governing body of Hamburg was confined to the more affluent citizen whose family had been established for some considerable time and who was a property owner. Women had no political rights.

Adolph Hinrichsen's sons' destinies were marked out at birth; following family traditions they were expected to enter their father's business and this is what they were trained for. But before they were old enough and given the considerable expenses entailed in bringing up four children, maintaining a good lifestyle and running a factory, Adolph needed help and further financial backing. In 1851 he took on an active partner. By 1862, when it became apparent that Robert, Adolph's eldest son, was well able to cope with his responsibilities, the partnership ended by friendly agreement.

1859: Robert Hinrichsen becomes a partner in the Adolph Hinrichsen corset factory

Robert had started working with his father some years earlier and became a partner at the age of 24, in 1859. The second son, Caesar, was not inclined to spend his life making and selling corsets and never settled down to business with any enthusiasm. He relinquished his partnership, settling for a private pension provided by his brothers Robert and Carl, and assigned his share in the business to them after Adolph's death. Caesar was an adventurer who travelled a lot. He lived in South America for some time, then in Moscow, and he spoke fluent French and Russian, as well as Spanish and Portuguese. He lived to be almost 80, dying in 1915 at the height of World War I. Eduard, the third son, appears to have been a sickly young man and died at 37 in 1876. Carl, the youngest son, became a partner in 1874.

Adolph Hinrichsen lived to see the changes he had always dreamed would one day become established. The legal emancipation of the Jews finally took place in 1870–1 – though this was in fact to be short-lived. By the time he died at the age of 79 in 1887, outliving his wife Bertha by exactly one year, Otto von Bismark had led Prussia to victory over France in 1871 and established a unified Germany; and Hamburg had become the major centre of German socialism.

The ageing Kaiser Wilhelm I of Prussia now ruled a domain – the Second German Reich – which was half as large again as it had been, with a population that had increased from 24 million to 40 million. Though there were many anomalies in the constitution, allowing the separate states a great deal of autonomy, in many respects Germany became the strongest and most important continental power. Between 1871 and 1878, 36 Jews were elected to the Reichstag, the governing body of more than six hundred deputies. Though many Germans still considered them outsiders, they were nonetheless outsiders at the very centre of public life. However, in spite of their being legally emancipated, anti-Semitism persisted. When the stock market crash of 1873 occurred throughout the continent, the Jews were once again blamed. Later, Jewish refugees from Russia were blamed for the 1892 cholera epidemic in Hamburg.

This was the sixteenth and most serious outbreak of cholera in Hamburg since 1831. Asiatic cholera arrived in Europe as a consequence of European industrial enterprise. In Hamburg, it was the incompetence of successive ruling bodies in handling each outbreak – which affected mainly the poor – that led to new epidemics flaring up. By 1892, the authorities were well aware that the causes were a lack of hygiene and contaminated water supplies in the poorer areas of the city. However, official response was slow. The epidemic of 1892 took as many lives in Hamburg as all the epidemics of the nineteenth century together; 13.4 per cent of the population died. By contrast, no other city in the whole of Western Europe suffered a major epidemic of cholera that year. The better off, like the family of Robert Hinrichsen, fled the city or isolated themselves, leaving contact with the outside world to their servants. Eventually, the city authorities gave priority to the recognition and erad-ication of the causes of cholera, thus finally saving the city from further epidemics. A major anti-Semitic movement had emerged in the 1880s, promoted by the *Deutsch-Soziale Blätter*, published in Leipzig. It slandered Hamburg Jews, accusing them of ruling Hamburg and of capitalizing on and being responsible for the cholera epidemic. This was of course non-sense – there were no Jews in the Senate at the time and they certainly didn't rule the city. The anti-Semites were supported by petty state employees, shopkeepers and white-collar workers, though most workers felt that the views they held were silly. In due course, the furore died down and truth and common sense prevailed. Political anti-Semitism diminished throughout Germany towards the end of the nineteenth century and was virtually at an end in Hamburg after 1907, though socially the situation remained much the same.

Adolph Hinrichsen died in 1887. When the corset business was taken over by his sons Robert and Carl, the same tensions prevailed in society and the same prejudices their father had faced since founding his factory remained to be fought. Sole ownership of Adolph Hinrichsen & Co devolved to Robert on 16 May 1895 on Carl's death. Carl, who had been married twice, did not long outlive his father and died at the age of 50 while his second wife survived him by 22 years.

1887: Robert Hinrichsen

Robert Hinrichsen, born in 1835, was a dour man who took his respon-sibilities extremely seriously and became a first-class businessman. In his efforts to integrate with the majority population, he embraced the

Fig. 6 Markus Leiser Abraham 1795–1872. Mayor of Danzig.

new Jewish Reform movement, celebrating the Sabbath on Sundays and celebrating Christmas as well as Hanukkah, whilst also maintaining the Jewish traditions to which he was born. He was popular with everybody who knew him and was one of the leaders of the Jewish community; for 24 years he devoted his spare time to his duties as chairman of the Temple Association. However, Robert considered himself to be first and foremost a German citizen and integrated to such an extent that, instead of purchasing a burial plot in the Jewish cemetery for his family, he purchased one in the Christian Ohlsdorf cemetery. The monument which he chose was not the customary evangelic-looking statue of a woman but a huge chunk of granite. He had found this whilst he was on holiday in Italy and had it shipped back to Hamburg at enormous cost; it was emblazoned with the name HINRICHSEN and subsequently mounted guard over four generations of Hinrichsen remains (Fig. 10).

1862: Robert Hinrichsen marries Betty Abraham

By the time my great-grandfather Robert became the sole owner of the family business, he was already middle-aged, had been married for

Fig. 7 Henriette Abraham (b. Herrmann) 1798–1867.

over 30 years and was the father of three sons. He had married Betty
Abraham from Danzig in 1862. Born in 1840, Betty was the youngest
of the seven children (five sons and two daughters) of Markus Leiser
Abraham and Henriette Herrmann (Figs 6 and 7). Their father was
the respected mayor of the seaport of Danzig (now Gdansk) which at
that time was a flourishing, intellectual and artistic city.

Jews, though not welcomed in Danzig, had been granted a 'general
privilege' to settle there in 1773 when 240 families, some 1,257 individuals, became Prussian subjects. Danzig was an attractive provincial
city, largely German in population, language and culture and involved
in the political concerns of the German state. Although their Prussian
status had been recognized legally for some time, Jews' rights were
often withheld and only grudgingly accorded to them by local officials. But by the first half of the nineteenth century, when the Jewish
population had increased to almost 4,000, they were participating in
the cultural life of the city and filling various positions in the city
administration and the merchants' associations. Leading Jews of
Danzig played an important role in the development of the local
economy in trade and banking, though the Jewish population had

Fig. 8 Robert Hinrichsen 1835–1917. Heir to the corset factory.
The author's great-grandfather.

fallen to under 2,400 by 1900. It was completely annihilated by the
Nazis after 1938.

Betty (Fig. 9) had grown up in this lively atmosphere and had
absorbed a deep interest and joy in all the arts. She had wanted to
marry a local German politician; both were very much in love.
However, her father forbade the match, as the politician was not
Jewish; and so the cultured and vivacious young woman was married
off to the tall businessman in Hamburg, Robert Hinrichsen (Fig. 8).
Robert had been brought up in Hamburg which was then very much
a commercial centre, lacking in cultural life. He was not remotely
interested in the arts. Betty found Hamburg and the world of commerce extremely dull and so she created her own salon.

Robert Hinrichsen had bought an elegant house at 9 Hallerplatz. It
was a house typical of the type inhabited by wealthy business people
and furnished in the best of taste. The lively Betty set the tone; she
entertained with great style and surrounded herself and her family
with guests from all walks of life. She was especially happy to entertain
people from the world of art and the theatre, and intellectuals. Her

Fig. 9 Betty Hinrichsen (b. Abraham) 1840–1919 Wedding pictures.
The author's great-grandmother.

great interest lay in what her sons teasingly called 'the ol' Greeks and
Romans'. Betty instilled in her three sons her love of the classics, literature, art and music and introduced them to a world far removed
from the commercial interests of their father.

Like his father before him, Robert Hinrichsen expected his three
sons to join the family business and ultimately to take it over. He was to
be disappointed – two of them were no more inclined to follow that
path than two of his own brothers had been. Max, the eldest, was born
in 1863 and escaped the paternal factory in order to study law. Law in
nineteenth-century Hamburg was largely centred on commerce and it
was not unusual for the son of a merchant family to enter the legal profession. This was generally to the advantage of his father's enterprise.
In due course Max became chairman of the Senate of the Provincial
High Court and Court of Appeal in the Free City of Hamburg until his
compulsory retirement at the age of 70 in 1933, allegedly because he
was over the age of 65. His dismissal was actually a result of the new Nazi
laws promulgated against Jewish judges. Hamburg embraced National
Socialism to the extent that the discrimination, sterilization and

extermination policies of the Third Reich were implemented more efficiently there than in any other part of Germany.

Max Hinrichsen was married to Alice Jacobi, one of four daughters of Leopold Jacobi and Clara Katz.[3] Max and Alice had two daughters: Anne-Marie, who married a lawyer with whom she had a son and then emigrated to the USA; and Elly, who married a non-Jew and had two daughters and a son and remained in Hamburg. Max Hinrichsen died in 1938, probably as a result of Nazi harassment. An official portrait of him had been painted to celebrate his seventieth birthday and was to have been hung in the Provincial High Court where he had spent 42 happy years in his position as a judge. However, a portrait of a Jew hanging in the Provincial High Court was unacceptable to the new Nazi authorities and so Anne-Marie took it with her to the USA. In 1957, she offered it to the Seventh Civil Senate and was delighted when they accepted her gift. The portrait was cleaned and hung in the courtroom of the Senate where it found its rightful place 35 years late and where it hangs to this day.

1868: Birth of Henri Hinrichsen

Robert and Betty Hinrichsen's second son, Henri, who became my grandfather, is the one who will take our saga forward into the twentieth century. He was no more inclined than his brother Max to devote his life to corsets. Henri Hinrichsen was born on 5 February 1868 in Hamburg. His formative years were spent in his parents' elegant house. As was customary in Hamburg at that time, young Henri first attended a private school, in his case the one run by Dr Otto. In due course he went to the *Realgymnasium des Johanneums* (the Johanneum Grammar School); this was, at the time, the city's only high school and only open to the brightest students. It was at this time that he first met and made friends with Paul Ollendorff – a friendship which was to have a deep and lasting effect on his life. Henri grew up with his two brothers as the middle child. Whilst the three brothers were totally different in every way, they nonetheless enjoyed a deep and lasting friendship and always remained in close touch. It was said that the young Henri, in contrast to his brothers, was always busy and very conscientious. After they went their separate adult ways, they made a point of spending a week together every winter in Braunlage, as long as possible throughout their lives, and all were devoted to their parents and to their home. The Hinrichsens remained a close-knit family.

---

3 By a strange coincidence Clara's younger sister Bertha was eventually to marry Waldemar Bendix and they became my grandmother's parents.

After leaving school, Henri entered the family firm of Adolph Hinrichsen & Co, Corset Factory, and undertook a course in business management studies. But with all the stimulation offered him by his mother's intellectual ideas, and his own widening outlook, he found he could not settle happily into his father's business. Together with his brothers, he had spent frequent holidays in Leipzig visiting his bachelor uncle, his mother's elder brother Dr Max Abraham, owner of the music publishing company of C. F. Peters, Leipzig. There he had been allowed to ride his uncle's horses. He had been taken to concerts at the famous Gewandhaus, had glimpsed the world of music publishing and had met some of the famous composers whose music he had heard. The intoxicating aroma of freshly printed sheet music had entered his life and displaced any residual interest in the restrictions of laces and stays.

Robert Hinrichsen had naturally assumed his second son would feel duty-bound to continue the family business. But, after only six months, young Henri knew he wanted something more culturally stimulating to challenge his formidable intellect. The world of music publishing in Leipzig offered the life he wished to embrace. He just could not see himself spending the rest of his days manufacturing and selling corsets. Henri Hinrichsen made the decision to devote his life to the world of music. In 1887, the 19-year-old respectful rebel turned his back on corsets for ever and embarked on his new path. It was to be a life of excitement, achievement, music, huge social responsibility, education and honour – followed by cruel persecution, tragedy and murder. Henri Hinrichsen could not have imagined, as he boarded the train to Leipzig on 20 September 1887, what a profound and far-reaching effect that step was to have – both on himself and on the city of Leipzig.

1914: Edmund Hinrichsen takes over the corset factory

It was ultimately Robert's third and youngest son, Edmund, only 13 years old when his brother left for Leipzig, who was to inherit the mantle of manufacturer of ladies' foundation garments. Born in 1874, Edmund joined his father's business a few years after Henri's departure and became a partner in 1901. Over the years the company was variously restructured and in 1914, when Robert was almost 80, he handed sole control to his youngest son.

Robert Hinrichsen died at the age of 82 in 1917. The corset factory which his father had founded with such enthusiasm in 1830, and which had been his own lifetime's obligation and livelihood, was to last under its new owner for only another 22 years.

In 1939, because the three owners were all Jewish, the company was confiscated by the Nazis and qualified to be Aryanized (to be 'sold' to a non-Jewish person). It was valued at RM 20,000. However, it was then compulsorily dissolved on 8 July 1939. Not only was the company obliterated but so, in due course, were all its archives and records which were taken into the care of the *Handelskammer* (Chamber of Commerce) of Hamburg. File number 5949 registered in the *Handelsregister* (Trades' Register) held in the *Amtsgericht* (District Court) of Hamburg was removed in 1939 'to be kept until 1979' and then destroyed. I arrived 15 years too late.

Fig. 10 Hinrichsen family tombstone in Hamburg.

CHAPTER SEVEN

1887–1900: Leipzig – Music Publishing and Society

The train that carried young Henri Hinrichsen from his home in the commercial Hansa city of Hamburg to the provincial railway station of Leipzig on 20 September 1887 was met by his uncle – his mother's brother, Dr Max Abraham. He was to become Henri's guardian, mentor, teacher, role model and ultimately his testator.

Henri arrived in a city with a long history. Leipzig, in the state of Saxony, lies at the crossroads of the main trade routes of Europe and its name goes back to the year 1050. An annual trades fair held since 1160 has been an international trades fair – the *Leipziger Messe* – since the fifteenth century. The University of Leipzig was founded in 1490. In the nineteenth century, Leipzig was at the centre of the Napoleonic Wars, with the *Völkerschlacht* (Battle of the Nations) at which Napoleon's troops were spectacularly routed, taking place in 1813. 1837 saw the publication of the world's first daily newspaper, the *Leipziger Allgemeine Zeitung* (Leipzig General Newspaper), which is in circulation to this day.

Long a centre for the fur trade, with the opening of the Leipzig–Dresden railway in 1839, commercial opportunities increased. To cater for Leipzig's expansion, between 1902 and 1913 the railway station was enlarged to create the largest rail terminal in Europe. The city became prominent for industrial development and was the cradle of the Workers' Movement.

Henri Hinrichsen was moving to the eighth largest city in Germany, with a population in excess of 100,000, in which the German Supreme Court was established in 1879. It is, however, for the production of music and books that Leipzig can lay its major claim to fame and these two powerful passions took over young Henri's life.

Leipzig was a centre for the book trade. As the hub of the printing industry, the city saw the flowering of many fine publishing houses. This resulted, in 1825, in the foundation of the *Börsenverein* (the Association for German Book Traders). This organization's many-sided efforts contributed enormously to the development of the entire German book trade. The Central Association for the entire book industry in Leipzig was founded in 1884 to encourage excellence in book production. Leipzig was the seat of the German Association of Book Printers and of the Book Trade Association founded in 1884, as well as of the Book Museum. Many major printing works produced books in many languages; cartographic institutions, graphic artists, type foundries, manufacturers of printing blocks and allied trades were situated in Leipzig. Before World War I, one in every ten Leipzig inhabitants was employed either in the book trade or in the graphic trade. There are academies for graphic art and the book trade, two technical colleges for librarians and a special technical college for the book and printing trade – *Deutsche Buchhändler-Lehranstalt.* In 1913, the *Börsenverein* founded the German Library in Leipzig, a reference library in the style of the British Library.

Called the 'city of music' by its inhabitants, Leipzig is famous throughout the world for its vibrant musical history, the most important association being with the name of Johann Sebastian Bach. The Gewandhaus Orchestra was founded in 1743. Its heyday began when the 26-year-old Felix Mendelssohn-Bartholdy became director in 1835. Mendelssohn's contributions to the musical life and heritage of Leipzig were incomparable. He resurrected the memory of Bach after almost 100 years of oblivion in the city which owed him so much and in 1843 he founded the Conservatory of Music, later renamed the *Mendelssohn Akademie,* as the first conservatory of music in Germany. Many composers were associated with the city amongst whom was Richard Wagner, who was born there in 1813 and received his musical training from the Thomaskantor Theodor Weinling. Robert Schumann was active in Leipzig between 1830 and 1844 when he founded the *Neue Leipziger Zeitschrift für Musik* (the New Leipzig Journal for Music); Albert Lortzing worked at the Stadttheater (City Theatre) from 1833 to 1845 and composed three of his operas during his tenure.

C. F. Peters, Music Publishers

Music publishing was a major industry in Leipzig and more than half the sheet music of the entire world was printed by Leipzig's music printers whilst nine out of ten of all music engravers in Germany worked there. Henri Hinrichsen's uncle, Dr Max Abraham, was the owner of one of the most important music publishing companies in the world, C. F. Peters, Leipzig, which was established in 1800 when it was called Bureau de Musique.[1] Dr Abraham saw to it that the firm of C. F. Peters was always at the forefront of new developments, both in a regulatory capacity and in the technology of music publishing. It was in part due to his striving for excellence at affordable prices that Leipzig achieved leadership in the music trade through the development of moveable type which replaced the hitherto expensive copper engraving.

The first 63 years of the company's existence had seen several different owners and directors. The music of Beethoven, J. S. Bach, Louis Spohr, Carl Czerny and other composers was published and the company was at the forefront of the new copyright legislation. Carl Friedrich Peters himself only owned the business for 13 years – from the time he bought it in 1814 until his death in 1827. However, the company was legally bound to carry his name in perpetuity, a decision which was to prove to be fortuitous a little over one hundred years later.

Dr Max Abraham

Dr jur. (Dr of Law) Max Abraham's arrival as a partner in the firm of C. F. Peters Leipzig, Bureau de Musique in 1863, stabilized this unsettled state; henceforth a sense of purpose marked its progress. He was to stamp his personality indelibly over the brilliant future of this publishing house. He brought not only a new spirit into the offices but also an entirely new tempo into the business. And he ensured a continuity of family ownership (Fig. 11).

Kürze ist Würze (brevity is the essence) was the motto by which he lived and by which he conducted his business. These few words encompass the character of Dr Abraham, who lived his life by the example he set: *Sein, nicht Schein* (reality, not appearance). For him the objective took priority over the person. The publishing house, and especially the Edition Peters which he founded, was all.

Born on 3 July 1831, Max Abraham was the fifth of seven children of Markus Leiser Abraham, businessman and mayor of Danzig, and his wife Henriette. He grew up in a cultured home where he learnt to love music, art and the theatre. After gaining a degree in law at Bonn, he studied banking in Paris and London before going to Berlin. He was working in Berlin, where he took an active part in its thriving musical

---

1 For a history of the company, see my book, *Music Publishing and Patronage – C. F. Peters: 1800 to the Holocaust.*

Fig. 11 Dr Max Abraham 1831–1900. Proprietor of C. F. Peters Leipzig,
Music publishing company. Brother of Betty Hinrichsen.

life, when he met Julius Friedländer, the new owner of C. F. Peters
Bureau de Musique, who invited him to become his partner. At the age
of 32, Dr Max Abraham embarked upon the venture that dominated
the rest of his life and which was to remain a lasting memorial to his
inspiration, making the name of C. F. Peters synonymous with the
concept of excellence in music long after his death. Friedländer did
not actively participate in the running of the company and Max
Abraham was able to buy him out in 1880.

Max Abraham's greatest passion was launched in 1867 when he
founded the now famous Edition Peters for the publication of new editions of the classics, which won immediate popularity. These enjoyed
phenomenal success as people recognized the quality of the engraving, the print, the paper, the format, and the affordable price, as being
something hitherto unobtainable. With the economic expansion of
the 1870s, the green covers (copyright-free works) and the pink covers
(original C. F. Peters copyright works) with their composers' names in
large capital letters soon became known, admired and purchased the
world over.

Edvard Grieg is taken on

New composers were taken on, including Franz Liszt, Richard Wagner, Johannes Brahms, Moritz Moszkowski, Christian Sinding amongst others and Max Abraham was always the first to publish music after the expiry of copyright, which at that time lasted for 30 years after the composer's death.

However, without a doubt the most important composer for the company was Edvard Grieg who, at the age of 19 in 1863, approached Dr Max Abraham with his *Opus 1*, asking whether the firm of C. F. Peters might care to publish it. Grieg became the glittering star in the firmament of this music publishing house. This unique relationship forged with the Norwegian composer was the major thread running throughout more than forty years of the company's history. More than the regular interaction between composer and publisher, it was a bond of friendship, support and mutual care, rare in business. [2] An idea of its depth can be gleaned from more than four hundred illuminating and personal letters from Grieg to his publishers. Correspondence took place from 1863 until the end of 1900 with Dr Max Abraham and from around 1890 until the composer's death in 1907 with Henri Hinrichsen. Grieg's letters were not only about his compositions but were also about his health, life, problems and concerts on his many tours throughout Europe and carried his opinions; they are an eloquent testimony to his character. [3]

As the relationship deepened over the years, Grieg grew to rely more and more on his publisher for advice – professional and personal as well as financial – and he came to regard Abraham as his 'adoptive' father. Dr Max Abraham was always delighted when the

---

2 One and a half chapters in *Music Publishing and Patronage* are devoted to the extraordinary relationship with Edvard Grieg.

3 The Grieg letters (apart from a few which found their way into other hands) were taken from Leipzig either by Henri Hinrichsen's son Robert in July 1939 or by his son Walter between 1945 and 1947. They were kept at Walter Hinrichsen's company, C. F. Peters Corporation, New York. In 1986 his widow, Evelyn Hinrichsen, sold them to the Norwegian state that presented them to the Grieg Collection in the Bergen Public Library. In 1930, Nina Grieg presented those letters which she still had from Dr Max Abraham and Henri Hinrichsen to the Bergen Library. The missing letters were lost or destroyed though copies of many are to be found in the C. F. Peters Copy Books in the Sächsische Staatsarchiv Leipzig. The complete letters, along with many replies in the original German, are published in *Edvard Grieg, Briefwechsel mit dem Verlag C. F. Peters 1863–1907* (Edvard Grieg, Correspondence with C. F. Peters Publishers 1863–1907), edited by Finn Benestad and Hella Brock, published by C. F. Peters Frankfurt, 1997.

Fig. 12 c.1900. 10 Talstrasse Leipzig.
Business premises of C. F. Peters and home of the Hinrichsen family.
Designed by Otto Brückewald. [Photo C. F. Peters].

composer came as a guest to stay at number 10 Talstrasse, Leipzig, the
offices of C. F. Peters, as well as the private home of the proprietors
(Fig. 12). Grieg nearly always travelled with his wife, his cousin the
singer Nina Hagerup Grieg. Dr Abraham gave his favourite composer
many presents over the course of the years and took him on many holidays. He always paid Grieg generously for his compositions and he
gave the composer the money to build his house at Troldhaugen.
Grieg was immensely grateful for all the help he received from his
publisher. It is a mark of Max Abraham's interest in everything new
that, in spite of being aware of Wagner's rabid anti-Semitism, he
invited his favourite composer to accompany him to the first performance of the complete *Ring of the Nibelungen* at Wagner's newly built
Festival House in Bayreuth.

Educational benefactor

Whilst music publishing was his overriding obsession, Max Abraham
was a pioneer for the betterment of women's position in society. In
support of his ideals for the education of women, he made the three

upper floors of his house at 26 Königstrasse available rent free for the *Frauen Gewerbeverein* (Women's Trade Association) which he also supported financially. This remarkable association offered education and training to working-class women at a time when this was unheard of. He supported many musicians through the *Holstein-Stift* (Holstein Trust) founded in Leipzig in 1878 in memory of the officer, poet and composer Franz von Holstein who had died that year. Max Abraham was the major benefactor of this trust set up to perpetuate Holstein's good work.

Abraham further granted scholarships to music students at the Leipzig Conservatory and at the College for Students in the Book Trade, to which institutes he also made regular generous contributions. He made allowances to various deserving people individually and to many good causes, being a major contributor to the Organization in Support of the Poor. In celebration of the centenary of C. F. Peters in 1900, he made a major contribution towards the building of a Home for Musicians in Jena. As Max Abraham's wealth increased, so did his generosity, but he preferred not to let it be known publicly. When he presented Max Klinger's exquisite sculpture of 'Cassandra' to the Leipzig Art Gallery, he did so anonymously and it was not until after his death that Henri Hinrichsen made it known who the donor had been.

Max Abraham was one of many Jews without whose immense contributions Leipzig's cultural eminence and advancement during the nineteenth and early twentieth centuries would not have taken place. It was in particular their creative endeavours in all areas of business, spiritual well-being and cultural life that contributed so much to the communal life of Leipzig. Whether as scientists, artists, medical doctors, industrialists or businessmen, the Jewish citizens of Leipzig proved themselves to be initiators and catalysts in the promotion of Leipzig's excellence. They served not only their own city but were instrumental in promoting its importance internationally.

1887: Henri Hinrichsen joins C. F. Peters

Sound business sense decreed that the inexperienced and untrained young Henri Hinrichsen should not immediately become his uncle's right-hand man. It was, and still is, customary throughout the music-publishing profession in Germany that the young heir to a business should first of all follow several different, but allied, apprenticeships before entering his father's company. Henri embarked upon his apprenticeship. His uncle had done the same thing thirty years earlier in the 1860s; three of his sons, my father and two of his brothers, would undertake similar apprenticeships in the 1930s; and their children, my American cousin and myself, would also follow the same path in the 1950s.

Henri was to acquire necessary business experience and become acquainted with and learn to understand his future clients, the retailers; he needed to learn about methods of publishing and about different types of retailing. His first apprenticeship was 20 months in Basel, where he felt ill at ease in the reserved and old-fashioned Swiss town; being German and a Jew were definite social disadvantages. In 1889, he went to Brussels for a year, where he was happier in this more relaxed atmosphere. There he forged deep friendships with a family on whom he was to rely during the last terrible year of his life some fifty years later. Then he spent some months in London, where he got an insight into the workings of C. F. Peters' agent in England, the music publisher Augener & Co., and forged lasting friendships with the Augener family.

On 15 May 1891, he finally entered C. F. Peters, Leipzig, as Dr Max Abraham's right-hand man. He took to the business with the enthusiasm of youth coupled with a profound interest in and love of music. He also involved himself eagerly with his uncle's philanthropic ventures. One of his first contributions, along with his uncle, was towards a splendid monument in honour of that great promoter of music in Leipzig, Felix Mendelssohn-Bartholdy. Mendelssohn was the grandson of the famous Jewish philosopher of the Enlightenment, Moses Mendelssohn (1789–1826). He had fought against religious intolerance and the anti-Semitic excesses of the eighteenth century. His son, Abraham (1776–1835), had worked in Paris as a banker and then moved to Berlin where Felix was born in 1809. In 1816, Abraham Mendelssohn had followed his brother's advice and had his children baptized, adding the name Bartholdy as an outward sign of Christian conversion. The family was affluent and followed a Christian lifestyle, enabling Felix to indulge in his passion for music and the arts.

It had taken many years to collect the huge sum of money necessary to construct the substantial and elaborate monument, which was unveiled on 26 May 1892. In his speech on its inauguration, the director of the Conservatory of Music said: 'This monument is presented to the City of Leipzig. She should take care of it in the gratitude, which the city owes to him whose name we speak with love and honour.' This was a worthy sentiment but one which was expressed in vain.

1894: Foundation of the Peters Music Library

Dr Max Abraham recognized his nephew's talents, and his dedication to the ideals on which he had built the reputation of C. F. Peters, when he named Henri Hinrichsen his partner and heir only four years later, in 1894. The new heir was granted Leipzig citizenship that year – a necessity for those wishing to make their home in the city.

1894 was an important year of philanthropy for Abraham and Hinrichsen. Leipzig had been acknowledged as a centre of musical life in Germany since the beginning of the eighteenth century and the city was the heart of the music publishing industry and of the book and printing trades. However, it was lacking one vital element – a really comprehensive and freely accessible music library. Dr Max Abraham was well aware of these shortcomings and had long wanted to improve the situation. When a splendid private music library came up for sale in 1891, he purchased it and, under the name of the Peters Music Library, made it available on indefinite loan to the Music Department of the Library of the City of Leipzig. The inspiration for this act of magnanimity came from Abraham's nephew, Privy Councillor Dr Edgar von Ubisch, a man to whom compiling a collection was a passion. Ubich became the Director of the Berlin Armoury in 1895, retiring in 1911, during which time he assembled the most comprehensive collection of medals in Germany for the museum.

Max Abraham had purchased 26 Königstrasse (now Goldschmidt Strasse) for his charitable women's institution in 1872 and now the ground floor would house the Peters Music Library. The festive opening of the Peters Music Library took place on 2 January 1894 in the presence of the mayor, many representatives of Leipzig's cultural institutions as well as musicians and music publishers. This was to be a free Reference Library, open to all, i.e., a public library. The opening caused a sensation both in Germany and throughout the world. It was the first such institution accessible to all, even to women, which at the time was not a matter of course. Both Max Abraham and Henri Hinrichsen subsequently added hundreds of books, manuscripts pictures and composers' letters to this splendid collection every year and assumed responsibility for its upkeep and for the salary of the Chief Librarian.

1898: Henri Hinrichsen marries Martha Bendix

Henri Hinrichsen was still a bachelor whose interests were concentrated in the business; romance had never entered his life. But one sunny day this solitary and dedicated life was to erupt into an unexpected passion. Henri met his bride, Martha Bendix, on 29 July 1897, whilst both were on holiday in the Bohemian spa town of Carlsbad. Henri was taking the waters with his uncle and Martha was there with her father. What initially attracted the 30-year-old to this fresh, innocent 18-year-old girl from Berlin would have been her blue eyes, set in

Fig. 13 Wedding of Martha (b. Bendix) and Henri Hinrichsen.
6 March 1898. The author's grandparents.

a peaches-and-cream complexion, surrounded by a halo of blonde, gently curling hair. They fell deeply in love and, on return to their separate homes, wrote to each other almost daily, Henri took every opportunity to visit Berlin. They had known each other barely five weeks when, on 4 September, they became officially engaged. Martha paid her first visit to Leipzig ten weeks later.

On 6 March 1898, Henri Hinrichsen married his charming and intelligent sweetheart (Fig. 13). Theirs was a love match from the outset and was to become a happy and rewarding marriage lasting more than forty years, and producing seven children – five sons and two daughters – their three eldest sons would follow their father into the business of C. F. Peters.

Martha Bendix was born in Berlin on 2 March 1879, the second of four children of Jewish parents. She had three brothers: Friedrich Moritz (called Fritz), Kurt and Otto. Their parents were Waldemar (1849–1924) and Bertha (born Katz) Bendix (1855–1920). Waldemar, like his father, was a leading member of the executive of the Reform Community; his wife, Bertha Katz, was the daughter of a banker.

Waldemar Bendix's orientation was a strange mixture of prophetic Judaism and puritan Presbyterianism, which had impressed him deeply when he had spent his apprentice year in Scotland. It was a source of pride in the family that Waldemar Bendix's sister Marie's husband, Hermann Senator, was a personal physician to the old Empress Augusta Victoria, wife of Emperor Wilhelm I.

The Bendix family name was originally Elkisch, after the town from which they came, Elkisch, near Krakau in Poland. They moved to Berlin around 1700 when Waldemar's grandfather, Bendix Joseph Elkisch (1777–1864), changed his surname to Bendix.[4] He owned a linen mill, Bendix & Co., located at Sorau a hundred or so miles east of Berlin, which he had bought in 1835 from a distant relative who had founded it in 1805. His son Moritz Bendix (1812–73), one of the founders of the Jewish Reform Movement in Berlin, inherited this business, which passed to his son Waldemar, Martha's father. The family had held German nationality from 1809 onwards.

Martha and her three brothers grew up in a home run according to strict ethical rules; all Jewish holidays were kept and synagogue was attended regularly. Her father was very much a family man – and he ruled his family. He was a proud man who instilled a great deal of pride into his children, especially into his daughter. Her mother, Bertha, was a refined and cultured lady who played the piano well and ran her household in an exemplary manner. She too was brought up strictly, by her older sister Clara (1838–1917)[5] and her husband Leopold Jacobi (1830–95), a banker in Hamburg, her parents having died when she was young. Clara and Leopold Jacobi had four daughters, one of whom, Alice, married Henri Hinrichsen's brother Max in Hamburg in 1892.

Waldemar and Bertha Bendix had a strong concern for those who worked with and for them and with the disadvantaged in general. This attitude of care and concern for others was a tremendous influence

---

4 The Berliner *Judenbürgerbuch* (Berlin Register of Jewish Citizens) in Berlin Stadtarchiv – Berlin City Archive tells us that he attained Berlin Civic Rights on 9.4.1809 under his complete name of Bendix Joseph Levy (Leib) Cohn (Kaz) Elkisch. He received a new Certificate of Citizenship on 20 January 1843 in the family name of Bendix and first names of Elkisch Joseph, this name having been legalized by Royal Cabinet Order of 22 May 1842 and legitimated by a certificate from the Police President's Office on 29 July 1842.

5 Clara and Bertha Katz's mother was Philipine Katz – born Mond – whose brother, Meyer Bär Mond, was the father of Ludwig Mond who emigrated to, England and whose son, Alfred Mond (1863–1930), became the first Lord Melchett. Another of the Jacobi's daughters, Flora, married Edwin Sachs and emigrated to England; their son became the Right Honourable Eric Sachs (1898–1979), a High Court Judge.

on their daughter Martha throughout her life. She always sought out people in need and, when financial help was required she had a way of convincing the recipients that they had done something important and that they had earned their 'reward'. Thus the gift was never considered to be charity.

The marriage of Martha Bendix to Henri Hinrichsen in Berlin was, as such events are, the occasion for a great family gathering. There were many relatives from Berlin. The groom's extended family came from Hamburg: his parents, Robert and Betty Hinrichsen, his uncles, his younger brother Edmund – who would inherit the family corset factory in Hamburg – and his older brother Max, the Hamburg High Court judge with his wife Alice and her relatives, the Katz family. (Two brothers, Henri and Max Hinrichsen, had now both married daughters of the two sisters – Bertha and Clara Katz; hence the Bendix and Hinrichsen families were twice related). Uncles and aunts came from Danzig, birthplace of Henri's mother Betty and her brother Dr Max Abraham, and elsewhere. All the employees from Bendix & Co. were invited; their spokesman made a charming speech in praise of the bride who had always been a welcome visitor to the factory. An indication of Waldemar Bendix's concern for others is that, not having been required to pay a dowry on his daughter's marriage, he decided to contribute the money thus saved towards the welfare of his employees. He established a fully paid health insurance scheme for them instead.

From then onwards, there was to be a close interchange between Leipzig, Hamburg and Berlin. The new and growing Hinrichsen family in Leipzig would frequently visit their relatives in the other two towns; and the unborn Berlin and Hamburg cousins were later to become frequent, welcome visitors in the loving home to be created by Henri and Martha Hinrichsen in Leipzig.

Henri Hinrichsen's upbringing, in contrast to his wife's, having been much more relaxed in religious terms, the new Hinrichsen household was not run according to Jewish beliefs. In all things, the Hinrichsen family belonged to the cultured German elite of Leipzig society; they had little contact with the 15,000 strong Jewish community, whose members were largely of East European origin. The new couple's first home was an apartment on the second floor of the elegant house, 8 Stephanstrasse in Leipzig, with its beautiful balcony and view over the Johannistal. Here, their first child, a daughter, Charlotte, was born on 27 December 1898.

In October 1900, the little family moved to live with Dr Max Abraham in the C. F. Peters Music Publishing house, 10 Talstrasse, occupying the second floor apartment. This was the property that Max Abraham had commissioned in 1873 when the success of Edition

Peters necessitated larger premises. The architect, Otto Brückewald, who also designed Wagner's Bayreuth Festival House, was commissioned to build him a suitable property, in classic style. C. F. Peters, Leipzig had moved into its new home at 29a Talstrasse (Valley Street) in August 1874. The street was subsequently renumbered making the address 10 Talstrasse.

By the time Henri and Martha moved in, Dr Abraham was already seriously ill. It was characteristic of him, in spite of his wealth which he distributed so generously, that he lived modestly, in almost Spartan-like rooms, furnished in great simplicity. Here, in the early years, he used to enjoy entertaining young musicians. But this pleasure declined as his illness, an advanced asthmatic condition with complications, combined with acute eye problems, became more severe, until the only person he welcomed was his nephew, Henri Hinrichsen.

The centenary celebration of the foundation of C. F. Peters took place on 1 December 1900. Dr Abraham, seriously ill, nevertheless took part in the celebrations. Delegates came from the Gewandhaus, the Leipzig Conservatory of Music, the University of Leipzig, the city of Leipzig council, as well as many professional colleagues, friends and suppliers; messages of congratulations were received from around the world.

1900: Death of Max Abraham – Henri Hinrichsen takes over C. F. Peters

On 8 December 1900, Dr Max Abraham, aged 70, the pain of his illness having become insupportable to him, died by his own hand. The official funeral was held at the Leipzig cemetery but the burial of a suicide was not permitted in consecrated ground. As he had expressed a wish to be cremated and as there was no crematorium in Leipzig at the time, his remains were transported to Gotha for incineration and burial. Some years later his ashes were exhumed and re-interred in Leipzig, in the family burial plot which Henri Hinrichsen was to purchase for his family in 1909 in the Christian South Cemetery. To honour his memory in a public manner, in 1910 the Leipzig town council authorized a street to be named after him – the Abraham Strasse. However, when the Nazis came to power, they could not leave even the memory of a dead Jew to rest in peace and in 1935 renamed the street Robert-Naumann Strasse.

The other tangible memorial to Dr Max Abraham was the sculpture that his nephew Henri Hinrichsen commissioned from the well-known sculptor, Carl Seffner. This was taken from Abraham's death mask and placed in the Peters Music Library.

When Dr Abraham died, the enveloping mantle of family tradition and responsibility settled on the slim shoulders of the 32-year-old Henri Hinrichsen. He had formidable antecedents. From his ancestor, the martyred Henrique de Milão of Lisbon, through the enterprising Alvaro Dinis, founder of the Jewish community of Glückstadt, through generations of court financiers in Schwerin, to his grandfather, Adolph Hinrichsen, founder of a corset factory in Hamburg and his father, a leading member of the Sephardic Community there and fighter for Jewish emancipation. Henri Hinrichsen's education and training had prepared him for the life ahead; he was able to step into his uncle's shoes as though they had been made to measure. With the business of C. F. Peters, Henri Hinrichsen also inherited monumental obligations and debts which Dr Max Abraham had run up to finance his huge publishing endeavours and his support of the Peters Music Library and many charitable organizations. The new owner was determined to honour all of his predecessor's obligations and it was to take many years before he could pay off all the debts, the worry causing him severe nervous problems throughout his life.

CHAPTER EIGHT

1900–1918: Stability, Citizenship and War

Henri Hinrichsen was a tall, handsome man, of upright posture. With his black hair and beard and his dark brown eyes, he resembled a Spanish nobleman. He was proud of having been descended from a Sephardic dynasty, though he was not a practising Jew. Born in Hamburg, he spoke an educated and attractive Hamburg dialect. He was well dressed and in his breast pocket would carry a silver toothpick which he would use after meals. He had been brought up to respect all people and was always courteous and friendly, whilst still maintaining a distinctive formality.

1901: Birth of Max Hinrichsen

In 1901, with the next member of their growing family imminent, the Hinrichsens incorporated the rooms of the first floor apartment into their home. Their second child and first son Max (my father) – named after his great-uncle, Max Abraham – was born on 6 July 1901 (Fig. 14). The united Germany into which Max was born, whilst not perfect, was certainly bearable, especially for the affluent Jews. His father felt distinctly hopeful that anti-Semitism no longer constituted a social barrier.

As a music publisher, Henri Hinrichsen emulated his uncle to perfection, so that Edvard Grieg wrote to him that he was 'truly the resurrected Dr Abraham personified'. Like his uncle, he was always ready to embrace the newest technology and ideas. When the *Genossenschaft Deutscher Tonsetzer* (Cooperative of German Composers) was founded in 1903 at the instigation of Richard Strauss, Henri Hinrichsen was the only music publisher to join this organization for the protection of composers' copyright. He gave as his reason that he always wanted to

Fig. 14 1903 Charlotte (b.1898) and Max (b.1901) Hinrichsen.
The author's aunt and father.

make the artist's life in general more bearable. This was certainly a credo he lived up to at all times.

C. F. Peters' composers continued to enjoy the cordial relationships established over the years with Dr Max Abraham without a break on his death, the new owner accepting all the existing responsibilities. Having known Edvard Grieg for some twelve years, it seemed natural for Henri Hinrichsen to take on the same role of 'adoptive father' and friend as his uncle had done. The friendship and confidence between the two men was as sincere as that between Grieg and Dr Abraham had been. Hinrichsen continued to pay for some of Grieg's holidays, and sometimes to go with him, and was generous with presents and financial support. The composer enjoyed his visits to his publisher's house that took on a new dimension which delighted Edvard and Nina Grieg whenever the Hinrichsens added a new baby to their family. Childless themselves, the Griegs took a great delight in the publisher's children and followed their lives with interest (Fig. 15).

In 1904, the year the Hinrichsen's third child (a daughter named Ilse) was born, Henri Hinrichsen became one of the founder members of the LBA – the *Leipziger Bibliophilen Abend* (Leipzig Bibliophiles' Evening). With his experience of printing and graphic arts and his interest in all aspects of the printing, publishing and book trades, he welcomed the formation of this society. The constitution of the society limited the number of members to 99 men – hence its nickname 'The Ninety-niners'.[1] Two thirds of these were either publishers,

---

1 For a more detailed account, see *Music Publishing and Patronage*.

Fig. 15 1903. Paul Ollendorf, Edvard Grieg, Nina Grieg, Martha Hinrichsen,
    Henri Hinrichsen in 10 Talstrasse, home of the Hinrichsen family.

proprietors of printing works, book designers, book dealers and anti-
quarians, worked as librarians or were professors. Henri Hinrichsen
counted several of these amongst his closest friends.

With a growing family and expanding business, a complete refurbishment and enlargement of 10 Talstrasse was put into effect in
1905. Henri Hinrichsen took the opportunity to commission a new
'Florentine' front door (Fig. 16).

Anti-Semitism amongst the cultured elite of Leipzig society in the
first years of the twentieth century was not a problem. However, the
Jewish middle classes, through their enterprise and desire for success,
were the butt of much jealousy and anti-Semitic feeling. Since the final
two decades of the nineteenth century, several Jewish entrepreneurs
had established department stores. These proved to be popular with
the citizens as a whole as they offered good value for money. They did,
however, become the cause of much envy to the German small shopkeepers, who complained that the Jews were depriving them of their
livelihood. Over 60 per cent of the Jews in Leipzig were in professions
– as lawyers, medical doctors and artists – but most were in business as
fur traders, shopkeepers or department store owners. Far from depriving other citizens of a livelihood, many of the Jewish entrepreneurs

Fig. 16 1905. New Florentine door for 10 Talstrasse. [Photo C. F. Peters]

gave much to Leipzig, for which the city owed them an immense debt of gratitude. Several of them were generous benefactors to various Leipzig institutions and projects, none more so than Henri Hinrichsen.

Like Dr Max Abraham, Henri had a profoundly developed social conscience, and was fully supported by his wife. As he became wealthy through the sound publishing policies that he was following with C. F. Peters, so he became more involved with the needs of people less fortunate than himself. As a member of the committee of several charities, he was a generous supporter of many worthy causes and gifted individuals and established himself as one of the leading citizens. The spectrum of Henri Hinrichsen's more than thirty years of voluntary activity displays the many-sided aspects of his political, social and cultural involvement with the city of Leipzig. Between 1900 and 1933, he was a member of more than eighty associations. This level of involvement was not uncommon amongst the better-off and socially conscientious educated classes of Germany at the time. His interests can be broadly encompassed in four groups: professional associations connected with publishing and printing, in which he was generally an active member of the committee; various associations connected with music and composers; many associations covering education and the arts; and charitable organizations, both Jewish and non-Jewish, to which he was a generous benefactor. Much of his involvement, other than that with professional associations, was with local organizations.

Local involvement and patronage

He was active in local politics as a long-term local councillor. Elected by the community on 2 January 1911, he remained in office until the end of 1919, during which time his business expertise was much in evidence. He was active on various sub-committees, such as the one covering unemployment benefit, and at various times was chairman of the Transport Committee and the Chamber of Commerce for Trade and Industry, amongst others. One of his major voluntary activities was as a judge in trade disputes. He was also active and generous in the support of Leipzig's poor.

Henri and Martha Hinrichsen were conventional, totally assimilated and definitely a part of the establishment – which in Leipzig was known as the *Bildungsbürgertum* (the bourgeois educated classes, or intelligentsia). They were also supportive of feminist ideals, which then were generally not regarded worthy of any consideration, and they had a great concern for the education of women at a time when this was generally considered to be of little importance. They saw education not only in academic terms but also for the less intellectual working-class women as the learning of skills. After Dr Max Abraham's death, Henri Hinrichsen continued fully to support the *Frauen Gewerbeverein* (Women's Trade Association) which his uncle had founded. He also sponsored a kindergarten in a working-class area of Leipzig which was free of charge – unique at that time in Leipzig.

Martha Hinrichsen, to whom her husband referred as 'the power behind the throne', had a great deal of sympathy with the problems of women's rights and needs. She took her place on the committee of the *Frauen Gewerbeverein* in 1899 and persuaded her husband to make further huge donations towards the upkeep of the house, 26 Königstrasse, and towards furthering the aims of this charitable association.

1907: Decorated by Kaiser Wilhelm II

Henri Hinrichsen, a fervent German patriot, was a great admirer of the Kaiser, which might be seen as a rare lapse in his otherwise excellent judgement. Kaiser Wilhelm II, born in 1859, became German emperor and king of Prussia in 1888. He dismissed Chancellor Otto von Bismark, the architect of modern Germany, in 1890 and began a long period of personal rule. He was bombastic, self-opinionated and a difficult man to deal with. Whilst he had a strong character, his personality was weak and, possibly as a compensation for his withered arm, he enjoyed dressing up in a variety of gaudy uniforms which he would design himself. He did not like Jews, whom he considered as the parasites of his empire, but he nonetheless used them when it suited his purpose and counted several prominent, wealthy Jews amongst his advisers and associates. He accepted their hospitality and socialized with them when he felt it would benefit him but he never invited their wives to accompany them when he issued the invitations.

When Kaiser Wilhelm II commissioned the *Volksliederbuch für Männerchor* ('Folk Song Book for Male Voice Choir'), also known as the *Kaiserliederbuch* ('Emperor's Song Book'), Henri Hinrichsen put in his bid.[2] It represented a huge financial investment for C. F. Peters but, with its publication, he was demonstrating his confidence in the German nation. It was one of his early and most prestigious publications. The book was superbly produced in the Edition Peters and was reasonably priced, which probably helped lead to its enormous popularity. The *Volksliederbuch für Männerchor* appeared on 6 February 1907 and was presented to the Kaiser at a special celebration in the palace in Berlin by seven of the gentlemen of the Commission for the Folk Song Book. As the publisher and investor, Henri Hinrichsen was invited to the Royal Palace in Berlin to take part in the presentation ceremony.

Full of the excitement of the event, he immediately telephoned Martha in Leipzig. The connection was poor; she was not satisfied with his telephone description and asked him to write it all down in a letter. Henri was particularly concerned that His Highness should not feel offended because, like the Kaiser, he himself was wearing a pince-nez. The letter described the entire event and the 20-minute speech given by the Kaiser. Wilhelm II had said that music was for him the highest and noblest of the arts and he noticed to his regret that in Frankfurt the ability to read music was diminishing and he was afraid that folk songs would become completely forgotten. This was the reason for which he had commissioned this book. He gave his opinion that the attraction of the common people to alcohol would be reduced through singing; if people had sung for three hours, however, they could certainly be rewarded with a few glasses of wine. Henri Hinrichsen was thrilled that the Kaiser then engaged him in a long conversation and presented him with a medal – the *Kronenorden* (Order of the Crown) Third Class; the third-class award was for Jews – gentiles received first-class awards.

---

2 Fully documented in *Music Publishing and Patronage*.

1907 also saw two events of family significance. Associated with the Hinrichsen family and with the firm of C. F. Peters for over 40 years, the composer Edvard Grieg died aged 64. It was a sad loss, both personally to the family and in business terms, as Grieg had been the publisher's most prized composer. However, the deep friendship between Henri Hinrichsen and the composer's widow Nina continued and he supported her financially until her death in 1935.

Life is constantly renewed and Martha Hinrichsen gave birth to their fourth child, a son whom they named Walter, within weeks of Edvard Grieg's death. Thirty-six years later, it was Walter who, as a US military officer, was to become the champion of his brothers and sisters after the Holocaust had devastated the family.

1909: Purchase of a family burial plot in the Christian Cemetery

Robert Hinrichsen, Henri's father, had purchased an elegant family burial plot in the Christian Ohlsdorf cemetery in Hamburg for his parents and his Hamburg descendants. Henri himself, being conscious of his citizenship of Leipzig and not being an active member of the Jewish community, decided to purchase his own family burial plot in the recently consecrated Christian Süd Friedhof (South Cemetery) in Leipzig in 1909. He was the first Jew to do so and, when his uncle Dr Max Abraham's remains were transferred from Gotha by special dispensation, they became the first Jewish remains to be interred there. In choosing to have an urn burial plot, Henri Hinrichsen was at the forefront of the new development of cremation at a time when less than 4 per cent of the population chose this method of burial, of which the Jewish Rabbinate did not approve. This would prove to be a prophetic choice at a time when cremation was still relatively rare. As one of the first to purchase a site and conscious of his position in society, he selected Plot No. 18, one of the most prominent. It was right next to the wide central pathway leading to the chapel and the crematorium, near the north entrance, which was overlooked by the Völkerschlachtdenkmal, then still under construction.

In recognition of his considerable financial contribution to the production of the *Folk Song Book for Male Voice Choir* and for his charitable work in many spheres, Henri Hinrichsen was honoured with the title of Kommerzienrat, on 29 May 1911. On 26 October 1916, this title was elevated to that of Geheimer Kommerzienrat (Privy Councillor), generally shortened to Geheimrat. It was the Kaiser who conferred these titles on distinguished businessmen, financiers and industrialists in

Fig. 17 1919. Henriette Goldschmidt 1825–1920. Founder of the first
All Women's College in Germany, sponsored by Henri Hinrichsen.

Germany.[3] Henri's title gave him a certain dignity and as a mark of
respect he was henceforth always addressed as Herr Geheimrat, which
honour confirmed his acceptance in German society.

My grandfather had a strong moral code which encompassed his
investment strategy. He would neither borrow nor lend money. He did
not invest in stocks and shares but in his own business. He committed
the profits that he made over and above his business and family needs
to the needs of others and to the many charities, individuals and organizations that he supported or sponsored.

1911: Sponsor of education for women

From the time of his arrival in Leipzig, when he came under the
influence of his uncle, Max Abraham, and even before he became
father to seven children, Henri Hinrichsen developed a deep interest
in and involvement with education, especially for women. Though he
was a business man and music publisher, he felt equally at home
amongst academics and intellectuals. He naturally inclined towards
belonging to the bourgeois intelligentsia – people who met to talk

---

3 The titles were no longer conferred after the Kaiser's abdication in 1918.

about ideas, philosophy, books, art, music, education and social welfare. It was as part of this group that he first came in contact with Henriette Goldschmidt (1825–1920) (Fig. 17) and became very impressed by her inspirational ideas on the education of women. By 1910, having been able to fulfil all of the financial obligations that he had inherited from his uncle, he had amassed a sizeable sum and was keen to invest it in an educational project for women. He became the founding benefactor and long-time sponsor of the first all-women's college in Germany: the Henriette Goldschmidt Schule.[4]

The plot of land at 18–20 Königstrasse that Henri Hinrichsen had bought for the construction of the college was along the same street as the Peters Music Library house, which was at number 26. The C. F. Peters' office and the family home at 10 Talstrasse were around the corner and the warehouse in the Lindenstrasse, around the next corner, was attached to this. In fact, the three roads bordered the properties, the gardens of all the properties adjoined and there was a constant communication between the different establishments.

The aims of the college were high: first, to give women a thorough grounding in the educational profession of motherhood; secondly, to equip them to devote themselves to the many-faceted general duties which they would encounter within the community, the state and society, in the broadest terms and with a full understanding for the requirements of the present. There were weekly open-evening lectures, which outsiders were invited to attend; Henri Hinrichsen made a point of being present whenever possible. Unfortunately, with the changes in society over the years, the college did not long follow in the ways in which Henriette Goldschmidt and Henri Hinrichsen had envisioned; though he did not welcome the changes, the publisher continued to support the college with generous donations. Later, both of his daughters would complete their education there, qualifying as kindergarten teachers.

Henri Hinrichsen's involvement with the education of women was only one expression of his desire to devote the profits from his publications to the betterment of the lives of others. He was as concerned for the interests of composers as he was for the correct conduct of business. He generously supported the workaholic, alcoholic composer Max Reger for the last ten years of the composer's life. He helped Christian Sinding and Hans Pfitzner, amongst others, with frequent payments well over and above what they had earned when he knew they were in financial need. And he cared for composers',

---

4 Fully covered in *Music Publishing and Patronage.*

colleagues' and employees' widows after their husbands' deaths. This support was particularly important to them during and after World War I when their resources were depleted and inflation was rampant.[5]

The Hinrichsens' fifth child, a son whom they named Hans-Joachim, was born in 1909 and their sixth, Paul, was born in 1912. (Hans-Joachim would eventually study law, whilst his younger brother wanted to farm in Brazil.) By then, Martha and Henri's four elder children had been at school for some years. When the first Jewish High School was opened in 1912, they made a conscious decision not to allow their children to be educationally segregated but to give them the advantages of the full German educational system.

1913: The Völkerschlachtdenkmal

Henri Hinrichsen was pleased when, as a member of the Leipzig town council, he met the Kaiser again, some six years after his first meeting. The occasion, which Kaiser Wilhelm II attended, was the inauguration of the Völkerschlachtdenkmal (the Memorial to the Battle of the Nations) on 18 October 1913, the centenary of the battle that had taken place outside Leipzig on 18 October 1813 when Napoleon's troops had been thoroughly routed. Other monarchs present included King Frederich Augustus III of Saxony, Archduke Franz Ferdinand of Austria, Grand Prince Kyrill Wladimirowitsch of Russia, Prince Wilhelm of Sweden – all of whose armies had taken part in the battle – as well as the princes of almost all the German States.

This colossal monument, the largest in the world at the time, grandiosely proclaims the might of the German empire. Everything about the Völkerschlachtdenkmal is on a vast scale. Three concepts were incorporated in the three main parts. The visitor is introduced to the events being commemorated at the foot of the monument: between the two supporting walls at either side there is a sculpture in relief measuring 19 metres high by 16 metres wide, depicting a battle scene; St Michael stands 11.6 m high at the centre. Gigantic sphinx-like heads of barbarians flank steep flights of steps at each side. The crypt is a memorial to the thousands killed in the battle of 1813. There was an eternal flame, destroyed during World War II and never replaced, huge statues watching over the dead and eight 5.5 m-high death masks. The middle section of the monument, the so-called Hall of Fame, houses four gigantic carved granite figures representing the characteristics of 'the German people during the war of liberty'; they

---

5 Some of these are well documented in *Music Publishing and Patronage*.

are 9.5 m tall and each weighs about 400 tons. There are also 96 carved human figures, each one different, framing the windows. A stone dome, measuring 28.86 m and embellished with 324 almost life-sized soldiers mounted on horses, is cast in concrete and finished in the finest detail. The third incorporated concept is shown in the circle of twelve 'watchmen' figures leaning on their swords, surrounding the outside of the dome, signifying the willingness of the people to fight for freedom; each figure is 12 m high and weighs 200 tons; they face in all directions. A 364-step spiral staircase goes from the crypt to the 91m high summit. Two hundred people can admire the view from the top. The whole structure took 15 years to build.

The inaugural festivities lasted several days. Hinrichsen was proud to have been a part of this grand patriotic venture to which he, like his uncle, Dr Max Abraham, had contributed financially – his name as a contributor was engraved on one of the brass plaques displayed inside the monument. His sense of patriotism did not end there. Some years later, he was able to combine this with his lifelong interest in art when he bought two paintings at auction commemorating the Battle of the Nations. He presented these to the City History Museum of Leipzig in 1927.

Autographs and paintings

Henri and Martha Hinrichsen had a hobby – they collected autographed letters of composers. All of their children became fascinated with their parents' collection and gradually each developed their own. Often Henri would give his wife or his children prized pieces on birthdays and special occasions. The Hinrichsens started their collections in 1902 with about a hundred of the letters that had been addressed to C. F. Peters and owned by Henri Hinrichsen. They included letters from Beethoven, Czerny, Spohr, Brahms, Grieg and Reger as well as from Meyerbeer, Weber, Wagner, Liszt, Mahler, R. Strauss, Schönberg and Sinding. These would be proudly and carefully shown to anybody who shared their owners' interest and enthusiasm in trying to read them. The collection was added to over the years by the purchase of rare and original letters and documents; some of the more choice items were from Gluck, Monteverdi, Gombart, Frescobaldi and Tartini. Later, in 1926, Henri Hinrichsen bought the entire collection of correspondence between the violinist Joseph Joachim and Brahms from Joachim's son (Dr Joachim of Göttingen) which he gave to his wife as a souvenir of the Handel Festival in Göttingen. An admirer of Hugo Wolf, in 1926 Henri Hinrichsen was delighted to be able to buy the complete collection of 230 letters from Wolf to Heinrich Potpeschnigg. When the opportunity arose in 1932 to buy a collection of about 40 letters from Hugo Wolf to Paul Müller, he bought that.[6] By 1933, the collection numbered about 370 pieces.

It was at this time that Henri Hinrichsen, always interested in art, started his collection of paintings. Whilst his interest was not exclusive, it centred itself on paintings by German masters of the nineteenth century and he became a discerning collector. He studied auction catalogues and bought wisely, not specifically for investment but for his own pleasure. He embellished his home with masterpieces by Adolph von Menzel, Adam Friedrich Oeser, Max Klinger, Hans Thoma, Wilhelm Leibl, Joseph Carl Stieler, Karl Spitzweg, Fritz von Uhde, Max Liebermann, Defregger, Feuerbach, Passini, and several others. Paintings by some more widely known painters included *Lucretia* by Lucas Cranach and a small painting by Gustav Courbet.[7] The collection included good portraits of the classical composers, which adorned the walls of the music room and Henri Hinrichsen's office, as well as some exquisite engravings and watercolours.

When the subject of a painting was a composer as closely linked to C. F. Peters as Ludwig van Beethoven, the publisher could not resist the opportunity to buy it. One particular portrait, however, had an even stronger claim to his interest, owing to a connection with Louis Spohr whose collaboration with C. F. Peters spanned some 50 years. This was the portrait of Beethoven painted by Joseph Carl Stieler in 1819–20 and is one of the best known of the many portraits of the composer. It was acquired by the brother of Louis Spohr at a raffle run by the Art Association of Brunswick. He valued the portrait highly because Stieler had assured him that he was the only painter to whom Beethoven had allowed sittings – and that only at the specific wish of

---

6 A competent accompanist on the piano and also a composer, Potpeschnigg was an Austrian dentist and close friend of Wolf's. The correspondence between Wolf and Potpeschnigg was edited by Heinz Nonveiller and published by the Union, Deutsche Verlagsgesellschaft, Stuttgart in 1923, before Henri Hinrichsen bought it. Müller was a grammar school teacher in Berlin, where he met Wolf in 1892. In 1895 he founded the Hugo Wolf Society in Berlin. Paul Müller (whose dates have not been ascertained) published *Erinnerungen an Hugo Wolf* (Memories of Hugo Wolf), which included extracts of some of the letters, in *Die Musik* Year 2 (1902/3), Vol. 12, pp. 428–40. He published a booklet, mainly about the Lieder, *Hugo Wolf*, in Berlin, 1904. *Ungedruckte Briefe von Hugo Wolf an Paul Müller aus den Jahren 1896–1898* (unpublished letters from Hugo Wolf to Paul Müller from 1896–1898) was published in the Peters Music Library Yearbook, Year 11, Leipzig, 1904.

7 The Lucas Cranach painting (the author is not certain whether this was Cranach father or son) was, like the others and the autograph collection, confiscated by the Nazis in 1939. The Courbet painting was taken out of Germany by Henri Hinrichsen's son Max in 1937, however, without a certificate of authenticity.

Fig. 18 Ludwig van Beethoven by Joseph Carl Stieler.
Purchased by Henri Hinrichsen in 1909.

the composer's friends and patrons, the Brentanos. It is understood to be a good likeness; only the hands had to be painted from memory as Beethoven could not be persuaded to sit any longer.

The Stieler portrait was treasured and well cared for in the Spohr household. Permission for reproductions was not given until 30 years after the painter's death and the firm of Hanfstaengl, who made lithographic reproductions, were not able to produce their 'Aquarel' print until 1907. On Spohr's death, the painting was inherited by his daughter Rosalie, the Countess Sauerma, a well-known harpist, from whom Henri Hinrichsen was able to buy it in 1909. It had pride of place as a symbol of the C. F. Peters tradition in his private music room in 10 Talstrasse.[8] (Fig. 18)

---

8 Carl Stieler's portrait of Beethoven was rescued from Leipzig in 1945 by Walter Hinrichsen and taken to the USA, where it hung in his office at C. F.Peters Corporation in New York. A copy was painted to replace it when the original was sold to the Beethoven House in Bonn in 1981, where it now hangs.

Fig. 19 c.1914. The Hinrichsen children
on the roof garden of 10 Talstrasse.

As one of the foremost music publishers and a music lover, Henri
Hinrichsen was a firm supporter of the Gewandhaus concerts and
always had a season ticket. However, he was extremely critical. If the
music did not please him, or if the performance was not up to the standard that he expected, he would leave. He abhorred wasting time. The
new Gewandhaus had been opened in 1884, just three years before his
arrival in Leipzig. The great Arthur Nikisch (1855–1922) was the
musical director of the Gewandhaus Orchestra, having taken over
from Carl Reinecke. Hinrichsen and Nikisch grew to have a good business relationship through the conductor's enthusiastic support for
Mahler, Reger and Richard Strauss whose music was published by C. F.
Peters. They also enjoyed a personal friendship, Nikisch being a frequent guest in the publisher's home. The performances under
Nikisch were of such a high standard that there was always a huge
demand for subscription tickets; it was jokingly put about that a
person's name had to be inscribed at birth in order to ensure a
season ticket in old age. The concerts themselves were not only artistic
experiences of the highest calibre but also impressive social occasions.
University academics, artists, scientists, intellectuals and publishers
would arrange to meet there. The audience would arrive punctually
to be in their places, settled and silently anticipating the concert,
minutes before the appearance of the conductor. Elegantly dressed,
they would parade in the foyer during the interval, conversing in rev-

erent whispers. But this genteel way of life was to be shattered with the outbreak of the Great War.

1914: Outbreak of World War I

When war broke out in 1914, more than ten thousand young German Jews were as keen to volunteer to fight for their fatherland as their non-Jewish compatriots were. By volunteering for war service before being called up, they hoped that they would finally be fully accepted into German society. Many of them were duly awarded for their bravery with the Iron Cross. Their hopes for full integration were fuelled by the Kaiser's speech in the Reichstag on August 4 when he proclaimed that differences of religion, political affiliation, class and ethnic origin no longer counted. Whilst the Jews were grudgingly welcomed in the army, they were not accepted as equals and there was considerable official anti-Semitism practised. The consequences of the war were disastrous for all the nations embroiled in it and it ultimately contributed nothing towards the full integration of the Jews into German society. As had historically been the aftermath of major disasters, much of the blame for the war was attributed to the Jews.

Henri Hinrichsen was 46 at the outbreak of war and hence too old to take part; his eldest son Max was only 13 but he helped towards the war effort as all children did. The staple diet in the Hinrichsen household as throughout Germany seems to have been swedes and turnips and the cook had to use all her ingenuity to present these loathsome vegetables in some palatable form. There was jubilation in the Hinrichsen household on the occasions when a very welcome parcel of butter and ham and other Scandinavian victuals would arrive from Nina Grieg to enhance the monotonous diet.

Nine months before the end of the war, Martha Hinrichsen gave birth to their last child, Robert, in February 1918. He was almost six years younger than Paul and nineteen years younger than his eldest sister, Lotte; his upbringing was more akin to that of an only child. He was not yet 15 when the Nazis were to come to power in 1933 and, as a Jewish child, he would be prevented from completing his schooling in Germany.

With the ending of the Great War, life was to change completely for everybody, not least for the family. The resulting political changes and attitudes formed with the advent of the Weimar Republic would lead to Henri Hinrichsen's role as a leading citizen of Leipzig taking on a different aspect.

Chapter Nine

1918–1933: The Weimar Republic and Patronage

By September 1918, Germany's defeat was inevitable, the country was impoverished, exhausted and on the verge of collapse. In November, the navy mutinied and an entirely spontaneous revolution occurred. The Kaiser, whose policies had contributed to the disaster of the war, fled to Holland and was forced to abdicate.

The uprising of the Workers' Movement, with its attendant strikes and demands for better working conditions, had far-reaching effects. Whilst Henri Hinrichsen was a good employer within the customs of the time, conditions in general for workers were poor, with long hours and low pay. The so-called November Revolution of 1918 was followed by changes in the relationship between proprietor and staff at C. F. Peters. Most of the employees joined the Union of Employees in the Book Trade and the Transport Workers Union. The introduction of the eight-hour working day led to the need for more staff, which doubled during the 1920s, though the turnover decreased. At the end of July 1919, the Union of Employees in the Book Trade called a strike for higher pay. The offices of C. F. Peters were closed for more than a week until the demands of the staff were met and all those who had been on strike were promised their jobs back.

1918–1921 was a period of revolution and counter-revolution, inflation and temporary stability, when the immediate consequences of defeat fell upon the German economy. The Kaiser's abdication in November 1918 was followed by the reluctant signing by Germany of the Treaty of Versailles and the allied ultimatum on reparations in May 1921. The worst inflation since the beginning of the war was in 1919. As usual the Jews were blamed for this and there were frequent clashes between Jews and anti-Semites, especially in Berlin. One of Germany's new political parties – the National Socialist German Workers' Party

(NSDAP), soon to be known as the Nazi Party – was formed and published its Manifesto in 1920 when the party had just 60 members. Point Four stated: 'None but members of the Nation may be citizens of the State. None but those of German blood, whatever their creed, may be members of the Nation. No Jew therefore may be a member of the Nation.' Nobody heeded this declaration of intent. One of the members who had drafted this Manifesto was a former soldier from the Western Front, Adolf Hitler. This rabble-rouser, who rose to become Chancellor of Germany and architect of the Holocaust, was at that time regarded as a political nonentity.

The year 1923 saw hyperinflation, followed by deflation; unemployment figures in Germany reached hundreds of thousands. The currency was valued at 1 billion marks to equal 1 gold mark. One US dollar equalled 4.20 gold marks. To put this into perspective, the first female employee at C. F. Peters, employed in 1915 when her weekly salary had been 20 marks, noted in her diary for Easter 1923 that she had received a salary of 80 billion marks for one week.

1923 is seen as the definitive year of the German inflation. When the Reichsbank eventually found itself unable to supply all the bank notes needed for the continuation of business, it was compelled to organize the printing of emergency money (*Notgeld*) by local authorities. The whole monetary structure of the Reich collapsed under a tidal wave of worthless paper. A new currency, the *Rentenmark*, was launched on 5 November 1923. All credit to the government ceased and the Reichsbank stopped discounting the treasury bills that had been the basis of the nation's finances since 1914. The disintegrating currency brought the first serious unemployment since the end of the war. By 1924, it was clear that big business was the principal winner in the inflation. The eight-hour day was suspended and rising unemployment strengthened the industrialists' advantage. During 1924–1928, the Weimar government promoted the interests of industry at the expense of the working class. So ultimately, on the restoration of stabilized monetary conditions, the main burden of reparations fell on the working classes.

C. F. Peters survived most of the problems brought about by the war and subsequent inflation, thanks to the astute forethought and planning of Henri Hinrichsen. In this he was supported by the collaboration of his suppliers on whom he had to rely for the promotion of his business. With the ending of the war and subsequent social revolution, the acumen of middle-class businessmen like Henri Hinrichsen was no longer welcome on town councils and so his term of office as town councillor came to an end. However, he was devoted to the city of Leipzig and placed his considerable talents to the benefit of other local organizations. Politically, like most Jewish voters, he supported the German Democratic Party (DDP) as a member, donating considerably more than the membership subscription. However, the gradual tendency towards the Right led, in common with many of the Jewish members, to his resignation in 1928. He had long supported many international trade organizations, which he continued to do.

A major focus of Henri Hinrichsen's voluntary activity was the Leipzig *Verkehrsverein* (Traffic and Transport Association). This body, founded in 1909 when it was concerned with flying and the flight trade, had as its objective 'Transport, especially tourism in Leipzig and general business services'. The concept of these organizations throughout Germany was to offer 'a mirror of the business prosperity of the city's population' in which the local businesses – in the case of Leipzig, the many book and music shops – trade unions and other organizations, were engaged.[1] During the 1920s, it was felt that stronger promotion of the *Verkehrsverein* was called for and so a magazine giving publicity to local events, theatres, concerts and reports on building projects, road works and cultural politics was circulated regularly. From 1924 onwards, Henri Hinrichsen was a member of the committee of management of the *Verkehrsverein* and he was still on the committee in 1930, even though he had offered his resignation in 1927, at the approach of his sixtieth birthday.

1920s: Family life in the Hinrichsen home

The 1920s probably comprised the period of greatest stability and assimilation that the Hinrichsen dynasty had known for 500 years. By the late 1920s, six of the Hinrichsen's seven children were in their teens and twenties (Fig. 20). By this time, they also had five cousins in Berlin and three second cousins in Hamburg of around the same age. The cousins were frequent and welcome guests in the large, friendly home in Leipzig. The household was quite formal and run to a routine. Martha and Henri each had their own study and children were seen by appointment. Martha would sit at her desk for many hours, attending to her charity and socially oriented activities. A couple of gentile women of reduced means would help with the secretarial work. She often appeared oppressed by the never-ending trail of paperwork on her desk. She also supervised the children's homework in this room and reviewed exercises prior to exams. In spite of her full schedule, she allotted a certain amount of time to be with each of her children separately every day.

---

1 The word *Verkehr* in German covers a multitude of concepts, including transport, traffic, business, company, socializing, contact, communication, intercourse, dealing, service, etc.

Fig. 20 1919. The Hinrichsen family in Leipzig.

She attended to her household and civic duties and shopping errands in the morning. Martha Hinrichsen dressed simply but had a certain style. She looked, though unfussy, every inch the Frau Geheimrat (Mrs Privy Councillor). Whilst she was firm and probably at times a bit too authoritarian, she was kind and loving and had a warm interest in everybody. The children and their cousins all adored and respected her. She was a very good hostess, though social life did not have the importance for her that it had for her husband. Most of all, she was intent on being fair and just. She loved to give presents. Martha Hinrichsen was always on the lookout to see how she could improve a person's life and stimulate further interest in them. She had a way of being able to encourage people, especially the young, to realize their full potential for their aptitude. She took great delight in helping her children, and her nephews and nieces who enjoyed her hobby of photography, to develop their talents. She can take the credit for encouraging Otto Bettmann,[2] a friend of the family, who went on to make a lifetime career in photography. He had fond recollections of Martha Hinrichsen, when he was in his nineties some seventy years later.

Henri Hinrichsen had his own private staircase from the family apartment and his office was jokingly called 'the inner sanctum'. It was quite large and well appointed. On the mantle stood the Beethoven mask sculpted by Max Klinger and over the fireplace hung Stieler's

2 Otto Bettmann (1904–1988) photojournalist, emigrated to the USA in 1935.
   He collected 'The Bettmann Archive' of over 12 million items and was Author of *The Good Old Days – They Were Terrible* and the autobiography of 1993, *Bettmann: The Picture Man*, and other works.

portrait of Beethoven. He was a man who enjoyed a well-ordered routine and precise ritual. Before the large midday family meal, he would embark on his morning constitutional, always well insulated against the vicissitudes of weather. At times he would invite one of his children or his guests, or some of the gentile ladies who worked for his wife, to accompany him. In bad weather he would walk on the roof garden and on rainy or stormy days he would march up and down on the large, covered terrace. He would walk briskly round and round the veranda, dressed in coat with upturned collar, hat and gloves, carrying his elegant cane.

Lunchtime in the Hinrichsen household had its own strict ritual. It was an ironclad rule that the children had to be home from wherever they had been at 1.15 pm when the hand-washing bell was rung and everybody made a mad dash for the bathrooms. Shortly before 1.30 pm, Mina the housekeeper sounded the big, brass gong and every-body – large and small – would repair to Henri Hinrichsen's study. There, he and his wife received them all for a few minutes before Mina would open the connecting dining room doors to announce ceremo-niously that luncheon was ready to be served. This meeting was usually the first occasion in the day when Henri met his younger children. He used to say jokingly that he could not tolerate children and guests before 1.00 pm. There were usually questions about the events of the day, some teasing and admonishing. Then all would march into the dining room in formal procession. Henri would sit at the head of the table, Martha to his right, guests and children seated according to their status and age; the youngest with their nanny or tutor would sit at the foot of the table.

The music room was the centre for much activity, especially when musicians or composers, like Edvard Grieg, came to visit. Another friend and frequent visitor was Arthur Nikisch, the popular conductor of the Gewandhaus orchestra, whose death in 1922 was mourned by all Leipzig. This was also where the family made music – each child learnt to play an instrument – and where Henri Hinrichsen enter-tained his music-loving friends. He loved playing the piano and one of his proudest possessions was the Steinway grand piano that he bought in 1921. He would regularly while away an hour or so each day on this beautiful instrument and he derived great pleasure from playing chamber music with his musical visitors and with his children. It was a great occasion for him when Gustav Mahler, on a visit to discuss the publication of his Fifth Symphony, sat down at the piano with his publisher and they played the four-handed version of a symphony by Bruckner together. Students from the Leipzig Conservatory of Music, several of whom he supported financially over the years, were regular visitors.

He was a member of the Committee of the Friends of the Leipzig Conservatory of Music and was generous with donations to the organization. When the Conservatory was suffering with dire financial problems in 1922, Henri Hinrichsen made a huge donation which was desperately needed if the Conservatory were to continue to function. In spite of this the Conservatory, mismanaged, was in a state of collapse in 1924 when there were new elections to the Board of Management. In recognition of the publisher's many years of involvement, financial support and business acumen, he was elected to the board. Although he deemed this an honour, he would not accept. He had already resigned from the committee, having suffered much unpleasantness because he felt that the ideals of the Conservatory had been eroded and that it was being totally mismanaged by several incompetent people. Unless the whole ethos of the Conservatory was to change, he had no further interest in any involvement. There was eventually an improvement, after which he accepted a place on the board.

Great music lovers that they were, Martha and Henri Hinrichsen held permanent subscriptions to the Gewandhaus concerts. The Gewandhaus was yet another of the institutions towards whom he extended generous patronage. Apart from lending financial support, in 1904 he commissioned a marble bust of Edvard Grieg from the highly regarded Leipzig sculptor Carl Seffner, which he presented to the Leipzig Gewandhaus[3] (Fig. 21).

Henri Hinrichsen also enjoyed his skat[4] evenings when card tables were set up in his office and in the music room. Drinks and snacks were served before the game which was itself followed by an elegant supper. Women and children were excluded from these totally masculine evenings.

The elegant and spacious family apartments were on the second and third floors over the business premises of C. F. Peters and so family and business life were closely integrated. The children grew up within the lively atmosphere of their father's business circle and of their mother's social concerns. Though there were servants in the household, these were regarded as part of the family and the children were brought up to respect all people as equals. The Hinrichsens were well off but they did not lavish money on their children and brought them up not to be wasteful. They imbued them with a social conscience which they each maintained in different ways throughout their lives.

All well brought up young people of the time attended dancing class. At home there were dances and suppers for the grown-up children;

---

3 Seffner's bust of Edvard Grieg was lost when the Gewandhaus was bombed during World War II.

4 Skat is a very popular card game.

Fig. 21 1904. Bust of Edvard Grieg by Carl Seffner, presented to the
Gewandhaus by Henri Hinrichsen. [Photo Gewandhaus zu Leipzig.]

they were called *Lämmerhüpfe* (lamb hops) and were only lightly chap-
eroned. The young people were mostly on their own with occasional
visits from their parents. By the time they reached their late teens the
children, as well as the visiting cousins, were included in the formal
dinner parties. At the end of the meal each person was served with a
finger bowl into which they would dip their fingertips and then deli-
cately brush their lips which they would then daub with huge napkins.

The garden, at some distance from the house, was a source of great
joy and relaxation to Henri Hinrichsen. Here he could lie in his
hammock, away from the cares of business and family and the jangling
telephone. Apart from a fish pond, there were fruit trees and a veg-
etable garden – a reliable source of provender for the large family that
sat at the table at 10 Talstrasse.

In 1917 Henri's father Robert Hinrichsen, owner of a corset factory
in Hamburg, died. His mother Betty, the vivacious and cultured lady
who had given her son his love of art and music, died in 1919; barely
a year later Martha Hinrichsen's mother Bertha died, leaving her
blind father, Waldemar Bendix, in Berlin. He was 71 and came to live
with the family in Leipzig. When he died in 1924, his ashes were
buried in the Christian South Cemetery in Leipzig alongside his wife's

in the Hinrichsen family burial plot. Within the space of seven years, the older generation had gone and Martha and Henri Hinrichsen took their place, as their own children grew to adulthood.

The 1920s were also a time of celebration. Relatives and friends from their Leipzig social and musical circle shared the Hinrichsens' celebration of their silver wedding anniversary on 6 March 1923. They were well aware of their good fortune and of the advantages and privileges they were able to provide for their children. In a typical gesture of generosity, they marked this family celebration by sharing some of their wealth with poor and disadvantaged children. Sending 500,000M to the mayor of Leipzig, Hinrichsen suggested that this could be spent on sending poor children to holiday-colonies during the long holidays, or on providing milk for them.

1920: Lotte Hinrichsen marries Dr Otto Sobernheim

The Hinrichsens' two daughters married during the 1920s. Charlotte (called Lotte), the eldest child, born in 1898, had enjoyed a conventional upbringing. At the age of 18 she attended the Henriette Goldschmidt School where she stayed for two years. She then went on an extended visit to her Bendix grandparents in Berlin where she met Dr Otto Sobernheim who was destined to become her husband. Otto was born in Berlin on 3 March, 1882, to Justizrat Dr Heinrich Sobernheim and his wife Elise, née Bütow. He had attended the French High School in Berlin and was in the Imperial Army during the Great War when his two younger brothers were killed on the Western Front in 1918. He studied in Freiburg, Baden, and received his doctorate of law. He chose a government legal career and after a few years became *Landgerichtsdirektor* (Supervisory Judge of the Prussian State Court) serving in *Landgericht I* in Berlin.

The wedding took place in Leipzig on 5 September 1920. The religious ceremony was interdenominational – Rabbi Goldmann, the chief rabbi of Leipzig, and a Protestant clergyman officiated. Lotte Hinrichsen said farewell to the parental home in Leipzig to create a new marital home with Dr Otto Sobernheim in Berlin. They had a son, Heinz, and two daughters[5] between 1921 and 1930.

1928: Ilse Hinrichsen marries Dr Ludwig Frankenthal

Ilse, the Hinrichsens' third child, born in 1904, also attended the Henriette Goldschmidt School, graduating as a qualified kinder-

---

5 Their names are withheld at their request.

Fig. 22 c.1926. Ilse Hinrichsen 1904–1987.

garten teacher. This was the start of an ongoing relationship with children which she maintained throughout her life. She often accompanied her father on trips abroad and to social occasions when her
mother was unavailable. Ilse was one of those people whose company
everybody enjoyed; she was always full of laughter and love for
mankind. On 8 November 1928, Ilse Hinrichsen married Dr Ludwig
Frankenthal (Figs 22 and 23) according to Jewish law in a ceremony
presided over by Rabbi Goldmann. Ilse and Dr Ludwig Frankenthal,
who lived in Leipzig, had two sons: Günther, born in 1929, and
Wolfgang, in 1931.

Ludwig Frankenthal, one of nine children, was born in Schwanfeld,
Bavaria on 27 November, 1885. He studied medicine at the universities of Munich and Berlin from 1906 to 1911 and qualified as a
medical doctor in 1911. After working in Hamburg and Berlin, he volunteered his services as a military surgeon in 1914 and was posted to
various military hospitals during the Great War where he was regarded
as a first-class surgeon and diagnostician. There he observed muscle
stresses and wrote numerous scientific papers on the treatment of
those buried alive and on oedematous diseases caused by gas which
led to his wide recognition and assured him a place in medical history.
He served at the Western Front without interruption from October
1914 until December 1918. The Kaiser awarded him the Iron Cross
First Class for his wartime military service in May 1915 and later he was
awarded the Iron Cross Second Class. (By then the Kaiser had
decided that the First Class award was only for non-Jews; Jews were to
receive the Second Class award.) He was also awarded the Hanseatic
Cross.

Fig. 23   c.1928. Dr Ludwig Frankenthal 1885–1944.

After the war, Dr Frankenthal took up a post in the largest surgical university clinic in Germany, in Leipzig, under the direction of Erwin Payr, during which time he published numerous papers. In 1928, together with the internist Pascal Deuel, he became the medical director of the new Jewish Hospital in Leipzig, founded by the Chaim Eitingon family. Both had received international renown. Frankenthal had by that time published over twenty important papers, which increased to around fifty by 1937. The work for which he will be mainly remembered is his disclosure in 1916–1918 of what is now known as the 'Crush Syndrome', appertaining to burial alive, resulting in muscle and kidney damage. He is regarded as the pioneer in this field. Martha and Henri Hinrichsen were happy to see their two daughters married to such fine and worthwhile men and hoped that their sons would also fall in love with the sort of women who would uphold their own high ideals. Sadly, hopes are not always rewarded.

1926: The Music Instruments Museum

Henri Hinrichsen continued to support the two causes close to his heart with tremendous enthusiasm and generosity: the Peters Music Library and the Henriette Goldschmidt School. They were at one and the same time educational and also designed to benefit people who would not otherwise have the opportunities offered by these institutes. They were also centres that contributed greatly to Leipzig's reputation as a focal point of culture and study. 1926 brought the opportunity for Henri Hinrichsen's third major sponsorship to benefit his adopted city of Leipzig: the purchase of the Heyer collection of 2,600 musical instruments to form the Music Instruments Museum and Music Research Institute of the University of Leipzig. This became the second largest museum of its sort in Europe. The Leipzig City Council could not afford the purchase price of 800,000M, of which one quarter (200,000M) was to be paid immediately, the rest being payable over ten years. So Hinrichsen offered to pay this sum if the council would fulfil the remainder of the obligation. In gratitude for his sponsorship, the main exhibition hall on the first floor of the Music Instruments Museum, which contained the rarest items in the collection, was named after the benefactor 'The Henri Hinrichsen Hall'. The grand inauguration of the Musicological Institute and the Music Instruments Museum of the University of Leipzig took place on 30 May 1929.[6]

Henri Hinrichsen's health was not good and, as was customary in Germany, he paid frequent visits to spa resorts where he received treatment for stress, for a delicate stomach condition and for his back problem. The responsibilities which he had taken on for many years were becoming too heavy, so he decided that his approaching sixtieth birthday was a suitable time to turn down further invitations to accept honorary duties and to relieve himself of some of those which he held. It was his contention that, after more than 30 years of voluntary service since 1894, he had more than fulfilled his civic duty towards his town and that it was now up to younger men to continue the good work.

However, he accepted the invitation onto the board of the Friends and Promoters of the University of Leipzig in May 1927 which he deemed a great honour and which would make no particular demands on his energies. As one of the foremost supporters, in 1930 he donated the money for the construction of a new Mensa (dining hall) at the university.

1928: Henri Hinrichsen's sixtieth birthday

In Germany, a sixtieth birthday has great importance. Resulting from Henri Hinrichsen's prominent position in Leipzig, in the musical world and as the centre of a large extended family, the festivities for his sixtieth birthday on 5 February 1928 were extended and multifaceted. The Mayor of Leipzig and Council sent fulsome congratulations and the town council commissioned an official portrait of him, for which the subject gave a number of sittings. The artist, Eduard Einschlag, born in Leipzig in 1879, was a well-known German portrait

---

6 The full story of the collection and of the Leipzig Music Instruments Museum is told in *Music Publishing and Patronage*.

painter. The portrait was to be hung in the Henriette Goldschmidt
School. There was a concert and speech day in his honour at the
school, which delighted him. Unhappily, when the portrait was finished he disliked it intensely and stayed away from the unveiling ceremony when the modernistic portrait was hung in the main hall. He
subsequently had it moved out of sight and commissioned a further
portrait, by Willy Geiger, at his own expense to replace it.

The staff at C. F. Peters laid on a celebration and produced a little
illustrated booklet entitled *Henri Hinrichsen. Ein Gedenkblatt zu seinem
60. Geburtstag* (Henri Hinrichsen: a Souvenir Booklet for his Sixtieth
Birthday). The birthday celebrations lasted for three days. There were
big formal gala dinners with speeches in his honour. The family celebrations included a performance by three of his nieces of dances to
Edvard Grieg's *Norwegian Dances.*

By 1928, the young adult Hinrichsens were no longer living at
home. Martha wrote to all her absent children regularly, telling each
what was happening at home, about the plays and concerts she and
their father had attended and her opinion of them, the books she had
read and who came to visit. She also told each one what all the others
were doing. In this way she laid the groundwork for sustaining a very
close-knit family. They maintained this concern for each other for the
rest of their lives; it offered them strength and it helped them to come
to terms with the horrors which they were to experience within the
next few years.

1929 saw Martha Hinrichsen's fiftieth birthday. With only the two
youngest children, Paul and Robert, still living at home, she had more
freedom to follow her own interests, reading and photography, and
she assembled an impressive archive of photographs of musicians
and composers. She could now also look forward to travelling with
her husband more often. To celebrate his wife's birthday, Henri
Hinrichsen took her to Paris in April 1929. In March 1930, they went
on the only cruise of their lives, to Rio, which they loved. And in May
1931 they went to London for a holiday. In earlier years holidays had
always been traditional family sojourns at seaside resorts in Germany,
or in the beautiful German countryside or mountains, when houses
would be rented and household staff accompanied the family.

1929: Honorary doctorate

1929 was a memorable year for Henri Hinrichsen. It saw the recognition of his thirty years of major sponsorship towards education in
Leipzig in the form of an honorary doctorate, awarded to him by the
Philosophical Faculty of Leipzig University on 27 February, 1929. The
citation reads:

With this certificate, the Faculty of Philosophy of the University of Leipzig names the proprietor of the Leipzig publishing house of C. F. Peters, Mr Geheimer Kommerzienrat Henri Hinrichsen, who has contributed so energetically to the improvement of education in Leipzig and who has done so much to further the development of musicology in Germany; who has earned himself untold recognition for the conscientious development of the famous Edition Peters, promoting German music throughout the world, an Honorary Doctor of Philosophy.

Leipzig, 27 February 1929.

The Dean,
Dr L. Lichtenstein.[7]

The new Dr h.c. Henri Hinrichsen was well aware of the great honour that had been bestowed upon him. He was the first German music publisher ever to have received this recognition. In his lengthy speech of acceptance he referred to this and added:

My connections with the Leipzig Alma Mater are not new. It is almost forty years since I, having been born in Hamburg, arrived in Leipzig. The day on which I became partner in the firm of C. F. Peters in 1894 was the day on which the then proprietor, Dr Max Abraham, opened the doors of the Peters Music Library, through which since then there has been a constant traffic of students of musicology. I have been watching over them for 28 years and delight in the lively participation of the students. This, my tie with the University, will from now on be an even stronger one, when the Music Instruments Museum – obtained from Cologne through the active participation of Professor Kroyer – names the *Cimeliensaal* [the hall containing the finest pieces] in my honour for all time. I will not refrain from expressing my most appreciative thanks also for this honour. . . .

Honours and hopes can be short-lived.

There was serious depression in Germany in 1929 and by 1932 six million people were out of work. The slump was to Adolf Hitler's advantage and his little-regarded National Socialist Party had grown in strength until in 1932 it was the second largest political party, with 107 deputies in the Reichstag (Parliament).

---

7 Dr Leon Lichtenstein (1878–1933), professor of mathematical physics.

1931: Max Hinrichsen becomes a partner in C. F. Peters

By this time the Hinrichsens' two eldest sons had grown up and
entered the business of C. F. Peters with their father. Max, the eldest,
born in 1901 and named after his great-uncle, Max Abraham, had
grown up with all the traditions of the family business in the full knowledge that this was to be his destiny. He felt very much at home with
this and always enjoyed being allowed to meet the composers and
others from the musical world who visited 10 Talstrasse. As a young
child, he sat on the knee of Edvard Grieg and, as a 15-year-old, he went
with Max Reger to meet friends after a visit to 10 Talstrasse, on the last
night of the composer's life. He had met Arthur Nikisch, Bruno
Walter, Arnold Schönberg, Gustav Mahler, Hans Pfitzner and many
more composers and musicians who visited the family home. Max was
educated at the Nicolai Gymnasium (Grammar School) in Leipzig
and for light relief his chosen instrument was the flute which he
played in an amateur orchestra.

Before entering C. F. Peters, Max underwent a long period of apprenticeship and training to acquaint himself with all the aspects involved
with music publishing and concert management. This started when he
was 18 when he went to Berlin. From there he transferred to Zürich in
1922. Then he went to the United States for four years, becoming
manager of the US distribution agency for C. F. Peters in New York from
1924 to 1927. His American experience taught him about the art of
advertising and publicity which he was able to apply to great advantage
after he joined his father in business. He would probably quite happily
have remained in the USA if Henri Hinrichsen had not sent him a
telegram urging him to return home to start work properly.

Once back in Leipzig, and after having found himself a bachelor
apartment, Max launched himself wholeheartedly into being his
father's right-hand man and took a lot of the work off his father's
shoulders. On 25 October 1928, he was officially granted power of
attorney to act for his father. He also became administrator of the
Peters Music Library and helped with the editing of the *Peters Music
Library Yearbooks*. Socially, Max had a circle of friends who comprised
the younger generation of publishers – the sons of his father's contemporaries; the friendly collaboration and rivalry which had existed
for so long following its natural progression continued with the next
generation. Never a sportsman, Max surprisingly took after his father
in that he learnt to enjoy horse riding, even to the extent of having to
get up early in the morning to get his ride in before work.

On the occasion of his thirtieth birthday on 6 July 1931, Henri
Hinrichsen took Max into equal partnership as co-proprietor of C. F.
Peters, Leipzig. By this time his father, who was 63 and in poor health,

Fig. 24 1931. The five Hinrichsen sons.
Standing: Robert, Paul, Hans-Joachim. Seated: Walter, Max.

gladly entrusted Max with more and more of the day-to-day running
of the business and came to rely on him in ever greater measure. Max's
business partnership with his father did not, however, make him his
father's sole heir. Under a family agreement, after Martha and Henri
Hinrichsen's death, their surviving children were to receive equal
shares in the business.

1931: Walter Hinrichsen joins the family business

Walter, the second of Martha and Henri Hinrichsen's five sons (Fig.
24), was born in 1907. Brought up traditionally like his brother Max,
his personality, however, was quite different. Whereas Max was quiet,
serious and introspective, Walter was outgoing, larger than life and
always the popular centre of attention. He and his sister Ilse formed a
close bond which was to be important to them in later life. After

leaving school, Walter spent a short while at the Leipzig Conservatory of Music before embarking on his years of apprenticeship in the music publishing business at the age of 20 in 1927. The following year he started his apprenticeship in Hamburg. He spent some months in Lausanne, after which he went on to Cologne in 1929. From there he spent a while in Paris, Brussels and London. On 1 March 1931, he joined his father and brother in the family business. Max was to be his professional mentor and adviser throughout his life.

Henri Hinrichsen's two eldest sons' training was to stand them in good stead and would assure the future of C. F. Peters, though not in the way envisaged at the time. The brothers could not have anticipated the cataclysmic changes which were to cause the family's well-structured plans to be destroyed and their world to be transformed into a nightmare of suffering, sorrow and loss. These later years of less responsibility for the elderly Hinrichsen couple, and more time for relaxation together, when Max was running the business, were to be short-lived.

CHAPTER TEN

1933: National Socialism and Education

The euphoria of the new Music Instruments Museum evaporated when Professor Kroyer left Leipzig in 1932. His vacant chair at Leipzig University became the subject of economies in the university budget. He was to be replaced by an associate professor whose salary would be considerably less. On 4 January 1933, the Dean appealed to Henri Hinrichsen who wrote to the Ministry of Culture, expressing his willingness to cover the difference in salary, so that the university could again employ a full professor. However, on 25 March, the Ministry turned down his offer without giving any reason. Adolf Hitler had been appointed Chancellor of the new Cabinet on 30 January. On 5 March 1933, he scheduled a new election. Persecution of the Jews took immediate effect.

With their state-inspired anti-Semitism, the Nazis were adopting a return to the attitudes prevalent towards the Jews in the Middle Ages but with one difference. Then, the motive was religious. With the Nazis it was a question of 'racial purity' and this time it signalled the end of the hard-won emancipation of the Jews in Germany. The persecution of the Jews by the Nazis was already under way before 1933 but, after the accession of the National Socialist Party, it rapidly escalated. At that time, there were around 500,000–600,000 Jews in Germany (representing 0.8 per cent of the population). Of these, 15,000 lived in Leipzig. From March 1933 onwards, one piece of anti-Semitic legislation after another was passed, with the aim of eliminating all aspects of Jewish influence from German life and of economically crippling the Jews and driving them from Germany. The first general manifestation of this came from the order of the directorate of the NSDAP, dated 28 March 1933. It was the officially sanctioned, organized, wild and excessive 'boycott' which took place on 1 April, intended 'for practical, planned implementation of the boycott of Jewish businesses, Jewish products, Jewish doctors and Jewish lawyers'. Jews and other critics of the regime were sent to the concentration camp of Dachau in their thousands from March 1933 onwards.

There had been Jews in Leipzig since the thirteenth century. Persecuted and driven from other countries, they had found tolerant refuge there. The largest contingent of Jews, the Ashkenazis, came from Poland and they upheld the East European Jewish traditions and ways of life; their main trade was in fur and they transformed Leipzig into the European centre for the fur trade. A much smaller group, whose lifestyle was entirely different, was the German Jews. Many of these were Sephardim, whose ancestors had originally been expelled from Spain in 1492. They were highly cultured people and had for centuries been assimilated into German life; many were in mixed marriages and without any particular religious affiliation. The Hinrichsen family, whose ancestors had acquired German citizenship in Glück-stadt in 1646, belonged to this group. They considered themselves to be first and foremost German. It was the persecution instigated by Hitler that made many totally assimilated Germans first aware of the fact that they were Jews; and as such, they were henceforth to be regarded as foreigners and enemies of the people. In Nazi terminology, as non-Aryans they were regarded as sub-human and equated with scum, pigs and vermin.

Legislation against the Jews

A new concept entered the German vocabulary as a term used to define the difference between a Jew and a Gentile. It was 'Aryan'. Though originally a linguistic term referring to the Indo-European group of languages, it had been distorted as a concept since the late nineteenth century to denote racial superiority over the Semitic races. 'Semitic' was itself originally a linguistic term referring to a language group which included Hebrew and Arabic. But Hitler redefined the term to fit his new racialism. 'Aryan' became synonymous with 'pure', while 'Semitic' became synonymous with 'Jew', thus 'impure'.

Germans were henceforth registered as either 'Aryan' (denoting German) or 'non-Aryan' (denoting Jew). Ancestry had to be proved back several generations in order for a person to be classified as 'pure Aryan'. With one Aryan and one Jewish parent, the classification was *Mischling ersten Grades* (first-degree mixed race). One Jewish grandparent denoted a second-degree mixed race; one Jewish great-grandparent, i.e., a carrier of one-eighth Jewish blood, was classed as third-degree mixed race. We will see how this affected some members of the Hinrichsen family.

One of the first pieces of legislation brought in by the Nazis was that all Jewish judges were sacked from their state appointments, and this included Dr Otto Sobernheim in Berlin, the husband of the Hinrichsen's eldest daughter, Charlotte. This took effect under the law dated 7 April 1933 which forcibly 'retired' civil servants of 'non-Aryan' origin; their pension rights were also withdrawn. Many in fact managed to retain their posts until the implementation of the Nuremberg Racial Laws of September 1935. One such was Henri Hinrichsen's brother, Max, in Hamburg who remained in office till then as president of the Hamburg Senate but died in 1939 as a consequence of the vilification and harassment to which he became subjected.

Jewish professors were sacked from the universities and deprived of their pension rights. Doctors' practices were limited by a decree of 2 April 1933 that barred all non-Aryan doctors from work at state-supported health clinics and hospitals. This did not initially affect the Hinrichsens' son-in-law, Dr Ludwig Frankenthal, who was chief surgeon at the Eitingon Jewish hospital in Leipzig, though it prevented him from treating non-Jews. Lawyers' practices were restricted and they were sacked from state appointments. Jewish students were expelled from the universities. The Hinrichsens' son, Hans-Joachim, was in the process of studying law and it was only with great difficulty that he was able to graduate and obtain his doctorate in 1934. His younger brother, Paul, was prevented from studying agriculture in Germany.

The visiting of museums by Jews was forbidden and they were not allowed to use swimming pools or to sit on park benches. Jews were not permitted to go to concerts, the theatre or the cinema. They had to give up their driving licences. They were forbidden from using public transport except to go to work – but they were only permitted to do menial work, until that too was forbidden to them. They had to give up their bicycles. They were not permitted to go to the hairdresser or to have their shoes mended by the cobbler; they should look like unkempt tramps. Many more such new laws made life progressively more difficult for the Jews. The Nazis created over four hundred laws and edicts against Jews in the first six years of their rule, which they executed zealously. Many laws were designed to humiliate and exclude Jewish children and to terminate friendships between them and their former 'pure-bred' friends.

Jewish children's lives were made a misery by Nazi-indoctrinated teachers until they were barred from attending non-Jewish schools completely. They had to transfer to Jewish schools. The Hinrichsens' youngest son, Robert, was 15 years old in 1933. He was dismissed from school and, as his father did not want him to attend a Jewish school, the boy was sent to complete his education at Gordonstoun School in Scotland, where he was desperately unhappy.

The small Jewish schools suddenly became overwhelmed with huge numbers of children but, as the Jewish teachers were also dismissed from the 'Aryan' schools, there were enough teachers, even if not enough room or equipment. Two of Henri and Martha Hinrichsen's grandchildren, Günther and Wolfgang, sons of their daughter Ilse and the surgeon Dr Ludwig Frankenthal attended the Carlebach School in Leipzig (Figs 25 and 26). This school of fewer than 100 children was founded by the Rabbi Ephraim Carlebach. In 1933, it was suddenly forced to accommodate over one thousand children and the rabbi summoned his newly graduated 22-year-old nephew, Felix Carlebach, from Lübeck to help run the school. He remained until the Nazis closed the school in November 1938, after which he managed to flee to England, penniless, with his wife.[1]

The Leipzig Bibliophiles Association

Henri Hinrichsen had been one of the founder members of the Leipzig Bibliophiles Association in 1904. When the National Socialists came to power in 1933, they ordered that all 'non-Aryan' members should be dismissed. As this constituted almost half the membership, the remaining 'Aryan' members agreed unanimously to disband the Association, rather than be dictated to and to allow the entire concept of their society to be changed. The LBA met for the last time in May 1933. The founder, Georg Witkowski, a major figure in literary scholarship in Leipzig and throughout Germany, was persecuted as a 'non-Aryan' and his lectures derided by the state; he was deprived of his pension. He escaped to Holland in 1939 and died of bronchitis within four months.

Nazi laws controlling music

Music was an important propaganda weapon in the National Socialist armoury of persuasion. It was intended forcibly to guide the taste of the population away from all 'foreign' influence such as avant-garde music and jazz. To this end, the *Reichsmusikkammer* (State Music Chamber) was formed on 15 November 1933. A thorough and ruthless policy of anti-Semitism was pursued, even before then, aiming

---

1 Felix F. Carlebach and his wife were best friends with Ilse and Ludwig Frankenthal. Felix gained an MA in England and became a rabbi, a minister of the South Manchester Synagogue, until his retirement. Charismatic and immensely popular, he was still in demand until around the age of 90 in 2000; he died in 2008.

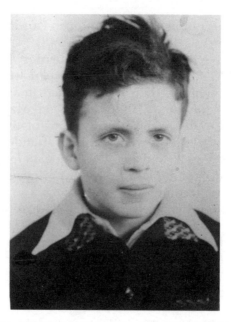

Fig. 25 Wolfgang Frankenthal 1931–1944.

to eliminate every possible Jewish element from German musical life. One of the first decrees of Hitler's Minister of Propaganda, Dr Joseph Goebbels, was the dismissal from their posts of all Jews holding important positions in any aspect of music-making in Germany. Amongst these was the conductor, Otto Klemperer, and Henri Hinrichsen's friend, the Gewandhaus conductor, Bruno Walter, who was summarily told on 16 March 1933 not to come for his rehearsal.

The *Reichsmusikkammer* issued a decree on 29 September 1934 prohibiting performing artists whose names sounded foreign. Its decree issued on 30 August 1935 forbade Jews and any other non-Aryans from playing in German orchestras. Another forbade Jews from teaching at music conservatories. Jewish musicians were not allowed to perform in Germany. Music magazines were taken over to promote the party message of purification of music from alien influences. Musicians such as Mendelssohn, Mahler, Weill and Klemperer were reviled.

There were rigorous rules preventing the performance of music published by a publisher who was deemed to be Jewish. This was financially devastating for Henri Hinrichsen.[2] Every kind of activity was affected, including key musical organizations with which he was involved, such as the German Music Publishers' Association and the

---

2 More detailed information is given in *Music Publishing and Patronage.*

Fig. 26 Günther Frankenthal 1929–1945.

German Music Dealers' Association, as well as the German Book Traders' Association. As a Jew, he was immediately expelled from all such organizations and his involvement as a committee member was instantly terminated. His son and partner, Max, was in Berlin attending the German Copyright Association annual meeting in March and was shocked that the very able Jewish members of the committee were vilified and dismissed. He noted on a further visit to Berlin in April that the mood was extremely oppressive and that the music trade had been especially badly affected as a result of the boycott. The fact that Jewish musicians were no longer permitted to teach and Jewish students were not allowed to study meant that the sale of sheet music dropped by 80 per cent. The firm of C. F. Peters was marginalized and membership of the important organizations, in which Peters had always played a major part, was barred – because the owner was a Jew. All appeals by Henri Hinrichsen to the highest authorities were met with indifference and no concessions were given. In June 1933, the mayor of Leipzig invited Henri Hinrichsen and other Jews on the Board of Management of the Conservatory of Music to offer their resignations.

In an effort to try and ease the disastrous economic position of the company, Walter Hinrichsen – Max's younger brother – embarked on a major round-the-world tour in August 1933 with a view to expanding the export business. The trip was combined with a holiday, which served to expand Walter's horizons and crystallize his ideas for the future.

The *Chronik*

For many years, people had been urging Henri Hinrichsen to compile a history of C. F. Peters and this task had been occupying him for some time. Martha Hinrichsen had, with great diligence, found pictures and photographs of long-dead musicians and others with which to illustrate this splendid tome. Entitled *Chronik des Hauses C. F. Peters. Geschichte des Verlagshauses C. F. Peters von seiner Gründung am 1. Dezember 1800 an bis zum 1. Oktober 1933* (History of the Music Publishing House of C. F. Peters from its Foundation on 1 December 1800 till 1 October 1933), it was prepared ostensibly for his family and completed on 1 July 1933. With the anti-Semitic changes that were taking place during 1933, Henri Hinrichsen felt the need to add some closing words:

> Recently I had the pleasure of seeing my eldest son, Max's, name enrolled in the Register of Companies as Partner in the company. Though I have entrusted to him the daily running of the business more and more over the last few years, I see myself as fortunate, during these commercially catastrophic years, in being able to continue to participate through daily conferences, contributing my many years of experience. Until my recent retirement from office, I have always promoted the interests of the Association of German Music Dealers and the German Music Publishers' Association in an honorary capacity to the best of my ability, so that I carry the certainty that the old, good relations which the firm of C. F. Peters has enjoyed with its friends will be maintained in the future, whereby the firm will hopefully be successful in surviving the current general crisis . . .
>
> It is my heartfelt wish that my son Max and later collaborating sons will continue to run our G e r m a n   b u s i n e s s in the spirit of its predecessors, because the publishing house has a l w a y s s p e c i a l i z e d in G e r m a n   m u s i c   f r o m its b e g i n n i n g s and has been d i r e c t e d   t o w a r d s this end during its e n t i r e e x i s t e n c e !

This depiction of the true German patriot which the 65-year-old Henri Hinrichsen had always been never even reached those whom it was meant to assure because the volume was never published. Beautifully leather-bound, typewritten copies, fully illustrated with photographs, were prepared for his sons, whilst the corrected typescript remained in the archives of C. F. Peters.

We will let Martha Hinrichsen have the last word on the *Chronik* in a letter to her son Walter, who was in the USA at the time, dated 7 October 1932.

NATIONAL SOCIALISM AND EDUCATION

I constantly see how useful such a chronicle is because it is through the chronicle that tradition is maintained. And even if Gustav Mahler, frustrated at the somnolent tradition at the Vienna Opera, shouts out loud 'Tradition is sloppiness', used in sensible measure with respect, it leads to blessing. Tradition means not blindly following in the footsteps of your predecessors. Approximately every thirty years there should be a shift in the business to let in new blood and to adopt modern ways of conducting business, which should be combined with the experiences of the past. And not to smash up everything which is there, but to continue that which is good – that is tradition. More than a lifetime ago, your father was the youngster who in his apprentice years rebelled against the ideas of Uncle Max Abraham, but he had the good luck to work with him for many years before taking on the full responsibility of the business . . . Your father changed many things, but he retained the tradition, that which was worthwhile and which Max Abraham constantly emphasized. This was why he maintained the publishing house as a small entity, to concentrate on the publishing, leaving the problems of printing, engraving and binding to others. Many of the larger firms, who did not do this, have now collapsed.

She went on to point out that Henri Hinrichsen had never speculated on the stock exchange and was thus able to save the firm through the war and inflation years. She said that he was now in a position to support himself during his retirement and that he had made provision to support the firm for his heirs. When Max Abraham had died, the obligations in his will were so high that not a penny remained for Henri Hinrichsen and that he even accepted responsibility for supporting several members of Max Abraham's family for many years. She concluded her letter with her wishes for the future of the firm in the hands of her sons: 'But it is my fervent wish that Max, you and Hanns should be as successful in being able to pass on the business to your heirs in as honourable and secure a position as it holds today.'

Martha presented a beautifully leather-bound copy of the *Chronik* to her eldest son, Max. She enclosed a brief note, dated 2 April 1935, which can be seen as a reflection of the times.

Dear Max,

I am delighted at last to be able to hand you the copy of the *Chronik*; it should serve you as a reference work. I hope with all my heart that the rumours which you hear whilst carrying out your duties, melt away to nothing, and that you can work with pleasure to maintain the position of the business, which is more difficult (especially these days) than to build it up.

With Love, Mother.

Fervent and heartfelt wishes are not always granted and these were to be denied in the most terrible manner. The rumours did not melt away. They materialized in the most tragic, gruesome, state-inspired, organized persecution and murder of the Jews – which subsequently became known as the Holocaust.

The donor banned from 'his' women's college

With the advent of National Socialism in 1933, the esteem in which Henri Hinrichsen had been held in the Henriette Goldschmidt Schule, the college of which he had been the founding patron in 1911, was replaced by a policy of humiliation and vilification. His name and very existence were to be expunged. This was also the stance adopted against the memory of Henriette Goldschmidt.

The college became subordinate to a new educational policy. Children's first obligation was no longer to their parents, but to the state. Parents were told: 'Your child belongs to us now! You will pass, but your descendants are already in the new camp. Very shortly they will only recognize the new community.' Henceforth 'students would be educated towards duty to the people and the family in professions promoting the spirit of National Socialism.' Those entitled to apply for a place in the college were girls who had completed high school education, were of pure Aryan descent and had proved their worthiness in the *Bund Deutscher Mädchen* (Association of German Girls), a Nazi propaganda and fitness organization, preferably as leaders. The director of the college was removed from her post and sent to a village to work on the land. On the second-floor landing there was a bronze plaque set into the wall with a dedication from the patron, commemorating the inauguration of the house on 29 October 1911; this was now covered with a picture which showed the quotation: 'You are nothing, your Nation is all.' Henriette Goldschmidt's birthday, which had been regularly commemorated on 23 November, was to be replaced with an outing for the students, without reference to her name.

Starting in August 1933, the Education Department, the mayor, the Leipzig town council and the governing body of the renamed *Sozialpädagogisches Frauenseminar* (High School for Ladies – cleansed of its founder's name) expended a great deal of time in discussion and in correspondence. The cause of all this paperwork was what was to be done with the sculpted bust and large portrait of Henriette Goldschmidt and the portraits of Henri Hinrichsen. It was no longer seen as fit that the participation of Jews in the founding of the First College for Women in Germany should be acknowledged. The correspondence points to innumerable moves of all four items, between the director's room, the library, the cleaner's store room and another house. (The students had been so indoctrinated that it was reported that one refused to take part in a discussion in a room where there was a portrait of a Jew.)

Henri Hinrichsen found the current developments terribly distressing. He was now totally excluded from the college which he had subsidized for over twenty years. His portrait had been replaced by one of Adolf Hitler, beneath which was a vile quote, directed at the benefactor: 'When the best fell at the front, one could at least exterminate the vermin at home, flush the perfidious brutes out of their hiding places and hang them from the highest gallows.'

The warped educational outlook was exemplified in the selection of reading materials available to the students. The library of educational books, which Henri Hinrichsen had donated, became 'cleansed' in 1936. Books by such authors as Freud, Horden and Fischhard were destroyed. The director, Frau Dr Braune, wrote to the Department of Education on 30 August 1937, asking for permission to remove the *ex-libris* label with the portrait of Henriette Goldschmidt from all the books. She received the following reply: 'I just cannot understand how a school in this National Socialist State could still possess a Trust which carries the name of a Jew. I regard it as intolerable that books in the Social Pedagogical Women's College, which originate from the Henri Hinrichsen Trust, should carry an *ex-libris* label with the portrait of Henriette Goldschmidt.'

It took four years for the authorities to reach a final decision on the portraits, which by then had been completely removed, whilst the correspondence as to their disposal continued. Their fate, and that of the other offending items, is given in a letter from the college director to the mayor, dated 10 November, 1937: 'The oil painting by Geiger and the bronze plaque have been sent to Dr Hinrichsen today. The *Ex-libris* labels will be removed and the painting by Einschlag will be destroyed.' The painting by Eduard Einschlag, a Jew, had been commissioned by the Leipzig town council in honour of Henri Hinrichsen's sixtieth birthday, in 1928.[3] The huge portrait of Henriette Goldschmidt was kept safely in store. Many years later it

---

3 Eduard Einschlag was transported to Treblinka concentration camp in 1938 where he and his family were murdered.

was re-hung. The sculpted bust of Henriette Goldschmidt was ultimately destroyed. The marble pedestal, too heavy to be moved,
remained. It still stands, as a memorial to those times.[4]

The authorities also had to make a decision on a huge collection of
educational material which the sponsor had given the school that
carried the name Henri Hinrichsen Educational Materials Trust.
Henri agreed to allow it to be incorporated into the general holdings
of the school. The authorities also felt the need to rename a number
of houses, including a kindergarten and a student's home, carrying
the name of Henriette Goldschmidt, which had been provided by
Henri Hinrichsen and were supported through his Trust. The name
was simply deleted. After the war, the houses were taken into DDR
state-ownership and allowed to fall into decay.

The Henri Hinrichsen Trust posed a larger problem for the authorities who desperately wanted to hold onto this substantial capital.
Eventually, political decrees and the Leipzig authorities caused the
Trust to be renamed 'Trust for the *Sozialpädagogisches Frauenseminar*'.
This was accepted by the Saxony Ministry of National Education in
Dresden, on 19 April 1941, by which time Henri Hinrichsen had long
ceased to have any influence on anything in Leipzig any more. When
a school inspection was carried out in February 1942, his name was not
mentioned in the report, which described the foundation of the
college thus: 'In the year 1911 a benefactor donated the building
which was named *Hochschule für Frauen* (High School for Women).'
After some years, even the new name of the Trust disappeared. Placed
in a general trust incorporating several redundant trusts, the funds
were frittered away by the eventual DDR authorities to become
untraceable.

The donor banned from the Music Instruments Museum and Peters Music Library

The acknowledgement of Henri Hinrichsen as the benefactor of
another major institution was similarly erased. He had been the
sponsor behind the purchase of the Heyer collection of musical
instruments in 1926, which formed the Music Instruments Museum in
Leipzig. Whilst the University of Leipzig valued Henri Hinrichsen's
support of the Music Instruments Museum, the government ministry
controlled policy. Only four years after the grand inauguration of this
fine museum, which without Henri Hinrichsen's generous financial

---

4 The pedestal remained empty for 70 years until 2004 when a copy of the original bust was placed on it.

contribution would not have existed, the sponsor was banned from further involvement in any aspect of the institution. In 1929, when the large notice reading 'Henri Hinrichsen Hall' in large, solid bronze letters on each side was hung in the centre of the hall holding the finest pieces, it was expected to hang there 'for all time'. Now it was thrown on a heap of rubbish in the cellar.[5]

Henri Hinrichsen was equally banned from the Peters Music Library which he had been financing for over thirty years for the benefit of Leipzig citizens. He had been the custodian and had chosen the chief librarian. But now he was banned from all further involvement – though his financial support was still expected. [6]

This was happening to a man whose absolute commitment was not to his ethnic background but to his chosen city of residence. For forty years he had been true to what he felt to be his obligation – to help the people and institutions that would benefit from his business acumen and generosity. Like many Jewish born citizens in his position, honoured in the city he chose to call home, he could not conceive of a time when that could change. He could not have imagined that the respect, in which he had for so long been held, was soon to turn to persecution and hatred.

Centuries of education and culture were to be annihilated. The first massive book-burning spectacle was organized in Berlin in May 1933 when more than 50,000 books by Jews and other 'traitors and degenerates' were ignited opposite the university. Similar book-burnings took place in other university towns throughout Germany. In Berlin the propaganda chief, Joseph Goebbels, led the ceremony and proclaimed 'the end of Jewish intellectualism.'

---

5 The sign was rediscovered almost 60 years later in 1991 when the author saw it in the cellar of the museum. It was restored and rehung.
6 The full story of the Peters Music Library is in *Music Publishing and Patronage.*

CHAPTER ELEVEN

1933–1938: Racial Purity, the *Kulturbund* and Emigration

1934: Dr Hans-Joachim Hinrichsen joins the business

Like his two elder brothers, Hans-Joachim (Fig. 27), who was born in 1909, attended the Nicolai School in Leipzig where he specialized in classics and from which he graduated in March 1928. He was the most academic and intellectual of the brothers and had decided to study law. His legal studies took him to the universities of Freiburg im Breisgau, Munich and Leipzig, followed by a period of practical legal instruction in the courts of Leipzig and Grimma. He was awarded a Doctorate of Law from the University of Leipzig on 20 November 1934. His thesis, which provided him with special-ized knowledge of which he made full use in the business, was enti-tled *Übertragung des musikalischen Urheberrechts an Musikverleger und Musikwertungsgesellschaften* (The Transfer of Musical Copyright to Music Publishers and Authors' and Composers' Societies). It was dis-cussed and praised in Belgian, Swiss, French, Dutch, German, Austrian and Italian professional journals and parts were translated for a French journal. A detailed reference was published in the Bulletin of the Permanent Bureau of the International Congress of Editors and distributed at the London Publishers' Congress.

Having decided at an early age that he would make his career in the family business, Hans-Joachim had already been actively involved since 1929. He started his apprenticeships in 1934 when he went to two companies in Vienna and then, like his brother Walter, spent a few months in Lausanne. He then went travelling for some months in 1935, representing C. F. Peters throughout Europe. After passing some time in London, he joined the company full time in October

Fig. 27 c.1935. Dr Hans-Joachim Hinrichsen 1909–1940.

1935, when he was granted official power of attorney. His speciality was in copyright and law and his work was to become indispensable over the next few years.

1934: Max Hinrichsen marries Marie-Luise von Siegroth und Slawikau

Henri Hinrichsen's eldest son Max, unlike his two sisters who had both married Jews, chose to marry a woman who, in Nazi terminology, was of pure Aryan descent. Max, his father's partner since 1931, was 33 when he met the 24-year-old Marie-Luise von Siegroth und Slawikau on 27 February 1934; they married on 28 June that same year, both having been baptized Evangelical (Protestant) a few days earlier (Fig. 28). The hasty marriage was necessary in order to circumvent the new 'racial purity' laws soon to take effect, forbidding intermarriage between Jews and Aryans. Intermarriage between Jews and non-Jews increased significantly in 1933 to 44 per cent; it fell to 15 per cent by 1935, after which it became outlawed. Both families warned against this ill-conceived match. The young couple would not be deterred in spite of the threat of a sentence to four months in prison, such as had been imposed on 14 June by a special court in Nuremberg on the Aryan wife of a Jew, guilty of being a 'race-defiling female'.

Fig. 28 Wedding of Max Hinrichsen and Marie-Luise von Siegroth
und Slawikau, 28 June 1934. The author's parents.

Born in Silesia, into an aristocratic Roman Catholic family dating
back to 1209, Marie-Luise had three older brothers. Her father had
been a strict Roman Catholic who died when she was only nine years
old; her mother was therefore able to bring her up in a much less
restrictive way than had been possible with her brothers. Her eldest
brother Hanns, a lieutenant and holder of the Iron Cross award, was
killed at the age of 19 in the trenches in France in 1915. Joachim, the
second brother was a major general in the *Wehrmacht* (the German
army) in 1934. Fearing that his sister's marriage to a Jew would jeop-
ardize his promising military career, he disowned her completely. He
refused to attend the wedding and he never spoke to her or had any
contact with her again.[1] Eberhard, her youngest brother, had no such
qualms and gladly accepted financial support from his Jewish brother-
in-law. Their mother, the widowed Baroness Elisabeth von Siegroth
und Slawikau divided her time between her home in Berlin and her
daughter's new home in Leipzig.

---

1 Major General Joachim von Siegroth und Slawikau was awarded the Iron
   Cross for distinguished military service. Taken prisoner by the Russians, he
   was killed in Siberia, probably in 1945. The sister whom he had spurned
   helped support his four little daughters for many years.

Fig. 29 1935. The newborn author with father
Max Hinrichsen and C. F. Peters' music.

Racial defilement

Max and Marie-Luise enjoyed a comfortable lifestyle and Max worked
hard alongside his father. The young couple were not initially worried
by the creation in 1934 of the Racial Office run under the auspices of
the local government but they were soon to experience its effects. On
8 April 1935, a baby was born whom they named Irene (Fig. 29).[2] She
was baptized Evangelical/Protestant yet, since the Nazis refused to recognize the baptism when her birth was registered, the racial terminology described her as *Mischling ersten Grades* (first-degree mixed
race). Life was embarrassing for the young couple. In August 1935, a
national newspaper campaign led by Julius Streicher, the fanatical
editor of *Der Stürmer* (often described as 'Jew-Baiter No. 1'), demanded legislation to prevent sexual relations between Jews and non-Jews.
The 'sexual question' played a decisive role in the Nazi campaign
against the Jews. Hitler devoted many pages to this in his book, *Mein
Kampf*, where he describes the Jew-boy lying in wait for the unsuspect-
ing Aryan girl whom he intends to violate. With the birth of Irene, Max
and Marie-Luise Hinrichsen were guilty of racial defilement.

---

2 The author.

Under Streicher's auspices, a special meeting of medical men had been held in Nuremberg in December 1934 which passed a resolution asking the Minister of the Interior to severely punish any attempted or completed physical intercourse between German women and Jews: in the case of a German woman, by taking away her German nationality and sending her to a labour camp and, in cases of completed intercourse, sterilizing her; in the case of a Jew, by taking away his German nationality, confiscating his whole property, sentencing him to at least five years of penal servitude, and afterwards expelling him from Germany.

The Law for the Protection of German Blood was passed in Nuremberg on 15 September 1935, forbidding all future marriages between Jews and German citizens or those of other blood. Such marriages were declared invalid even if they were conducted abroad in order to circumvent the law. The authorities did their utmost to persuade Aryans who had married Jews to divorce their spouses. Many did. Those Jews who remained married to their Aryan spouses were, to a certain extent, initially protected from the worst excesses of the Nazi regime in order not to alienate their Aryan in-laws. However, when food rationing was introduced in which Jews only received half the rations of non-Jews, it was extended to those in mixed marriages too.

The virulently anti-Semitic *Der Stürmer* led the campaign for the vilification of Jews. The slander and libel of Jews in the press and in public were now condoned; in practice, they had no redress. Those few who dared to bring a charge against such untrue allegations and lies faced the probability that it would be dismissed. A Jew was considered to be a second-class human and ranked socially lower than a pig.

On 1 January 1935, a decree was issued, obliging all Jews to be officially identified if their names did not appear on a list of 'typically Jewish' names issued by the Minister of the Interior. Jewish shops and businesses were gradually closed down and 'Aryanized', that is, assigned to people classified as Aryans (and generally members of the Nazi Party). The purchase price – a fraction of the true value – was never paid to the owners but withheld as one of the many taxes imposed on Jews. The concept of Aryanization will be explained below, in terms of how the firm of C. F. Peters and Henri Hinrichsen were affected. 30,000 far-sighted Jews left Germany in 1933, by which time a Reich's refugee tax was already in operation. A further 30,000 left the following year because of the deteriorating situation and, in 1935, 20,000 decided to make their homes elsewhere. These were all able to leave with relative ease, though necessarily forfeiting most of their wealth in line with the new Nazi requirements. The refugee tax, which was supplemented by other taxes, increased over the years to a crippling extent; emigrants who could not get out before 1939 left penniless. Those emigrating after 13 May 1938 were not permitted to take any valuables and had to provide a complete list of all personal property which they wanted to take with them for the imposition of an export tax. Henri and Martha Hinrichsen never had any plans to leave their homeland.

Not content with the defamation and persecution of the Jews and of depriving them of their professions and driving them out of their homeland, on 15 September 1935 the Nazis passed the Law of Citizenship. This law contains three short clauses; Clause Two runs: 'Only a German subject of German or related blood who proves by his attitude that he is willing and fit to serve faithfully the German Nation and Reich is a citizen. The right of citizenship is acquired by the grant of a citizen letter patent. Only a citizen is vested with full political rights according to the law.' Having already declared that Jews were not German citizens, the Jews were now deprived of all political rights. The fact that they were deprived of the right to vote stood in their favour; they obviously would not have voted for Hitler and anybody who did not vote for Hitler was generally penalized.

1936: Walter Hinrichsen emigrates to the USA

To the great distress of Martha and Henri Hinrichsen their second son, Walter, decided to emigrate. He did not like the situation in Germany and also realized that if he remained at C. F. Peters in Leipzig he would always be in second position to his brother, Max. The round-the-world business trip, which he had undertaken in 1933, had introduced him to the potential advantages of settling in the USA. There he would represent C. F. Peters and eventually form his own company. Walter Hinrichsen was 29 when he left Germany on 3 March 1936, separating himself from the situation that would destroy his family. He never saw his parents or two of his brothers again. The fact that he managed to get to the USA, where he eventually obtained citizenship, was ultimately to the best advantage of his remaining family.

1937: Max Hinrichsen emigrates to Great Britain

The eldest son, Max, felt a tremendous sense of responsibility to his father and to the family business with which he had grown up. He was joint managing director of C. F. Peters and administrator of the Peters Music Library, involved in the editing of its famous *Yearbook*. He did not want to desert his father. However, his wife Marie-Luise, under threat from the authorities because of her marriage, could foresee a worsening situation and urged him to emigrate. Max's preference was for a life in the USA but he joked that the country was not large enough for both him and Walter. In reality, the brothers felt that C. F. Peters would be better served if they each founded a company on opposite sides of the Atlantic. Wisely wanting to put the sea between himself and Nazi Germany, he chose Great Britain instead.

On 27 October 1937, business formalities were officially completed when Max Hinrichsen resigned as joint managing director of C. F. Peters, Leipzig. His brother Walter having emigrated, it was their younger brother, the lawyer Dr Hans-Joachim Hinrichsen, who took his place. Whilst rejoicing at the fact that his third son was now officially his partner, Henri Hinrichsen was devastated at Max's decision to leave.

The bureaucratic formalities required of Jews wishing to emigrate from Nazi Germany took several months to complete. On 12 November 1937, Max, Marie-Luise and Irene Hinrichsen left Leipzig for England where Max Hinrichsen founded Hinrichsen Edition Ltd in March 1938 and eventually Peters Edition, London. Henri Hinrichsen never forgave his eldest son for leaving and refused to communicate with him from that moment onwards – a heartbreaking tragedy that was to haunt Max for the rest of his life. Contact was maintained with Hans-Joachim and, in her letters, Marie-Luise urged him to leave Germany and to persuade his parents to do likewise. The now 70-year-old Henri Hinrichsen refused even to consider leaving, saying that he owed it to his uncle, Dr Max Abraham, from whom he had inherited the business in 1900, to remain with the business in Leipzig. Also, he shared the conviction with so many German Jews that things could not get any worse and that surely this could not herald the end of almost 2,000 years of Jewish presence in Germany.

Since the departure of his two elder brothers, Dr Hans-Joachim's position in the company had risen rapidly. His position as managing director was entered in the commercial register on 28 May 1938 and two months later he was granted permission to work as a music publisher by the Ministry for People's Enlightenment and Propaganda. However, this was to be of short duration as the discriminatory measures against Jews had been escalating since the beginning of the year.

The *Jüdische Kulturbund*

Jews were forbidden either to work as musicians or to attend musical functions. However, having deprived Jewish musicians of their livelihood, Goebbels was faced with a great deal of international criticism. His answer to this was that his Ministry of Propaganda proposed the formation of a *Jüdische Kulturbund* (Jewish Culture Association) which would offer employment to Jewish musicians. Throughout Germany this attracted approximately 180,000 people and the Association thrived until *Kristallnacht* in 1938.

The *Jüdische Kulturbund* was founded in October 1933 in Berlin under Kurt Singer, the dismissed director of the Berlin City Opera who was to die in Theresienstadt concentration camp in 1944. Following its formation, attempts were made to launch something along similar lines in Leipzig. But repeated applications for permission, submitted to the Leipzig authorities as well as to the regional authorities, were met by brusque refusals. In the interim, the Jewish religious authority endorsed the formation of the *Ausschuss für Kunstpflege* (Committee for the Cultivation of the Arts) which was permitted to organize concerts.

The inaugural concert of chamber music took place in Leipzig on 31 October 1933 under the direction of Henri Hinrichsen's friend, the choral conductor Barnet Licht. This musician had always been especially interested in the cultivation of music in the workplace; he had also arranged for music students and the unemployed to have free entry to concerts and rehearsals, as well as providing music in prisons. Born in Wilna, he had grown up in New York where he had early contacts with choirs before coming to Germany to study and live. A practising Jew, and a socialist, he became chorus master of the Temple Synagogue Choir in 1925 and worked as a music reviewer on the *Leipzig Illustrierte Monatschrift für Kultur* (Leipzig Illustrated Monthly Magazine for Culture).

As with all the early concerts of the *Kulturbund*, the emphasis was on German music with other, mostly classical and romantic, music also being represented. The Leipzig *Kulturbund* was finally inaugurated towards the end of 1934 under the chairmanship of Konrad Goldschmidt, a lawyer. The membership soon reached 625 and eventually attained 900, which was about 10 per cent of the Jewish population of Leipzig. Members mostly belonged to the cultured middle class and included doctors and lawyers, publishers, dismissed scientists and many business families. From 1935 to 1938, there were about 30 performances per year; these were mostly musical, but there were also theatrical performances, song recitals and poetry evenings with performers coming from Berlin and Hamburg, as well as from Leipzig. There was usually an attendance of 400–500 for these events, which were the only public entertainments that Jews were permitted to attend.

Jewish musicians who were still in Germany by 1935 found that their only chance of performing, was as members of the *Jüdische Kulturbund*; they were banned from all other musical activity. Goebbels boasted in November 1935: 'The *Reichskulturkammer* is cleansed of Jews today. There is not a single Jew practising in the cultural life of our people.'

One of the prime sponsors and promoters of the *Jüdische Kulturbund* in Leipzig was Henri Hinrichsen. In the spring of 1936, the government brought in an embargo against all performances of the *Kulturbund,* which they were trying to force into liquidation. However, Hinrichsen managed to get permission for a proposed concert with the violinist Carl Flesch, whose music was published by C. F. Peters and who was already living in London at the time. Hinrichsen financed the concert and Flesch was a guest with the family in 10 Talstrasse.

The work of the *Kulturbund* took place in isolation from the rest of the musical life of Germany and was totally supervised. No performance could take place without permission being granted at least four weeks in advance by the Gestapo in Leipzig and later in Berlin, nor without an official from the police or from the Gestapo being present and taking notes. Permission could be withdrawn at any time and performances could be cancelled without notice. In 1936, the Dresden Gestapo forced the resignation of the chairman of the Leipzig *Kulturbund,* whose place was taken by a member of the committee, a medical doctor, Hans Abelsohn. The committee saw itself being forced more and more to perform works by Jewish writers or musicians only and to eliminate works by Germans.

Jewish ghettoization became more pronounced with the wave of 'Aryanizations' of 1938 and the emigration of many members and musicians, together with dwindling financial resources. The *Kulturbund* issued a small monthly programme magazine, called *Monatsblätter,* that tried to offer encouragement but in what was to be the last issue in October 1938 expressed its loss of hope: 'The times have indeed become bitter serious.' The *Jüdische Kulturbund* effectively ceased to exist after *Kristallnacht* when 550 Leipzig Jews were arrested, many of them members of the association. Some managed to emigrate, others were transported to the east where they perished in the concentration camps. At the age of 71, Barnet Licht (whose wife was not Jewish) was one of the last Jews to be transported from Leipzig when he was sent to Theresienstadt concentration camp in February 1945. He survived there as a musician until the liberation, upon which he returned to Leipzig in July 1945 and formed a new choir, which he conducted until ill health forced him to retire in 1950; he died a year later.

The *Jüdische Kulturbund* was finally officially dissolved on 11 September 1941, with a letter from the Gestapo in Berlin to the headquarters of the organization in Berlin.

The vilification of Felix Mendelssohn-Bartholdy

Long-dead musicians of Jewish background became the victims of anti-Semitic persecution in similar measure to those still living.

Perhaps the most surprising and the most seriously vilified was Mendelssohn who had died almost ninety years earlier.

Felix Mendelssohn–Bartholdy (1809–1847) was, like Henri Hinrichsen, born in Hamburg. There were in fact several coincidental parallels between the two men. Although Jewish, both were non-practising. As young adults, both chose to make their homes in Leipzig. Both contributed greatly to the institutions of the city of Leipzig and worked tirelessly for its reputation as a 'Music City' and they were both awarded honorary doctorates by the Faculty of Philosophy of the University of Leipzig. They were both to suffer from all the prejudices engendered by the anti-Semitic Nazi state. Another, stranger, parallel is the fact that twenty years after Mendelssohn's death, and one year before the birth of Henri Hinrichsen, the firm of C. F. Peters, under the direction of Dr Max Abraham, moved its offices into what had been Mendelssohn's apartment. This was in the house in which he had lived for the last two years of his life: 12 Königstrasse (now Goldschmidtstrasse).

According to the criteria of the Nuremberg Racial Laws, Felix Mendelssohn-Bartholdy, in spite of the fact that he had been baptized a Christian, was a 'full Jew'. The fact that he had been dead for almost 90 years was of no consequence. A Jew was a Jew, and as such was considered unworthy of a memorial or even of a place in the history books and encyclopaedias.

The construction of the Mendelssohn monument in 1892 was described in Chapter 7. Four mayors of Leipzig were to come and go during the lifetime of the monument, including Dr Karl Rothe (1865–1953), whom Henri Hinrichsen held in great respect whilst he held office from 1918 to 1930. Dr Carl Friedrich Goerdeler (1884–1945) was elected mayor in 1930. His political stance was an enigma which has yet to be fully clarified.

Complaints were registered in 1936 to the effect that the Mendelssohn monument was offensive. The NSDAP made several demands for its removal but Dr Goerdeler steadfastly refused to allow it to be touched. However, there were two officials who were determined to get rid of the monument and, despite all of Goerdeler's protests, they used the opportunity of his absence from Leipzig on business to destroy it on 9 November 1936 – exactly two years to the day before *Kristallnacht*. It was done in secret, the press was not informed and it was hoped that the news would not be leaked abroad. Naturally, news of the destruction of this important monument to one of the world's greatest composers was nonetheless widely publicized and complaints flowed in from around the world. The London Philharmonic Orchestra threatened to cancel its planned concert in Leipzig but Goerdeler managed to persuade them to play after all. However, the members of the orchestra registered their disgust by playing in their everyday clothes instead of changing into evening dress.

Henri Hinrichsen's friend, Dr Helmuth von Hase, proprietor of the music publisher Breitkopf und Härtel, who was not a Jew, was the chairman of the Gewandhaus organization. On receiving an enquiry from Switzerland regarding the destruction of the Mendelssohn monument, he replied truthfully, laying the blame on the Leipzig town council. In fear of reprisals, he resigned his office. Following the destruction, Dr Goerdeler handed in his notice on 25 November 1936; but he remained in position until the end of 1937. Becoming disillusioned with Hitler's policies, he joined the group who attempted to assassinate the Führer, and who failed. For this, he was executed in 1945. There were to be no further objections to Nazi policy. The next mayor, Kurt Walter Dönicke, who held the post from 1937 to 1939, was the district leader of the NSDAP. SS Group leader Alfred Freyberg was the final Nazi mayor.

Several individuals and organizations wanted to have the monument for safekeeping and offered to buy it. Amongst these was Carl Hein, the director of the New York College of Music, who offered one and a half times the value of the monument, plus several original Wagner manuscripts. All such offers were turned down. For a long time it was rumoured that the monument had not been destroyed and was hidden away somewhere; however, it has never been seen since that night in 1936. All memory of Mendelssohn was to be eradicated. His name, like that of other Jewish composers and musicians, was deleted from musical reference books. Joseph Müller-Blattau, professor at the University of Freiburg, wrote in 1938 in *Geschichte der deutschen Musik* (History of German Music): 'It is not the duty of a German music history to concern itself with his overtures, symphonies and oratorios, his songs and his piano music.' In the Study Guide of the Conservatory of Music, which Mendelssohn had founded, his name was not even mentioned.[3]

1938: Jews forced to re-register their names

A new wave of Aryanizations started towards the end of 1937. The annexation of Austria in March 1938 marked the beginning of a

---

3 Information on the Mendelssohn monument was abstracted from *Auf dem Wege zum Holocaust: Der Abriss des Mendelssohn-Denkmals* (On the Way to the Holocaust: Destruction of the Mendelssohn Monument) by Thomas Schinköth, Leipzig, 1995. A new monument to Mendelssohn by Jo Jastram was erected in 1997. It is planned to recreate the original monument.

radical stage in the persecution of the Jews. In April, there was a decree ordering Jews to register their entire wealth over RM5,000; in July, there were more professional restrictions. Further discrimination was introduced with the decree of 17 August 1938, forcing additional names on Jews. They had to re-register their birth certificates, adding the middle name 'Israel' for a man and 'Sarah' for a woman. Martha Hinrichsen was forced to add the name 'Sarah' on 24 December 1938. Her driving licence had been withdrawn the day before. Henri Hinrichsen's registration of the additional name 'Israel' was entered in Hamburg on 25 January 1939. Martha and Henri Hinrichsen had to apply – and pay – for their re-registered birth certificates. Then telephones and radios were removed from Jews and Henri Hinrichsen's beloved Steinway piano was confiscated.

Jews were then forbidden from employing non-Jewish maidservants. The Hinrichsens and their housekeeper Mina were devastated at this new punitive measure. She had been a part of the family for over thirty years and had helped care for all of the seven children from birth to adulthood. The Hinrichsens' was the only family home she knew where she herself was now being cared for. To her great distress she now had to leave and enter an old people's home.

The Swiss aided and abetted the Germans in identifying Jews. On their insistence, from 5 October 1938 onwards, all Jews were obliged to have their passports stamped with a large red 'J'. This would prevent any of them from immigrating illegally to Holland, Belgium, Switzerland and other overland countries.

Jews were forced to sew large yellow star-shaped patches on their clothes; punishment for failure to wear the star in a public place could mean death or immediate transportation to the concentration camps. Henri Hinrichsen steadfastly refused to wear the star and hence, for his own safety, he did not go out of the house. Many Jews left Germany but many stayed on, thinking it could not get worse. After the mid-1930s, when larger numbers of Jews wanted to emigrate, visas for admittance to another country became difficult to obtain. Penalizing taxes were inflicted on Jews and they had to register all their assets and property. In the summer of 1938, all Jewish owners of shops and other businesses were ordered to paint the Star of David, as well as their names in large white letters, on their windows, thus making the premises easily identifiable to the Germans who could then boycott or vandalize them. In October, Goering declared that the wealth of the Jews belonged to the state and should not be squandered as a source of maintenance by corrupt party members.

The first mass deportations from Germany of 18,000 Polish Jews took place on 28–9 October 1938; 5,000 of these were from Leipzig. The German Jews, like the Hinrichsens, comforted themselves, thinking that they were not involved. Up until November 1938, Henri Hinrichsen still pursued his belief that things would not get worse for him and his family and that they would be spared the ultimate anti-Jewish excesses. He felt that his prominent position and his many fine and generous gifts to Leipzig institutions would stand to his credit. But Nazis, intent on carrying out every new law and stricture against the Jews with fanatical obedience, had replaced most of those city officials and bureaucrats who had known him for many years. The event which signalled the desecration of everything he had believed in and worked for over the course of more than forty years was the *Reichskristallnacht Pogrom*, the Nazi state-sponsored Night of the Broken Glass on 9 November 1938. It was a licence to terrorize Jews and destroy their property.

CHAPTER TWELVE

1938: *Kristallnacht*, Sachsenhausen, Buchenwald and Panic

On the night of 9–10 November 1938, the three younger Hinrichsen sons – Dr Hans-Joachim, Paul and Robert – were at home with Mina the housekeeper. Their parents were on an overnight visit to Vienna for a concert. Around 3.00 am, the young men were awoken by terrifying sounds coming from the streets; the screams of bewildered people were accompanied by the shattering of glass which heralded the onslaught of the terrible *Reichskristallnacht* – the Night of the Broken Glass.

Hearing noises below, they hastily pulled on their clothes. Creeping down the stairs, they encountered the frightening spectacle of armed Nazi thugs who had broken into 10 Talstrasse. In mortal fear of the mob who threatened them with crowbars and sledgehammers, they could do nothing but hide with Mina. The thugs ransacked the apartment, vandalizing and looting the family's possessions, smashing what they could not remove, or did not want. They broke into the offices of C. F. Peters and destroyed everything they could lay their hands on. They threw furniture, books, files and sheet music out of the window and made a bonfire in the courtyard. They ransacked the huge stockroom and threw all the sheet music by Felix Mendelssohn-Bartholdy onto the bonfire – a Nazi member of staff helped them in this act of senseless destruction. By the time their parents returned on 10 November, the brothers and Mina had tried to clear up some of the mess, though the wanton vandalism was all too evident.

But the Hinrichsens were not alone in their suffering. The shattering of glass, of the windows of shops belonging to Jews, the looting of their homes, the desecration of synagogues, the brutality and ferocity directed at innocent Jews were unleashed by the Nazis throughout Germany. All Leipzig synagogues, Jewish shops, offices, businesses

and institutes were vandalized and looted, many being completely
destroyed. Bonfires were lit in the Jewish areas and prayer books,
Torah scrolls and books on philosophy, history and poetry were
burned. The United States consul in Leipzig, David H. Buffum,
reported that the three main synagogues were set on fire simultaneously. At the Jewish cemetery in Leipzig, the Nazis practised tactics
which approached 'the ghoulish, uprooting tombstones and violating
graves. In the city itself,' Buffum wrote 'having demolished dwellings
and hurled most of the effects into the street, the insatiably sadistic
perpetrators threw many of the trembling inmates into a small stream
that flows through the Zoological Park, commanding horrified spec-
tators to spit at them, defile them with mud and jeer at their plight.'
Twelve out of the thirteen synagogues in Leipzig were burnt down;
one remained undamaged only because it formed part of an 'Aryan'
home.

Throughout Germany, 7,500 homes and businesses and 275 synagogues were destroyed. Over the course of 24 hours of violence in the
streets, almost 100 Jews were killed. The Jews were fined a billion
marks for the destruction which the Nazis had wrought on their property, levied by the compulsory confiscation of 20 per cent of the property of every Jew. They were ordered to clear up the mess immediately
at their own cost. The insurance companies refused to pay any compensation. The excuse for this long-planned act of terror on the Jews
was the shooting on 6 November of a German diplomat in Paris by a
Polish-Jewish student.

Dr Henri Hinrichsen and Dr Hans-Joachim Hinrichsen arrested. C. F. Peters confiscated

Jewish men were rounded up. Dr Henri Hinrichsen and his son
Dr Hans-Joachim Hinrichsen were arrested. Possibly as a mark of the
respect in which he had once been held, Henri Hinrichsen was
released after a week in the Leipzig jail but Hans-Joachim disappeared
for several weeks – he had been sent to Sachsenhausen concentration
camp.

Following *Kristallnacht*, the business of C. F. Peters was confiscated
from Henri Hinrichsen, as was his entire collection of paintings and
prints and autographed letters. Martha Hinrichsen, in understand-
able panic, wrote to her son, Walter, in the USA on 20 November:

> The dice have fallen. The business was confiscated from us on
> Thursday afternoon, with immediate effect. None of us may enter
> the office . . . I would have written of it to you immediately, but I
> wanted to wait until Hans returned. That seems to be taking a

longer time, we have no idea where he has been taken, we only know that he is no longer in Leipzig, it is eight days since they came to fetch him. Ilse and Lotte are in the same state of ignorance about their husbands. Father is finding it terribly difficult to make the decision to emigrate, but it will be impossible to remain here, even he said that this morning. The whole affair is terribly difficult for Father, who sees his life's work collapse like this – through no fault of his own . . . I cannot write in greater detail, I have to be careful because Hans is being held as a sort of hostage, that is why none of you must take any action on account of C. F. Peters.

Hans-Joachim Hinrichsen endured the hell of Sachsenhausen concentration camp, where the SS amused themselves by torturing prisoners, for six weeks. One of their frequent specialities was 'making sport'. In the euphemistic language of the SS, this command meant an excessive semi-military training – crawling in the dirt and tortuous exercises. This torture carried the expectation that it would kill weaker or older prisoners and it would continue until this aim had been accomplished. Those that remained would be chased back into the barracks and subjected to 'playing hares' – they were commanded to hop about on their knees. Anybody who disobeyed would be kicked or beaten with rifle butts. Daily tortures like these resulted in major injuries for most prisoners. Punishment, at the whim of an SS officer, was to hang the prisoner by the wrists tied behind his back until he died in agony. There were many deaths in the camp as a result of inhuman treatment, hard labour and starvation.

During his incarceration, Hans-Joachim was sent a letter, dated 15 November 1938, from the *Reichsminister für Volksaufklärung und Propaganda*, Goebbels' Propaganda Ministry, informing him that he was forbidden to practise his profession:

As from today, I exclude you from membership of the State Culture Chamber and also from the State Music Chamber. This decision is irrevocable. Through this decree you lose the right to exercise any activity in the sphere of the State Culture Chamber and at the same time lose the possibility of exercising all rights which as partner in the music publishing company of C. F. Peters you have exercised.

Goebbels had engaged SS Standartenführer G. Noatzke of Berlin to take over the custodial direction of C. F. Peters. His job was to confiscate the company; he was to be an interim custodian until the firm could be 'sold' to a suitably qualified Aryan person who understood music publishing. Many companies owned by Jews and taken over were to be liquidated. The Ministry had no intention of liquidating

C. F. Peters, rather to continue to benefit from it as a profitable source of foreign revenue for the Nazi state and also as a demonstration of pride in German culture. They did not want to run it as a state-owned business, which might not attract foreign trade, but wanted it to be sold 'legitimately'. There were several opportunists wishing to 'buy' what was arguably the finest music publishing business in Germany. It was Noatzke's job to weigh up the merits of the various applicants and to make his recommendations. The selling of the business to an Aryan would then constitute its 'Aryanization'.

Henri Hinrichsen did not feel himself to be capable of handling this grotesque situation on his own. With immense courage and in danger of being arrested again, he demanded that Hans-Joachim be released so that they could together oversee the compulsory handover of the business to Noatzke, who knew nothing about music publishing whatsoever. He said that unless his son was released, he would not cooperate. It must be credited to his determined stand that the 29-year-old Hans-Joachim was released from the incarceration and tortuous regime of Sachsenhausen. Emaciated and battered, he hid the true extent of his suffering from his mother and father.

All the most important Jewish men in Leipzig and many more had been arrested on the morning of 10 November 1938. Most of these were sent to Sachsenhausen or Buchenwald. Throughout Germany, some thirty thousand Jewish men, ranging in age from 16 to older than 60, were rounded up – around ten thousand of these were transported to Buchenwald concentration camp.

Dr Ludwig Frankenthal arrested

Having heard the terrible sounds of shattering glass during the night, the Hinrichsens' son-in-law Dr Ludwig Frankenthal got up, dressed and went straight to his hospital at 5.00 am, fully expecting to find many new patients. He prepared himself for an operation but was prevented from completing it. At 7.00 am he was fetched from the operating theatre by Gestapo officers. He was released the same day but rearrested the following day and taken straight to Buchenwald. When someone phoned Ilse from the hospital an hour later, she was warned that her life was also in danger as many Jewish women and children were being arrested. She was advised to take the two children and go into hiding; Günther was nine years old and Wolfgang was seven and they were terrified. They hid in their caretaker's home at first but returned to their own apartment after a few days. After ten days, Ilse met somebody who had been released who told her that she had to do everything possible to get her husband out because otherwise he would surely die there. In mortal fear for his own life, he outlined the brutal and inhuman conditions of Buchenwald which Dr Ludwig Frankenthal would be experiencing.

Buchenwald concentration camp

The prisoners were kicked and pushed into overcrowded railway trucks by brutal SS guards. Older men fell and those who tried to help them were kicked and pummelled by the guards who screamed insults at them. They were told that they would be shot if they tried to escape. When the train arrived in Weimar, the nearest station to Buchenwald, they were told to get out '*schnell, schnell, schnell*– [quick, quick, quick]'. The thugs from the SS Deaths Head Corps had formed two lines on the station platform. The prisoners had to run between them whilst dogs snapped at them and the guards whipped, beat, kicked and lashed them with belts, straps, whips and sticks, forcing them to run through to the waiting trucks to the sound of shrieked curses and insults. Any injured Jew who could not go on was shot. They were told to run back and forth and then stand against the wall; anyone who moved would get beaten. They were then crammed onto trucks and, once arrived at the camp, they again had to run the gauntlet past SS officers who beat them with bars. Suitcases burst open and the SS guards helped themselves to whatever valuables took their fancy. Some prisoners were forced to crawl in the dirt or were ordered to beat each other whilst the SS men stood by and dowsed them with icy water. The thousands of people who had been transported there that day were milling about, being told to go from one place to another; to lie down on the ground, to get up for no apparent reason and then to register. This inhuman treatment served to cow them into instant obedience. By nightfall, searchlights, machine guns and barbed wire surrounded the prisoners. Throughout the night they were registered, recorded and registered again. They were screamed at, beaten, herded from place to place and ultimately their heads were shaved. Sixty-eight Jews went mad that first night and were clubbed to death; some were suffocated in latrine buckets, others were torn to pieces by dogs. The subsequent days and weeks were horrific. Given very little food, the men had to work 12 to15 hours a day quarrying stone. There was terrible overcrowding and filth and they had to contend with disease, constant abuse and torture.

The Frankenthals flee Germany

Hardly able to believe this horrific description of what her husband was suffering, Ilse was determined to secure Ludwig's release from Buchenwald as quickly as possible. With tremendous courage she went to the Gestapo every day, enduring their insults, to negotiate his release. Finally they told her that her husband would be released if she arranged the family's emigration within 14 days. That posed considerable difficulties, as they had never made any applications for visas to leave Germany and there were huge waiting lists. For some years Ludwig had been the only Jewish doctor left in Leipzig, indeed in the whole of central Germany, and he had never wanted to desert Jews who were forbidden from consulting non-Jewish doctors. It had always been emphasized by the Nazis that nothing would happen to veterans who had fought at the front during World War I, especially those who had been awarded with the Iron Cross for bravery, as Ludwig had been. Now these assurances counted for nought. Ilse was a determined and single-minded woman. She went to the American Consulate in Berlin immediately where her application for visas received the number 53,086-9. This signified that the process would drag on for months, not eased by the fact that her brother Walter had sent an affidavit from Chicago. However, the Gestapo insisted that they must leave Germany within 14 days or Ludwig would not be released.

It was useless to expect any speeding up of the US visa process, so Ilse immediately broached another possibility. Three of Ludwig's brothers had previously obtained sanctuary in Holland and, through their intervention, she was able to obtain visas for the family to emigrate to Holland. With this permission, she went to the Gestapo again and secured Ludwig's release from the hell of Buchenwald on 27 November 1938. He was in a terrible condition and couldn't stop crying; he had nightmares at night and complained of terrible pains in his nose. Through her medical connections, Ilse managed to get Ludwig into hospital where he underwent two operations. He was petrified that he would be sent back to Buchenwald; he would not talk of his terrible experiences to anybody for fear of further reprisals. In order to leave Ilse free to make all their emigration arrangements, Ludwig remained in hospital until the family left for Holland on 15 December.

The demand for passports and entry visas to other countries escalated and the problems faced in getting out of Germany attained horrific proportions. All the Hinrichsens had applied for visas for the USA but would settle for any country granting them an interim visa. The embassies and ministries providing the various documents were mostly in Berlin. So the home of the Hinrichsens' eldest daughter Lotte and her husband Dr Otto Sobernheim became a family meeting point. As a result of her determination and superhuman efforts with the Nazi authorities, Ilse and Ludwig and their two young sons were the first to leave.

Before they could do so, however, Ilse had to make all the arrangements for the transportation of their household goods to the USA and to pay 100 per cent duty on their value. They had to sacrifice their entire life savings and insurance policies and deposit RM95,000 as Jewish refugee tax. Like all would-be émigrés, they also had to pay Jewish wealth tax, emigration tax, religious community tax, income tax, higher income tax and others. They fled Germany penniless and spent their last night in Berlin with Lotte on their way to 's-Gravenhage.

Martha wrote to Walter on 13 December about the difficulty of obtaining visas and the various plans which his three younger brothers were pursuing to escape Germany:

> This should be the Christmas letter . . . Father puts a brave face on things, at least in public, but the thought that he has to give his whole life's work away, just like that, has depressed him terribly. Above all is the uncertainty as to how he will lose the business. He has not been permitted to enter the business premises since the 12th of November, and has been forbidden to say anything about the running of the business . . . We want to make sure that Hans and Robert get out of German territory as soon as possible, and until then we will not know what remains to us from the business, and they must have something to live on. We and Hans cannot get at our money, and Robert hasn't any. We have enough to live on here . . . Max moved heaven and earth to try and get Hans out for us. He sent a Peruvian visa for him, which made no impression because it has no value without the various papers which are demanded to accompany it and which take a long time to procure. He also sent an invitation for Hans from a friend in England, which also had no effect on the authorities because he had to have an entry visa for London . . . Robert has written to Sidney, Melbourne and New Zealand, offering himself and Hans, and has a tiny ray of hope . . . Paul is now also here; he is helping Robert with the organization of our emigration so that everything will be running smoothly by the time they leave. Paul is still hoping to be able to leave on 29 December; they hand out the first visas on the 22nd and he is planning to stand in the queue in Berlin all night. Then I will take him to the ship in Hamburg.

None of Martha's hopes or her sons' plans were realized. Paul was not able to leave on 29 December and neither were Hans-Joachim nor Robert able to leave. Martha was right to worry about whether any part of the considerable Hinrichsen fortune would be left to herself and her husband.

Paul Hinrichsen's trauma

Born in 1912, Paul was the Hinrichsens' sixth of seven children
(Fig. 30). Following his three elder brothers, he had been educated at
the Nicolai School in Leipzig but his whole worldview set him apart
from them. Unlike his brothers, his main interest was not in cultural
and city pursuits and he did not incline towards a career in the family
music publishing business. He was a nature-lover whose early dreams
veered towards a life at sea, though as he matured his heart turned
towards the land; he wanted to go to university to study agriculture.
He studied at the University of Thüringen from 1932 to 1934 but as a
Jew was not permitted to complete his doctorate. Thus he enrolled at
an agricultural college in Denmark where he pursued his studies with
great success. Paul's ambition had long been to go on to study at a
colonial college in the USA and then to buy a farm in Brazil where he
would settle down and raise a family.

In choosing Brazil for his new home, Paul was unaware of his
family's connection with that country some three hundred years
earlier. The brother of his ancestor, the Portuguese Henrique de
Milão, burnt at the stake in Lisbon in 1610 and two of Henrique's sons
had settled there for some years. Paul was not only contemplating life
in a distant land with a family connection of which he was probably
unaware but he would also need to learn the language that his ancestors had spoken so long ago.

He had been able to realize his ambition in part when, at the age of
25, he went to Brazil in the spring of 1937 on a study visit which was
financed partly by his parents and mostly by his brother, Walter, in the
USA. He spent his time profitably touring the country and studying
various aspects of agricultural work, making copious notes that he sent
to his family in the form of long and informative letters. Brazil fully
lived up to all his youthful expectations and confirmed in him his original desire to buy a farm and settle in the country. He had already earmarked his chosen 300 hectares of jungle in southern Brazil.

Paul had intended to return home to his family for Christmas 1937,
settle up his affairs there and officially emigrate to Brazil in the spring
of 1938. Conditions in Germany had become considerably worse for
the Jews during his absence and his family and friends all urged him
not to return home, but to remain abroad. Following their advice, he
tried to extend his six-month visitor's visa to Brazil and, when this
failed, tried to exchange it for a legal immigration visa. This proved
not possible either and he tried all other available means to be allowed
to stay; he was swindled out of a sizeable sum of money on the promise
of a visa. Obliged to leave Brazil on 23 November, Paul sailed for
Hamburg from Rio de Janeiro on the steamer *Antonio Delfino*. He

Fig. 30 1937. Paul Hinrichsen 1912–1943 pictured in Brazil.

arrived back in Leipzig in time for Christmas 1937 but was unable to obtain a visa to return to Brazil in the spring.

Paul invested in a bond of entitlement to some land there with the Berlin branch of the British Railway and Settlement Company. He received confirmation from the company in London, in September 1938, on the condition that he claim his land in Brazil by 9 September 1939. He hoped to find a wife in Germany who would enjoy the hard life with him on the farm they would carve out of the jungle. He told all his friends and travelled throughout Germany to look for a suitable wife but could not find anybody with whom he would have been happy to share his life. Paul was an idealist. He happened to mention his plan to Almut, the 20-year-old, half-Jewish daughter of one of his Hamburg cousins. She, seeing it as a way out of her unhappy home situation and also as a way out of Nazi Germany, suggested that they get married. She was a cultured city girl who, he realized, would be totally unsuited to the arduous life she would have to face; he did everything he could to try and dissuade her but she was determined to accompany him. They had always liked each other and were prepared to support each other through a very difficult situation.

Paul's fiancée was a *Mischling ersten Grades* (first-degree mixed breed). Her mother was Henri Hinrichsen's niece who had married a gentile man during World War I, when such marriages were becoming more acceptable. As the wife of a gentile, Almut's mother had been protected to a certain extent from deportation to the concentration camps. The Nazis did not wish to upset the gentile relatives of the spouses in such marriages. However, her husband had died in 1933 and she was an invalid, which put her in a precarious situation. She was eventually to perish in 1943. Almut, along with her 17-year-old brother Carl-August and 18-year-old sister Ragna, was not at first in danger of transportation, though that would change. However, their lives were intolerable as they suffered the same restrictions as full Jews. Like them, they were only allowed half rations, they were not allowed to attend university or take a decent job. They were only permitted the lowest paid jobs and were in constant fear of the Gestapo. They moved from place to place, surviving as best they could. Ragna managed to get a visa for England to do domestic work – the only work which the British government would allow female refugees from Nazi Germany to undertake at the time.

The Hinrichsens and Almut's mother were opposed to this unlikely match but the engagement was celebrated by all the family in Leipzig on 23 February 1938. Though she was half-Aryan, Almut would automatically have been registered as a full Jew on her marriage to Paul. A Jew was not permitted to marry a non-Jew and she could have been imprisoned as a 'race-defiling female' – a similar situation to the one in which Paul's elder brother, Max, had found himself. Her future parents-in-law therefore wanted her to take classes and convert to Judaism – a foolhardy line of action for anybody in her situation to contemplate in Nazi Germany. She took the classes and also, for self-protection in the Brazilian jungle, learnt jujitsu. She had fittings for suitable clothing for the jungle and bought several pairs of boots, all of which Henri Hinrichsen paid for. Paul went through the countless, expensive, bureaucratic formalities required of Jews who wished to marry at that time and travelled around the country introducing himself to all of her relatives. Then quite suddenly, after a few months, she called off the engagement because she felt that they were not really suited to each other. Paul was devastated but all the relatives heaved a sigh of relief. It was a long time before Martha and Henri Hinrichsen would forgive their niece's high-spirited daughter; and she subsequently lived with the feeling of guilt for the rest of her very long life. When she subsequently fell in love with a devout Christian, they had to wait seven years, until the end of the Nazi regime, before they could marry.

Like his brother Robert, Paul had an autographed collection of composers' letters which he had to have valued and which was then forfeit to his desire to emigrate. The total value was set at RM2,330. Much later, in December 1942, these letters were to be auctioned and were offered first to the *Sächsische Landesbibliothek* (the Regional Library of Saxony) in Dresden. Almost a year later, on 28 October 1943, the director offered a lower price for several of the items. These included the letter from the Jewish composer Mendelssohn, who was reviled by the Nazis, which had originally been valued at RM50, for which the director now offered RM10, saying that he felt that was a sufficient sum, bearing in mind the lack of interest in the person. All but one item of Paul's autograph collection, unbeknown to him, went to the Dresden Library where it has apparently remained. The letter from Wagner, which had been valued at RM100, was sent to Berlin and on the orders of the Führer, Adolf Hitler, was transferred to Munich. (Hitler revered Wagner and wanted the letter for himself.) A 'Statement of Cultural Property originating from Jewish ownership', dated 6 March 1944, was sent to the *Reichskammer der bildenden Künste* (the State Chamber for the Decorative Arts), which also received 10 per cent of the sum realized. Paul did not receive any of the proceeds.

An international conference was convened at Evian on 6 July 1938 to discuss the future reception of refugees. By then, Brazil had accepted 8,000 Jews, Denmark 150, Great Britain 8,000, Palestine 40,000, the United States 55,000, Belgium 2,000 and other countries had accepted many more thousands. As the number of Jews wishing to leave increased considerably after *Kristallnacht*, the restrictions on their being accepted by other countries also grew. Paul was to feel the effects of this.

On 23 January 1939, in accordance with state requirements, Paul had to have his birth certificate re-registered in the name of Paul Israel Hinrichsen. He was 27. This new birth certificate was duly translated into Portuguese and registered with the Brazilian Consul General in Hamburg. He had still not been able to obtain his immigration visa to Brazil but he wrote optimistically to his brother, Walter, on 29 January that he hoped to get it by August. Walter had offered to pay all the various taxes, customs duties and miscellaneous payments required of Paul in Brazil which amounted to some US$1,600 from the USA because it would have been quite impossible to have the money transferred from Germany. Without this promise, there would be no hope of an immigration visa for Brazil. The sum was high due to the fact that Paul had purchased everything in the way of household goods, tools, agricultural tools for the jungle, a tent, a sewing machine, clothes and everything he might possibly need for basic survival, and all this was subject to customs duty. He was very well prepared for any hazard and full of optimistic hopes for his future, having already used his contacts in Brazil to secure himself some work experience for the first year or two.

But time was passing, and once again he had to relinquish his passage which he had booked on the steamer, *General St Martin*, for 3 February. By March 1939, he was still awaiting the promised visa which, he was informed at every enquiry, would be available 'in about four to six weeks'. He wanted to believe that this time he really would get his visa when he wrote to Walter on 10 March 1939. At the end of his four-page letter, he emphasized that his first concern was still for his parents: 'However, until the parents have left, which will probably take at least another two months, I am in no hurry to get out. But as soon as the parents and our brothers and sisters are out, I will try to get to another country, which I am sure, as a farmer, will not prove to be too difficult.'

Paul was a realist and understood that his Brazilian visa might not be issued for some time. What he did not know was that Brazil had issued secret instructions to its consulates that all Jews were to be denied visas. Paul tried to cover his emigration for all eventualities and so applied for a transit visa to Denmark. He had a guarantor there with whom he could stay for as long as he liked. But Denmark insisted on some form of guarantee from Brazil that he would be issued with a visa; this Paul could not supply because the Brazilian authorities stead-fastly refused to furnish him with any sort of documentation. He also had an invitation to Sweden but Sweden would not issue him with a visa unless he could deposit a sum of money in a Swedish bank which, of course, because of the German regulations he was unable to do. He was told that he might be able to get entry visas for Cuba or Paraguay but he knew enough about those countries not to want to apply for visas and the conditions of his entry would have been too disadvanta-geous. He investigated an offer from the Republic of Dominica, which would admit Jews, but only on deposit of US$500 and under certain conditions; and he also considered the Republic of Venezuela. Obtaining a visa for most Latin American countries was largely only possible through bribery and many visas thus obtained were not hon-oured on arrival and their bearers were sent back to Nazi Germany where they ultimately perished.

Throughout all this, Paul retained his optimistic outlook, his sense of humour and his unwavering belief that he would one day be able to get to Brazil and take possession of the land for which he had already paid. A young man, a gentile, who had been in Brazil for about four years and had a farm there himself and whom Paul had met in Brazil, was keeping an eye on his land for him. For all his optimism,

Paul was a practical young man and made provison in the event that he should die before ever taking possession of his land. He wrote to Walter, who had supported him so generously, on 5 April 1939: 'In order to make my gratitude to you still more plausible, you should receive by the next, or next but one, post a legally witnessed certificate stating that, in the event of my death, you will inherit my entire possession in the North of the State of Paraná.'

At the beginning of April, Paul received a letter from the Railway and Settlement Company from whom he had bought his land in Brazil. They said that they had been promised a number of entry permits for families who were professional farmers and that a 'family' should consist of at least two men and one woman. They said that they would try and help him but could promise nothing. He was still pursuing all avenues. Paul's applications for visas had been rejected by Holland, Denmark and Sweden. He did not want to go to England because from there he could only go to one of the British dominions and not to Brazil. So he settled on Venezuela as his second choice, in spite of the fact that that would commit Walter to a deposit of US$500 which would, however, be returnable after two years. He had done a great deal of research into all aspects of the economy, the ecology and farming in Venezuela and felt that it would provide him with a satisfactory way of life if he could not get to Brazil.

Paul went to the Consulate in Berlin, to see whether they could offer help in finding a suitable couple to whom he could become attached, and with whom he could then travel to Brazil. He stayed with his sister Lotte for a while. Feeling frustrated at not being allowed to work, he volunteered to help in the soup kitchen run for Jews by his aunt in the building that used to be the Reform Synagogue in the Johannisstrasse before all the synagogues were destroyed on *Kristallnacht*. He had some contacts and the situation looked hopeful but he had premonitions of his own mortality when he wrote to his parents on 12 May 1939: 'But I believe in fate, and I am convinced that I cannot escape my fate. If fate decrees that I should suffer an unnatural death, more accurately said an abnormal death, then it really doesn't matter where I happen to be. So long as I have the opportunity to enjoy nature and the open air.' He wrote much the same to Walter on the same day and added, 'from a totally logical point of view I feel I am entitled to think optimistically and to look forward to a peaceful and better future, which will compensate me for all the thousandfold wrong which has hurt me so deeply recently.'

Paul was 27. In spite of all his efforts, he was unable to procure a visa for anywhere and he returned to Leipzig to help his brother Hans-Joachim settle his parents' affairs.

CHAPTER THIRTEEN

1939–1940 – Dispossession and Aryanization

On 3 December 1938, a new decree was issued which concerned the 'planned de-Judaizing of our Economy'. It outlined the deployment of Jewish wealth, a ban on the purchase of property and land by Jews,

Fig. 31 1935. Martha Hinrichsen 1879–1941.

compulsory deposit of stocks and shares and official sales places for valuable metals and jewellery in Jewish ownership. Jews were forbidden to purchase valuables or to pawn or sell those which they possessed, except to government-controlled depots.

The Nazis take over C. F. Peters

C. F. Peters had been confiscated from the family following *Kristallnacht*, 9 November 1938. Henri Hinrichsen wrote to SS Standartenführer G. Noatzke, the custodian for C. F. Peters, asking what his position was. Noatzke's reply of 30 December from the Propaganda Ministry in Berlin informed him that neither he nor his son Hans-Joachim were permitted to be in any way involved with the day-to-day running of C. F. Peters. They were not to exercise any influence concerning the sale of the business and, if any prospective buyers approached them, they were to refer them to Noatzke immediately. He ended the letter with a veiled threat: 'I am convinced that your interests will be best served if you refrain from interfering in any way with the transfer of the business into German hands.' As a Jew,

Fig. 32 1935. Dr Henri Hinrichsen 1868–1942.

Henri Hinrichsen was no longer considered to be a German. In the meantime, the staff of C. F. Peters carried out their normal duties, without anybody officially at the helm. Noatzke had told the chief editor to run things as best he could whilst the business was being Aryanized and he himself would come every three weeks to see how things were going. Hinrichsen's position was in no way unique; on 1 January 1939, legislation had been passed for the complete elimination of all Jews from German business life.

Max Hinrichsen had placed applications with the British authorities on 17 November in respect of the Hinrichsens and their three sons for leave to take up residence in the United Kingdom. A letter to Henri Hinrichsen from the solicitor R. Shapiro & Co. of London, dated 18 January, states: 'Such application was supported by a very strong guarantee, and there is every reason to believe that there will be a favourable decision . . . Unfortunately there are so many cases under consideration that some time must elapse before your case receives approval.' Every country sent the same message to the Jews wishing to get out of Germany after *Kristallnacht*: 'So many applications . . . some time must elapse.'

The 5th of February 1939 saw Henri Hinrichsen's 71st birthday. Keeping him from total depression were letters from his son Walter in the USA whose sense of humour and efforts to try and secure entry into the USA for his parents gave them constant jolts of optimism. Responding to his son's cheerful birthday letter on 10 February, Hinrichsen also outlined some of his current concerns:

> Until we have an entry permit to the USA, as a mature man I will set aside all other plans. I am sure that this permit will be a long time coming . . . So, in the meantime we are trying London, but that will also take a long time. But first the business has to be Aryanized, which will take place in a few weeks. We don't know who will get it . . . I am attempting through tax, atonement fines, emigration tax and the like to reduce the fortune acquired through half a century of hard work. Hopefully there will be some left at the end. It really is a difficult time for an old man.

Henri Hinrichsen heard nothing from Noatzke, though he had repeatedly tried to get an appointment to see him; but after ten weeks he felt he had to take some action. On 26 February 1939, he wrote to Staatsrat Hans Hinkel,[1] Noatzke's superior at the Propaganda Ministry.

---

1 Hans Hinkel (1901–1960) SS Reich Organization Leader of the *Kampfbund für Deutsche Kultur* (Fighting Society for German Culture) and manager of the *Reichskulturkammer* (Reich Culture Chamber).

At the end of last year, the custodian of my publishing company informed me that my interests would best be served if I refrained from trying to have any influence on the transfer of my business into German hands. I followed this suggestion, even though – as I have recently discovered – originally the opportunity was to be granted to the owner of a company to come to some agreement with a prospective purchaser. In the meantime, the accounts for 1938 have been approved. I was promised an interview with the custodian, which has now, after ten weeks, been refused. I am approaching you today with the request that you inform me of the current situation. I can only successfully pursue my preparations for emigration if I know what will remain to me abroad from the sale of my publishing business. To what extent may I take my collections abroad with me, bearing in mind my decades of work promoting German music to the world, my trusts for the general good, such as the Music Instruments Museum, the Peters Music Library and the *Sozialpädagogisches Frauenseminar* [the Henriette Goldschmidt School]? I have no means to call on abroad and, after 50 years in the music trade and at the age of 71, I am not in a position to earn a living and support my wife. It can only be to the disadvantage of C. F. Peters, whose export business under my direction during the years 1932–1937 brought approximately 3 million marks in foreign currency into Germany, if it lacks a director for very much longer.
Henri Israel Hinrichsen.

The publisher who eventually presented himself to Staatskommissar Hinkel and SS Standartenführer Noatzke at the Propaganda Ministry in Berlin was Dr Johannes Petschull. He required capital and chose as his prospective partner Dr Kurt Herrmann, a book dealer. Herrmann's connections were most advantageous; he was a friend and hunting partner of Reichsmarschall Goering and had been awarded the title of Staatsrat (Councillor of State) sometime after 1934. Together Petschull and Herrmann put in a bid for C. F. Peters.

Dr Johannes Petschull, born in 1901, had worked in music publishing at B. Schott Söhne in Mainz since 1927. Dr Kurt Herrmann, born in 1888, the son of a labourer, trained as a building engineer and married the daughter of Bernhard Meyer, a rich industrialist, in 1914. From his father-in-law he inherited three aeroplane factories, a motor factory, a publishing house and a printing works and he maintained a lavish lifestyle, also owning hunting estates. He became the owner of several Jewish businesses, including jewellers and substantial properties which he 'bought' at extremely advantageous prices and Aryanized. Both men were full card-carrying members of the NSDAP (the Nazi Party). (There were approximately 10 million members of the party – one fifth of the adult population of the German state.) Certain definite obligations were entailed in membership, not the least of which was the swearing of an oath of allegiance to the Führer, Adolf Hitler.

The transfer of ownership, called *Arisierung* (Aryanization), as well as *Entjüdung* (de-Judaizing) was a special, complicated process completely outside of normal market practice. Neither sales nor purchases could be freely entered into; the dispossessed owners were not allowed any influence and were not allowed to recommend any particularly suitable Aryans to become their heirs; in the same way, the buyers were reduced only to announcing their desire to purchase the company. Everything else was regulated by the Propaganda Ministry and the Ministry for Trade and Industry. Every purchase was subject to the personal approval of Dr Goebbels. He had the prospective purchasers thoroughly investigated from the point of view of political loyalty and professional competence. The Aryanization process dragged on for over a year.[2]

Meanwhile, Hans-Joachim Hinrichsen could not get permission to leave Leipzig until the Aryanization of C. F. Peters was complete; he had to register regularly with the police department. Well-known throughout the relevant circles in Europe for his doctoral thesis on *The Transfer of Musical Copyright to Music Publishers and Authors and Composers' Societies*, he tried to find himself a job, and hence an entry permit, in another country. In April 1939, he wrote to some of his contacts in legal and copyright associations throughout Europe, offering his services and asking for references and introductions. He received many glowing testimonials and letters of admiration and appreciation. They all recommended him, not only for the excellence of his thesis but also for his thorough practical grounding in all aspects of his subject, and suggested that he would be a great asset to a future employer. Hans-Joachim had all these testimonials translated into English by an official translator in Leipzig and set about applying for jobs abroad. In spite of all the appreciation, he received no offer of a job.

In view of the Hinrichsens' applications for exit permits from Germany, in July the Foreign Exchange Office of Leipzig ordered the new (Nazi) head librarian of the Peters Music Library to take all of Henri Hinrichsen's collection of autographed letters into custody and have them valued, at the owner's expense. By August 1939, their

---

2 The Aryanization of C. F. Peters is fully detailed in *Music Publishing and Patronage*.

emigration plans had not progressed. All officials were exercising frustrating delaying tactics and hence all the paperwork was delayed.

Ration cards were issued on 27 August 1939 – Jews received half the rations that Aryans were entitled to; they were also only permitted to shop late in the day when the food that remained was what nobody else wanted. Hitler announced the annihilation of the Jewish race if war were to break out. In October and November, Leipzig Jews were moved out of their homes and herded into 47 'Jewish houses'. The Nazis would thus have better control over them and could easily round them up for deportation. Exceptionally, the Hinrichsens were able to stay in their home – albeit illegally. They never went out and friends brought them such meagre rations as they were able to obtain.

The Sobernheims flee Germany

Lotte's husband, Dr Otto Sobernheim, who had until his dismissal in 1933 been a supervising judge of the Prussian Court System, refused to talk about his horrendous six weeks' experience in Sachsenhausen concentration camp. Like his two brothers-in-law, he emerged from concentration camp emaciated, starved, brutally injured and petrified.

On her husband's release, Lotte Sobernheim had a struggle similar to her sister Ilse to get entry visas for herself and her family to emigrate. In spite of contacts abroad who sent affidavits guaranteeing their support, all her efforts to keep her family intact were in vain. Her son and her two daughters were to find themselves on opposite sides of the Atlantic. An entry visa to the USA for her 17-year-old son Heinz had been granted in early November 1938. He was due to leave by train for Holland on the evening of 10 November – the day after *Kristallnacht*. After a traumatic day during which he was hidden from the mob and the Gestapo by non-Jewish friends, he managed his escape. On 12 November, the boy sailed to the USA and freedom. His passport was stamped with the obligatory large red 'J'. Heinz had been attending school in Switzerland where his great friend was an English boy, Kent Nowell. Thanks to this schoolboy friendship, his two young sisters, aged fourteen and nine, were able to escape to England the following year with the help of the boy's Methodist parents. They arranged for the girls to be brought to England on the *Kindertransport* in July 1939, and guaranteed to provide maintenance for them and their parents. The *Kindertransport* was a scheme organized by the British Jewish Refugee Children's Movement in conjunction with the Red Cross that saved the lives of 10,000 children up to the age of sixteen, 90 per cent of them Jewish, in 1938–9.

It was not until 25 August 1939, just a week before the outbreak of World War II, that Lotte and Dr Otto Sobernheim could themselves leave for England. Had it not been for the Nowell family's vigorous efforts and guarantees on their behalf, they would not have survived. They were subject to the same financial strictures as Ilse had been and left Germany totally penniless; they owned nothing but their lives and the clothes they were wearing. Their son Heinz eventually found his way to San Francisco, where he married Ursula Koninski, also from Berlin. When he joined the US Army in 1943 and was sent to Europe, he changed his name to Henry Stanton.

At that time Lotte's youngest brother, Robert, was still in Leipzig. The whole family was desperately trying to get out of Germany. Walter tried to obtain visas and guarantees from the USA and Max was trying to facilitate arrangements in England. The visa application process was complicated and by that time required a guarantor from a host country to make an application. The American Consulate was so inundated with applications that they could not easily trace one before it came to the top of the pile.

Robert Hinrichsen flees Germany

Robert Hinrichsen, the seventh and last child of Martha and Henri Hinrichsen, was born in 1918. When the Nazis came to power in 1933 he was 15; as a Jew, the school doors were soon closed to him and his parents sent him to Scotland to complete his education at Gordonstoun School. Returning to Leipzig, he was unnerved at his necessarily abrupt entry into adulthood. His parents urged him to take immediate steps to secure his emigration from Germany. Robert went to Berlin in March 1939 to attend to formalities before he could be permitted to leave Germany. The regulations regarding currency and possessions were considerable and the complex bureaucracy delayed the issue of his passport several times. To the great relief of the family, he was finally granted a passport and visa and emigrated to England in July 1939. Had his papers been delayed by a further six weeks, when war broke out on 3 September, he would not have been permitted entry to Great Britain. His carefully packed and listed luggage, on which he had had to pay 100 per cent duty, never left Germany; it was confiscated by the Gestapo and he never saw his possessions again.

After war broke out on 3 September 1939, the British Home Office banned virtually all immigration from Germany and declared all previously issued visas to be invalid.

Henri Hinrichsen in prison again

Henri Hinrichsen was arrested on 8 November 1939. He was incarcerated in the Leipzig police prison in cell number II with several others for six weeks until his release on 19 December. The reason for his imprisonment was given as 'political'. Dr Hans-Joachim Hinrichsen was arrested on 10 November for the same reason as his father and placed in the same cell. He was also released on 19 December.

The authorities wanted to strip Henri Hinrichsen not only of all he possessed but also of his honorary doctorate from the University of Leipzig. In order to emigrate, it was necessary to apply for a *Heimatschein* (a certificate of domicile), which he had done. In respect of this, the director of the electoral register department of the city of Leipzig wrote to the university on 28 November 1939 pointing out that Henri Hinrichsen was a Jew and asking whether he was still entitled to use the title of Doctor. Bräunlich, the Dean of the Faculty of Philosophy of the University of Leipzig, bravely replied on 1 December, stating:

> In reply to your enquiry of 28 November 1939, I inform you that the Geheime Kommerzienrat Dr phil. h.c. Henri Israel Hinrichsen, born in Hamburg on 5 April* 1868, is still entitled to use the title of Doctor of Philosophy awarded to him by our Faculty. According to the regulations in force, the fact of his Jewish descent does not justify the withdrawal of his doctorate.
> Heil Hitler!

Everything is confiscated

Henri Hinrichsen had a splendid collection of German paintings that he was obliged to sell at a price well below the market value. Before this sale could be effected and whilst he was in prison, Martha and Paul received a letter from the authorities demanding that they hand over the entire collection of paintings, drawings and autographed letters for 'safe-keeping'. The communication concluded with the words: 'The costs of this order are to be met by the person affected. The right to complain to me against this Safeguard Order is given, but it will have no effect. Any contravention of this Safeguard Order will be punishable by arrest and in particularly difficult cases by long-term imprisonment.' Against such an order, there is no resistance for an old lady. Not only were Henri Hinrichsen's collections being confiscated but he was also expected to pay the costs of such action.[3] Henri Hinrichsen received nothing of the money that was due to him from

---

* The writer had written April in error. Henri Hinrichsen was born on 5 February 1868.
3 The details are fully documented in *Music Publishing and Patronage*.

the sale of his valuable collection. The Finance Department did not sanction its release to him.

The Hinrichsens had already been denied one entry permit to Belgium which they had not been able to claim in time because of all the bureaucratic delays. The Aryanization process of C. F. Peters and arrangements for the compulsory sale of Henri's paintings and autographs were complete, so he wanted to hasten his departure from Germany. He was fighting against time, exacerbated by a sense of being harassed by bureaucracy. It would mean certain death for himself and his wife if they were unable to use the visas that they had been granted for entry to Belgium by the due date. He wrote to the Director of Finance in Leipzig on 7 January 1940, detailing the arrangements he had completed and enclosing a copy of a letter from the Consulate of Belgium in Leipzig. He wrote:

> From this you will see that the right to a visa for Belgium will be lost to my wife and I and to our son if we are not able to present our passports to the Consul in Berlin by 19 January. I would respectfully request you to treat our affair with urgency, in order to avoid our losing an entry permit for the second time.

The letter from the Belgian Embassy in Berlin to the Belgian Consulate in Leipzig was dated 3 January 1940:

> The Belgian Ambassador in Berlin has the honour to inform the Belgian Consulate in Leipzig, in reply to his letter of 29 December 1939, B.13, No. 7237/650, that the transit visa for Belgium must be collected by the beneficiaries within thirty days of their being informed by the diplomatic representative. In this case the couple Hinrichsen and their son must collect the visa before 20 January 1940

On 8 January, Dr Hans-Joachim Hinrichsen wrote to C. F. Peters along the same lines and enclosed a copy of the letter from the Belgian Ambassador. He begged Dr Petschull to help expedite matters:

> As you well know, we have already lost an opportunity of an entry visa abroad, which we had obtained with the greatest difficulty, because our passports were withheld owing to the business. Now, after great effort, we once again have the opportunity of an entry visa, this time to Belgium. We have no hope of receiving another offer of an entry visa if we cannot make use of this one in time. Therefore I ask you to expedite the processing of our affairs. Without the acknowledgement of the various authorities that my

parents will be able to receive the sum promised to them abroad, they do not dare leave. Apart from that, they will not be given their passports until the Finance Ministry and the Religious Community have issued the document certifying that they have no taxes, loans, etc. outstanding. This is on the assumption that you have transferred the sum of RM550,000 to pay for the *Reichsfluchtsteuer* (refugee tax), *Judenvermögensabgabe* (Jewish wealth tax), *Auswander-Abgabe* (Emigration tax), *Gemeinde-Anlage* (Religious community tax), etc. Please will you effect the transfer without delay and impress upon all the authorities the necessity for immediate settlement of the arrangements made with Dr Franz . . .

Martha and Henri Hinrichsen flee Germany

Enough papers were gathered together for passports to be issued to Martha and Henri Hinrichsen and for them to be able to claim their visas for Belgium. But their financial security was not assured and there was still a great deal to be organized in connection with their departure. Before leaving, Henri Hinrichsen wrote a letter to the staff of C. F. Peters on 27 January, taking his leave of them:

> Dear Ladies and Gentlemen!
> Before we leave Leipzig, I would like to say goodbye to you in the name of my wife and son. As much as it was always my pleasure to work with you in the steady growth of the Edition Peters, in which we enjoyed considerable success, it is my pain that the conditions now prevailing have caused a sudden severance.
> I hope that you are all able to enjoy many years under the new management in the old established company and thank each one of you for your faithful collaboration.
> With kind regards,
> Henri Hinrichsen

The next night, Henri and Martha Hinrichsen crept quietly out of their house, 10 Talstrasse, Leipzig. Shutting the door behind them for the last time, they put their keys through the letter box. Without money and with nothing but hand luggage, they made their way towards the railway station with their son Paul to see them off.

Paul, who was 28 by then and no nearer obtaining a visa for anywhere, was living in the *Isrealitisches Kinderheim* (the Jewish Children's Home) at 7 Jacobstrasse in the Jewish ghetto in Leipzig where he helped with the children and drove the horse-drawn cart. Hans-Joachim remained in Leipzig for a further six weeks, in hiding, alone in 10 Talstrasse trying to organize his parents' financial affairs and make some sort of provision for his and his parents' future. Paul brought him food.

Paul helped Hans-Joachim pack their parents' household goods and personal possessions – other than their valuables, which they had had to forfeit – for despatch to the USA. They worked from five o'clock in the afternoon, right through the night, preparing the obligatory list. The customs official came at 8 am the next morning to check everything as it went into ten packing cases. The list was four pages long and included every single item from table linen, dish cloths and egg cups to pictures (of little value), sheet music and 'about 100 books'. It was in German and English to make it acceptable to the US customs. The cases were sent for despatch via the port of Bremen. They never left Germany. Confiscated by the Gestapo in 1942, the contents were sold in a so-called 'Jewish auction' for the benefit of the state.

Hans-Joachim's appeals go ignored

The various officials who were supposed to give acknowledgement that the taxes demanded of Henri Hinrichsen had been paid were singularly disinclined to make themselves available. Time was running out for Hans-Joachim whose entry visa to Belgium would expire for a second time if he did not leave Germany soon. He had to appeal to Dr Petschull to try and expedite matters and wrote to him covering all the points on 12 February 1940: 'Following our discussion of last week, I sent a detailed petition to the Finance Department. I was once again given the reply that an assessment could only be undertaken when the amounts in question had been settled. As I have already told you, the amount of refugee tax cannot be established until receipt of the tax assessment.' He went on to explain that he had not accompanied his parents when they had left, even though they had needed his help, but had remained in Leipzig in order to clarify the tax matters. He now realized that his presence has been entirely useless unless Dr Petschull immediately agreed to transfer the amount in question for the Ollendorff[4] pension and the taxes paid on his own behalf by the company to his father's blocked account number 17039 at the Leipzig branch of the Deutsche Bank. He continued:

> My father undertook to commit his entire private fortune to cover the taxes and officially required payments. For the publishing

---

4 Paul Ollendorff, former Business Manager and editor at C. F. Peters to whose widow Henri Hinrichsen was paying a pension.

company alone he has paid RM650,000, irrespective of refugee tax, Jewish wealth tax, emigration tax, religious community tax and other taxes. Clause 2 stated that RM550,000 was to be paid to my father immediately on completion. It was specifically agreed that only the compensation requirements of the custodian had to be met by my father. For this reason alone, my father cannot be held responsible for the Ollendorff pension or for the taxes paid on my behalf, quite apart from the fact that the business was taken over with 'all existing active and passive assets' except for the personal accounts of the partners. There is therefore no doubt at all that my father is not responsible for the Ollendorff pension.

The same is also true of the taxes paid by the business on my behalf. Apart from the reasons detailed, my father really cannot be held responsible for this because the purchase price of RM550,000 is to be paid exclusively to my father and not to my father and I. In addition, I could not possibly have been in a position to pay the taxes because my capital and net profit were paid to the business to cover my taxes (income tax RM12,127; higher income tax RM2,676; Jewish Wealth Tax RM4,800). For this reason, I could not have been held responsible for the amounts, unless I had known that the custodian had agreed the settlement of my tax debts through the business with Dr Franz. Apart from this, the contract states specifically: 'Any payments made to the partners after 17 November 1938, need not be refunded.' Finally, the taxes were paid from the business on someone's own initiative, against my wishes, whilst I was in prison. I myself only asked that an appeal should be registered against the taxes that I was required to pay – income tax, higher income tax and wealth tax.

As more than six weeks have passed since the day the company was transferred, I would like to ask you to undertake the necessary steps. You know that a great deal depends upon this for us, quite apart from the fact that I am very much afraid that I will lose my entry permit for the second time. Please, dear Dr Petschull, do not again say that you can make no decisions or that the whole matter will be cleared up within a few days. Please give the bank instructions immediately so that I can at last reach a conclusion with the Finance Department. Please accept my grateful thanks for your efforts.

Dr Petschull did not react to this plea of desperation. Hans-Joachim wrote to him again three days later, on 15 February, emphasizing the urgency of the matter and pointing out that he had to leave Germany very shortly. It was a further six days before Dr Petschull spoke to him, on 21 February, as noted by hand on both letters. There was further procrastination and nothing was settled.

Dr Hans-Joachim Hinrichsen flees Germany

Dr Hans-Joachim Hinrichsen left for Brussels on 6 March 1940.
Dr Petschull wrote to him on 9 March, telling him that Noatzke had
not appeared for an appointment and that therefore the matter was
still not settled. He was going to Berlin the following Tuesday to meet
Dr Möhring, the lawyer, and Noatzke. In the meantime, Dr Möhring
had written to Hans-Joachim who wrote to Dr Petschull on 18 March,
pointing out that Möhring had been available for discussion at any
time and that the whole matter could have already been settled. Hans-
Joachim regretted that he had risked his life pointlessly by staying in
Leipzig to try to sort everything out personally. He was, however,
still willing to make himself available through correspondence. Dr
Petschull replied on 28 March saying that everything possible had
been done from his side to settle things before Hans-Joachim's departure; it had not been possible to see Noatzke and Möhring before
12 March. In order not to complicate anything further, he would not
write any more about the matter but would leave the correspondence
to the lawyers.

There were now no Hinrichsens left at 10 Talstrasse, the house in
which the family had lived for forty years and which had been confiscated from them. Paul was the last of the family living in Leipzig, in
the Jewish Children's Home, in the Jewish ghetto. Dr Petschull wrote
to him there, on 1 April 1940, asking him to return the house keys
which were still in his possession. He also wanted to be informed when
the cupboard on the first floor would be collected. A hand-written
note on the copy letter baldly states 'settled.'

With this last act, the Hinrichsen family were deprived of virtually
everything except for the clothes that they were wearing.

CHAPTER FOURTEEN

1940–1945: The Holocaust, Exile and the Final Solution – Holland, Belgium, France, Latvia and Auschwitz

C. F. Peters continued in Leipzig under its new 'proprietors'. The Hinrichsens had been deprived of everything and had received nothing by way of compensation. Because of Nazi policy, the members of the family who had not managed to obtain visas to leave Germany were at gravest risk of losing their lives in the most terrible manner. Henri Hinrichsen's enormous contribution over the course of forty years, both financial and as a socially conscientious citizen, devoting his considerable business experience to the benefit of the citizens of his chosen city of Leipzig, meant nothing to the Nazi authorities.

Martha and Henri Hinrichsen in Brussels

Martha and Henri Hinrichsen arrived in Brussels on 30 January 1940 after a difficult journey from Leipzig. They had packed three trunks, preparing the necessary lists of contents and paying the required duty, intending to take them to Brussels in the luggage compartment of the train so that they could travel light with just one suitcase. However, the day before their departure, a new regulation forbidding Jews leaving Germany from taking anything except hand luggage had been introduced. So they had to transfer as much as they could to hand baggage. This now became so unwieldy that their son Paul decided to accompany them on the night train to the border at Aachen in order to help them carry the luggage which amounted to eleven separate bags and packages. Every piece had been sealed by the customs in Leipzig and all enclosed items had been detailed on the obligatory list. By the time everybody's luggage had been checked the train, which had been delayed, arrived two hours late in Cologne, causing the Hinrichsens to miss their connection to Aachen. As this was the only train going directly to Brussels, they remained overnight in Cologne. The next morning, Paul saw them and their numerous pieces of luggage safely onto the express train, where they should have been able to stay until arriving in Brussels.

On arrival at Aachen, the German officials announced that body searches would be made. Non-Jews were permitted to stay in the train but Jews had to descend with their entire luggage and submit to searches and complete examination of their possessions. By the time that all Jewish passengers were assembled in the station hall, the train had left. Once the search was complete, the Hinrichsens had to wait another two and a half hours for a slow train to Herbesthal. As this train also left late, they again missed the connection to Brussels and had to wait another hour. They finally arrived, exhausted, almost a day and a half late, in Brussels. Martha did not break the habit of a lifetime and wrote to her children the next day, detailing the trials of their awful journey.

My grandparents found accommodation in the front room of a small boarding house at 42 rue de la Loi, a busy main road. Coming from the beautiful house in the quiet Talstrasse in Leipzig, where they had fourteen rooms, the contrast in lifestyle was considerable. The noise of the trams thundering past every few minutes made sleeping difficult. However, as it was a main tram route, they were glad that it also made transport around Brussels very convenient. They were alive, and they were safe, and for that they were grateful. Not having been allowed to take any money with them, they lived in straitened circumstances, somewhat eased by money that their son Walter was able to send them from the USA. Their three trunks, to their great amazement, were delivered three weeks after their arrival. And they hoped to find their other ten packing cases when they arrived in the USA.

Martha had been unwell and very weak for some considerable time, partly due to her diabetes for which, as a Jew, she was forbidden insulin. She had to learn to control the effects with a special diet which, given the conditions under which they were living, was difficult to maintain. However, she had a positive outlook and took everything as it came without grieving over what was lost, only looking forward to settling in a permanent home where she and Henri could see out the rest of their days together. Their strength lay in the fact that, after forty years of marriage, they were still deeply in love with each other. Getting away from the terrible stresses and responsibilities, which their life in Leipzig had engendered over the previous few years, they were able to relax a little. This is apparent from a rare letter which Henri wrote to their youngest son, Robert, who was in England, on 6 March 1940, where he also displayed his dry sense of humour:

Good that you are able to save a few shillings; I'm afraid I cannot do that, though we are not starving. To celebrate mother's birthday, we went to the opera for the first time in one and a half years, when we saw the famous opera *Faust* by Gounod, with a superb ballet. During the day, I showed mother Brussels – with what little time she had to spare from letter writing. As I lived here for almost a year, fifty years ago, I know this lovely city which has beautiful parks and boulevards and wonderful air in view of its proximity to the sea. So your old parents have recuperated well and are adequately comfortable in their one room. It is anyway far simpler than 12–14.

Henri Hinrichsen was in fact feeling remarkably well for his 72 years and would walk a great deal and welcome the freedom to be able to read the great works of French literature for which he had never before had the time. He also had a number of friends in Brussels with whom he and his wife would share social occasions.

The Hinrichsens were delighted when their son, my uncle Hans-Joachim, finally arrived from Leipzig on 7 March, having been sadly unsuccessful in sorting out the paperwork concerning his parents' money. Whilst still in Leipzig he had not only been working on their behalf but had been helping all those Jews who sought his assistance with the legal requirements for their departure from Germany.

Hans-Joachim had even travelled to Hamburg to help his aunt Lili and uncle Edmund Hinrichsen, owner of the family business that his brother Henri had turned his back on in 1887, Adolf Hinrichsen Korsett Fabrik. The factory had been confiscated and 'Aryanized' by the Nazi government which meant that Edmund was obliged to sacrifice all he had and was forced to pay a fine of RM400,000 for 'excessive profiteering'. Edmund and Lili Hinrichsen had found it difficult to accept and to adapt to the changed circumstances brought upon them by the Nazi regime. They were so attached to their possessions, their beautiful home in Hamburg and their luxurious lifestyle that they had hoped that the situation in which they found themselves would just go away. Hans-Joachim attended to all the legal matters for them and persuaded them to emigrate and thus to save their lives. They managed to get to England in 1939, shortly before the outbreak of war.

Hans-Joachim was able to bring his entire luggage with him, and many files and documents about the business, the disposal of the art and autograph collections and the Aryanization of C. F. Peters. He found a room about fifteen minutes' walk from his parents, at 9 rue de Toulouse, in a quiet side street in which he settled happily. However, within a month the house was sold and on 15 April he moved to 33 rue Marie Thèrese, a quiet street just around the corner from his parents.

On 10 May 1940, German forces attacked Belgium, France and the Netherlands. Within days, the Germans had fully occupied Belgium and the Netherlands. Those Jews who had fled to these safe havens were now at risk.

Hans-Joachim Hinrichsen disappeared. His parents paid for his room for a further two weeks. But when they had heard nothing from him by 1 June, they packed all his trunks and files and moved them with the help of the local coal merchant, in his lorry, to the friends who were storing some of their own luggage. At the end of June, they moved to another boarding house, at 21 rue de Suisse, hoping to remain there until their departure for the USA.

1940: Dr Hans-Joachim Hinrichsen heads for the Pyrenees

Just ahead of the Gestapo entering Brussels, Hans-Joachim had made his escape to France. Heading for the Pyrenees, he hoped to get to Spain and then to Portugal and from there to get on a ship anywhere that would take him away from Europe. Whilst Spain under Franco was closely allied to Nazi Germany at the start of World War II, in time she became neutral. Any Jews escaping the Gestapo who were caught by the Spanish were interned and not deported. However, freedom tragically eluded Hans-Joachim; he was never able to reach Spain. The French police arrested him close to the Spanish border and interned him in the camp of St Cyprien near Perpignan. The camp was taken over by the Germans who deported some Jews there directly from Brussels.

During the interwar years, France had welcomed Jews from Poland, Romania and Germany but in 1939 the French government imposed restrictions on Jewish immigration and set up internment camps for refugees. There were approximately 350,000 Jews living in France when Germany defeated France in 1940, more than half of them refugees from Germany who had fled during the 1930s. Whilst northern France was under German occupation, southern France remained unoccupied but its Vichy government collaborated with Germany.

Conditions in St Cyprien and the other French internment camps, which eventually held about 45,000 Jews as well as criminals, political prisoners, women, children, the insane and many others, were appalling. Prisoners were housed in leaky, filthy, vermin-ridden, badly constructed huts which they were constantly trying to maintain. Ninety-six people were accommodated in two tiers in huts 50–60 metres long. The internees slept on straw that was rarely changed Clothing was minimal and never changed, hygiene was virtually non-existent, the water supply was insufficient, lavatories were surrounded by mud and stank horribly, disinfectant was rarely used and the flies and mosquitoes spread contagious diseases. Rodents attacked the meagre food reserves and the prisoners were on starvation rations of around 800 calories per day. At St Cyprien camp, which was subsequently closed, 85 per cent of the internees simultaneously succumbed to dysentery. The hospital in Perpignan was not equipped to cope.

Under such sordid conditions, it is hardly surprising that the death of Hans-Joachim Hinrichsen should be listed amongst the thousands who died from typhus in the French internment camps. As a Jew, he was denied medical care. This industrious and intelligent young man, beloved by so many people, died on 27 September 1940, just six months after leaving Leipzig.

Dr Hans-Joachim Hinrichsen, Martha and Henri Hinrichsen's fifth child, was 31 years old. He was buried in the Jewish corner of the Haut Vernet Cemetery in Perpignan. His parents and his brothers and sisters, separated by the circumstances forced upon them in Germany, Holland, Belgium, the USA and England, were devastated. None could attend the funeral. The Jewish community of Perpignan, unbeknown to the family, undertook to see to it that he had a proper burial according to Jewish law. This, at a time when they must have been suffering their own problems, was a generous act of brotherhood to a fellow Jew who was a stranger to them. Walter Hinrichsen in the USA subsequently commissioned a gravestone to commemorate his brother. Had Hans-Joachim received medical treatment and been cured, his fate would have nonetheless been sealed only days later. Those thousands of Jews in the French camps who did not succumb to typhus were subsequently transported to Auschwitz and gassed. The good Jews of Perpignan were shortly to have cause to envy the more-or-less natural death of one of their fellow kin. On 4 October 1940, the Vichy government issued its appalling *Statut des Juifs* – racial laws similar to the Nuremberg Laws against the Jews promulgated in Germany between 1935 and 1938.

1941: The Final Solution first mentioned

Martha was devastated at her son's untimely death and her own health deteriorated. She and Henri continued to live modestly in Brussels and were grateful for the food parcels which their daughter Ilse sent from Holland and the money which Walter sent from the USA. They were sustained by letters from their children and with the memories of forty years of stimulating life in Leipzig to look back on.

The German authorities in Belgium introduced anti-Jewish laws on 28 October 1940. Many Jews who had fled Germany now tried to flee

Belgium. Many could not face what they realized would be their inevitable death at the hands of the Nazis and they committed suicide. My grandparents could only wait for their hoped-for American visa.

It was on 20 May 1941 that Goering first referred to the 'final solution' of the 'Jewish question'. On 31 July 1941 he instructed Heydrich 'to carry out all the necessary preparations with regard to organizational and financial matters for bringing about a complete solution to the Jewish question in the German sphere of influence in Europe'.

As the war progressed, communication became difficult and it was not possible to correspond by mail with Great Britain. So it was through the Red Cross Message Bureau, part of the War Organization of the British Red Cross and Order of St John, that my uncle Robert Hinrichsen, who had by then joined the British army, was able to keep contact with his parents. The department that dealt with this type of communication was the 'Prisoner of War, Wounded and Missing Department'. Only 25 words were permitted on a printed form from an 'enquirer', who had to be related to the addressee and was obliged to state his relationship. These brief communications took well over a month to reach their destination and a reply limited to only 25 words was permitted. The forms went through censors and via the Red Cross in Geneva and had to be collected by the addressee. So, for example, the 'enquiry' dated 13 February 1941 from the 'son' in England was despatched on 1 April with the number 2466 and date-stamped again on 2 May. It was some time before the addressee received it and was able to reply on 18 July. It is not clear when the reply was finally received.

Martha and Henri Hinrichsen continued to hope for the miracle of their American visa. But they also realized that they might not live to receive it and made new wills. Martha foresaw their probable fate when she wrote to her children on 2 August 1941. 'We are now standing in the dark forest whose path is rugged and it is time to concern ourselves with our lives after our deaths.' Then she outlined what should be done with the contents of all of their trunks and with their possessions.

1941: Martha Hinrichsen takes to her bed

Martha's health was deteriorating and she was suffering from heart disease, diabetes and lung problems. On 27 September, the anniversary of the death of her son Hans-Joachim, she suffered a thrombosis from which she did not recover. She died on the night of 7 October and was buried three days later in the cemetery of Saint Gilles in the village of Calevoet in the southern suburbs of Brussels. Henri Hinrichsen attended his wife's funeral alone, their six remaining children being scattered throughout a war-torn world. When my uncle Walter Hinrichsen received the news of his beloved mother's death, he arranged for a memorial service for her at the Reform Synagogue in Chicago. Within the traditional Jewish memorial service was included a performance of the *Cradle Song* which Max Reger had composed in 1907 in celebration of Walter's birth and which he had dedicated to Martha Hinrichsen.

Henri Hinrichsen took over the correspondence with his children that his wife had so assiduously conducted over many years. Friends in Brussels took care of him and Walter continued to send money. After Martha's death, grandfather moved into lodgings in 109 rue St Georges with a Jewish lady, Mrs Wolf. However, in order to hide from the Gestapo, she decided to enter a convent and he moved again, this time to a boarding house at 176 avenue Hippodrome.

On 25 November 1941, the Eleventh Ordinance of the Reich Citizenship Law was issued in Germany, stipulating that the property belonging to Jews 'whose usual place of residence is abroad should pass to the ownership of the Reich upon loss of citizenship'. The Hinrichsens' ten packing cases had never left Germany and had been in the dock in Bremen for almost two years; now the Gestapo confiscated them. A so-called *Juden Auktion* (Jewish Auction) was held in Bremen on 19 June 1942 when all their possessions – clothes, linen, household goods, books, music, etc. – were auctioned off. The sum realized, RM18,315.20, was paid into the German State Treasury. Young Robert Hinrichsen's trunks were similarly disposed of.

Heydrich announced plans for the 'Final Solution' at the Wannsee Conference on 20 January 1942. These were to be carried out by Adolf Eichmann who would organize all the trains to be used in the transportation, or 'resettlement' as it was euphemistically called, to the concentration camps and the gas chambers. Implication was immediate, the first mass deportations of Jews taking place the day after the conference.

1942: Martha Hinrichsen's three brothers transported

With her death, Martha Hinrichsen was spared the knowledge of the terrible deaths suffered by her three brothers. In 1942, her brother Otto Bendix and his wife were transported from Berlin to Riga in Latvia. Like many thousands of other Jews, they were driven in lorries to pits in the Rumboli forest and shot, after which the pits were filled in. Their 17-year-old son Peter had managed to escape to England in 1939; like his cousin Robert Hinrichsen, he in due course joined the British army – and fought against his motherland. Martha's brother Fritz Bendix and his wife were transported to Reval in Lithuania where they were shot. They had three adult children. A 25-year-old daughter, Eva, escaped in 1939 and settled in England and a 21-year-old daughter, Lilo, came first to England and then emigrated to the USA. The 30-year-old son, Walter, emigrated to the USA.

Martha's third brother Kurt, who was married to a gentile, committed suicide in order to avoid the fate of his brothers. Their daughter Ellen, 28 in 1939, was a *Mischling* (half Jewish and half Aryan). By all accounts, she appears to have been a woman of dubious morals and a strong instinct for survival. In 1938, she had apparently blackmailed her uncle Otto Bendix. She survived the war in hiding, making out as best she could with her mother in Berlin. After the war, like many impoverished and starving survivors, she was involved in the black market. She never married and lived on what little she could earn and whatever money she could persuade her kind-hearted relatives in exile to send her until her death at the age of 71 in 1982.

1942 Dr Henri Hinrichsen says farewell to Brussels

There had been Jews in Belgium for several hundred years and by 1900 there were around 10,000. After 1933, the Jewish population increased to around 100,000, a quarter of them being refugees from Nazi Germany. There were 30,000 in Brussels alone. When the Germans invaded Belgium in May 1940, many Belgian Jews fled to France. Most did not get as far south as had Hans-Joachim Hinrichsen and were caught by the Germans and returned to Belgium. The Germans instigated many repressive measures against the Jews. Amongst other regulations was a curfew from 8.00 pm until 7.00 am and the confiscation of telephones. Jews were only permitted to live in designated areas – and those only in Brussels and three other cities. They were not permitted to practise as doctors, dentists or midwives and they were obliged to wear the hated yellow star.

On 4 August 1942, the first 998 Jews were deported from Belgium, via the Dossin camp in Malines to Auschwitz. Deportations continued until 31 July 1944. A total of 23,838 Jewish men, women and children never returned. Their names are inscribed on a monument to the Jewish Martyrs of Belgium, in the rue Carpentier in Brussels.

There was no further news of Henri Hinrichsen after August 1942. The Gestapo arrested him on 13 September. It was not until April 1945, after the war was over, that Walter Hinrichsen could go to Brussels and find out for himself the terrible fate of his father. This is perhaps best described in the original words in English of Berthold Kirstein, an old friend of my grandfather's who, at Walter Hinrichsen's request, addressed a letter to him with which he could pursue official confirmation of his father's death.

Brussels, April 15, 1946.

Dear Mr Hinrichsen!

I confirm to you that after the death of your mother your father, Mr Henri Hinrichsen, changed his lodgings and took a furnished room at the residence of Mrs Wolf until this lady went into a convent in order to escape the grip of the Gestapo. Then Mr Hinrichsen moved to a boarding house. I was told that early one morning in September 1942 officials of the Gestapo came to this boarding house in order to search for a man who had left several months previously. The officials then asked whether there were any Jewish residents in the house, and got the answer in the affirmative. These six, amongst which was our friend Mr Hinrichsen, were at once arrested and sent to the Jewish camp at Malines. In September 1942 a transport was put together in Malines and your poor father was on it. I do not know where the sealed vans were sent. But I was told that this transport had the number 10 and your father the number 901. I might add that, on arriving at the Jewish camp in Malines, everyone was deprived of his card of identity so that these persons lost for ever their names and became mere numbers.

Yours very truly,

Berthold Kirstein.

The *Aide aux Israélites victimes de la guerre* (Aid for Jewish War Victims) bureau in Brussels confirmed on 20 June 1947 that Henri Hinrichsen was deported to the Jewish camp at Malines on 15 September 1942 on the transport number X and that he was given the number 901. A letter of further confirmation, from Antwerp, dated 20 January 1948, was written by a man who was on the same transport and survived, N. Jakubowitz:

I can inform you that your father was deported in the same transport as I was; I even looked after him in the train, in my capacity as medical orderly. We arrived in Auschwitz on 17 September 1942 and all those who were over 50 years old, as was your father, were loaded onto lorries and driven to Birkenau, where they were killed by gas on the same day.

Henri Hinrichsen took his final choking breath in the gas chambers of Auschwitz concentration camp in Poland on 17 September 1942. The acrid fumes of Zyklon B gas had supplanted the fresh heady smell of printer's ink which he had inhaled with so much pleasure on his arrival as a young man in Leipzig 55 years earlier.

1943: Paul Hinrichsen goes east

Henri Hinrichsen's sixth child Paul had been forced to remain in Leipzig, living in the Jewish ghetto. Not only had the visa for his emigration to Brazil, which he had striven so hard to acquire, not been issued, he had not been able to obtain any other visa either. On 15 January 1941, he was transported to Neuendorf, Fürstenwalde, to work as a slave farm labourer. He was fit and healthy and loved the outdoor life so, apart from the starvation rations, this did not distress him too much. His last letter, still full of optimism for the future, was written to his 'adopted' uncle and aunt, Barnet Licht, a Jew, and his non-Jewish wife who were still in Leipzig. It was written on 5 April 1943, shortly before his transportation to the east. No further word was ever received from Paul Hinrichsen. Following sworn statements made by the businessman Salo Looser of Leipzig on 5 June 1946 and 7 April 1948, the Berlin *Landgericht* (county court) issued a death certificate on 13 April 1948. Paul Hinrichsen was in the concentration camp of Auschwitz at the beginning of September 1943, where he met his death by gassing. He had survived the typhus epidemic of June 1943 which ravaged the 100,000 slave workers and 7,000 SS guards in Auschwitz and he had borne the horrors of this terrible concentration camp for just over five months. The date of his death was established as 15 September 1943. Like his brother Hans-Joachim, who had predeceased him in the internment camp in Perpignan by three years, he was 31 years old.

CHAPTER FIFTEEN

1940–1945: Medicine, Murder and Rebirth

With the advent of Nazi rule in Germany in 1933, many Jews had gone to live in Holland which at the time appeared to offer them a haven. Ilse Frankenthal-Hinrichsen, Martha and Henri Hinrichsen's third child, had managed to obtain visas for herself and her family because three of her husband's (the surgeon Dr Ludwig Frankenthal) brothers had already been granted refuge in Holland and were able to vouch for them. However, Holland proved to be no more of a haven after the Germans entered in 1940 than Hamburg had proved to be for Ilse's ancestors in 1618 after the Inquisition had caught up with them.

The Frankenthals in Holland

Ilse with her husband and their two young sons, Günther and Wolfgang, arrived penniless in the Netherlands on 15 December 1939. The Frankenthals settled in 's-Gravenhage, the Hague, where they existed on what little money Dr Frankenthal's brothers were able to spare them. Those three brothers, as well as two further brothers and a sister, were subsequently transported to concentration camps, all to meet their deaths by gassing. (Of all the nine Frankenthal brothers and sisters, only two survived the Holocaust.) Dr Frankenthal was not permitted to earn any money so, in order to mitigate his feelings of extreme depression, he volunteered his services as a doctor without pay.

From 15 May until the end of the war in 1945, Jews were hunted down for transportation to the death camps. At the beginning of the war, there were 156,000 Jews living in Holland; around 106,000 of these perished in the Holocaust. When the Germans took possession of Holland, many Jews fled or committed suicide. The Frankenthals considered this latter option but discarded it on religious grounds. At the beginning of September, the Germans ordered them to leave The Hague. They found an apartment in Bennekom, Gelderland, at 42 Veenderweg where they survived under very difficult conditions from 6 September 1940 until 8 April 1943; friends shared what little they had with the family and Ilse sold her remaining jewellery in order to buy food. As Jews, the children were not allowed to attend the village school and Ilse taught them at home. As Jews, they had to give up the four bicycles which they had purchased with great difficulty over the past few years and this made getting about in the countryside immensely difficult. They lived in great fear of being arrested by the Gestapo and Ludwig was petrified of repeating his terrible experiences at the hands of the Nazis in Buchenwald concentration camp.

Their constant efforts to obtain visas for the USA were finally rewarded; they had all their necessary papers by May 1941 and were due to leave on the next transport for freedom. Then came the biggest blow: the United States of America entered the war and all the Frankenthals' expectations were dashed. The large sum of money which they had had to lay out was gone. They tried to get to France and had their luggage packed but that also fell through. They tried to get to other countries but all attempts ended in failure. No country would make exception to its immigrant quota to save Jews from murder by the Nazis. Even an eminent surgeon such as Dr Ludwig Frankenthal, in spite of many excellent recommendations and guarantees, was refused a visa to enter any other country.

1943: Westerbork concentration camp

The family was sent to the concentration camp at Westerbork where a doctor was required. Each was allowed to take only one large rucksack and a blanket. This meant leaving behind their entire household and possessions which they had brought with them in 13 trunks over four years earlier. After their departure, the Germans blew up the house and destroyed or stole everything.

The Frankenthals were in the Westerbork concentration camp from 8 April 1943 until 4 September 1944. Ludwig worked seven days a week in a well-equipped modern surgery, operating on and curing hundreds of people who would subsequently be transported to the gas chambers. Ilse worked from morning to night cleaning the hospital wards and surgery. Günther, who was 15 by then, had to work as a metalworker.

1944: Theresienstadt concentration camp

One day, thirteen women arrived in the camp. Dr Frankenthal was ordered to sterilize them. He refused, as it was against his religious principles. His refusal amounted to a death sentence for himself and his family. At 5 o'clock in the morning of 4 September 1944, Dr Ludwig Frankenthal, Ilse, Günther and Wolfgang were amongst 3,000 Jews herded into cattle trucks at Westerbork concentration camp for an unknown destination. On 6 September they arrived in Theresienstadt (also known as Terezin), the transit concentration camp in Czechoslovakia. There they had to do hard labour on a starvation diet. Ilse did heavy work in a potato cellar, dragging barrows of potatoes eight hours a day. Dr Ludwig Frankenthal, the surgeon, had to sweep the streets. They were in Theresienstadt for six weeks when they were suddenly summoned for transportation.

Auschwitz concentration camp

On 12 October 1944, the family was again transported by train for two days and two nights without food or water. When the train stopped, their first sight was of thousands of metres of electrified wire fencing. Ilse and her family had arrived in Auschwitz, where she remained from 14 October until 1 November 1944. The report Ilse wrote of her terrible ordeal in the concentration camps was used in the Nuremberg Trials after the war. An extract is reproduced in translation below:

> My husband immediately saw what our lot was and took his leave of me for life. Order: Nothing to be taken from the train, no rucksack, no food, men and women were separated. That was the last time I saw my two boys and my husband. A doctor stood there and selected the people. Boys had to go with the father and girls with the mother.
> Then the young and the old were selected. From one transport of about 2,000 people, only 200 remained. We, the remaining ones, were driven into the bath halls. We had to stand there naked for hours. Everything was taken from us; we were not allowed to take anything with us. I had to give up my wedding ring and my spectacles and all my things. All the hair on our heads and bodies was shaved off and after showers and selection we received very little to wear and it was very thin. It was most probable that one would be gassed if one's body did not look perfect. My body was covered in bites from the bugs in Theresienstadt. The man who selected me kicked me with his heavy boots through the entire bath hall, which

meant that I had not passed the selection. He said that I had
syphilis. The others, who were selected as good, were put on a work
transport to go to work in factories.

I was sent to the sick barrack. I was lucky; on Monday, 40 sick
people had been sent to the gas chambers, and I arrived on
Saturday. Four of us slept together on one narrow bed with one
thin blanket. We were terribly afraid; at any moment a lorry could
have come to fetch us to be gassed. After ten days, I had myself dis-
charged because I couldn't stand being amongst all those dying
people. Now there was another selection for a work transport; and
another 'fail' for eight others and myself. We were kept separate
for five days in a horse stable with hay. After five days of terrible fear,
we heard that a work transport of about 3,000 people was planned.
We mingled with the milling crowd whilst nobody was looking. We
desperately wanted to get out of Auschwitz. I had managed to
obtain some ointment to hide my scars. Again we had to endure a
selection my heart stood still; the doctor lifted his arm and let it
descend slowly: that meant: 'Saved'. After tortuous baths, we were
again given poor clothing but we were not yet permitted to get
dressed. We were lashed with whips by women who beat us out
into the ice cold night. There we were allowed to get dressed. We
stood outside for twenty-four hours for roll call, without getting
anything to eat or drink, in the cold, in the rain, near the burning
furnace chimneys. Then we received bread for three days and a
piece of sausage for the journey. The journey was desperately sad
because we didn't know what had happened to our husbands and
wives.

Fate of Dr Ludwig Frankenthal, Günther and Wolfgang

Ilse was not able to find out the fate of her family definitively until
1948. According to a notification from the Amtsgericht Berlin-
Zehlendorf to Ilse Frankenthal dated 31 March 1948, her husband
Dr Ludwig Frankenthal, aged 58, and her two sons, Günther, aged
fifteen, and Wolfgang, who was only twelve, were gassed in Auschwitz.
The date was presumed to have been 15 October 1944, the day after
their arrival. The horror of these deaths is compounded by the fact
that, less than a month later, gassing in Auschwitz was halted and the
gas chambers and crematorium were blown up by order of Himmler.
Two months later, on 27 January 1945, the camp was liberated by
the Red Army. However, information received from the Arolsen
International Search Service, dated 16 February 1988, states that
Günther was not gassed with his father and brother. His date of death
was given as 28 February 1945 'in the area of Auschwitz'. There were

at least 14 satellite camps around Auschwitz to house inmates working in local factories. Günther, by then a metalworker, would have been employed in a factory and would have died in one of those camps.

Ilse's account continues.

Bergen-Belsen concentration camp

On 1 November our work transport left in sealed, ice cold cattle trucks, which travelled for days and nights to Bergen-Belsen concentration camp. We didn't have to work, which is a far greater punishment, because the everlasting roll calls with insufficient food can drive one insane. But at first we slept in tents, until 16 November, when the storm was so strong that it blew the tents away. The barracks were full of bugs and there were many rats, which caused many people to die of typhus and starvation, especially many Dutch. I asked a man for shoes once; the reply was that I would be thrown into the pit three times over. I don't want to recall all these terrible things but I will never forget the lashings with the whips in Bergen-Belsen.

Ilse survived Bergen-Belsen concentration camp from 3 November to 15 December 1944. A work transport of 200 women left that day; many believed it would go to Auschwitz and certain death, so they remained sick. But Ilse, who had lost a great deal of weight through permanent diarrhoea, did not hesitate. The train journey was as terrible as the previous ones had been and she arrived at the concentration camp of Salzwedel on 18 December. Salzwedel, in the post-war former German Democratic Republic, was the female sub-camp of the Neuengamme concentration camp. Her report continues.

Salzwedel concentration camp

There were fifteen hundred of us women in the concentration camp of Salzwedel, near Hanover. These were Jewish women from Czechoslovakia, Austria, Hungary, Poland and Germany, etc. We had to go to a munitions factory every day. I worked on a measuring machine, filling cartridges. It was such dangerous work that my colleague, a Greek woman who worked nights, died by accidentally shooting herself. We worked 12 hours a day and then we had to shovel shit and empty the night-soil buckets. As well as all the bugs, I was suffering from typhus fever because of the chronic diarrhoea, but I worked with enormous energy. I did not dare remain in bed or I would have been transported to Auschwitz. One supervisor always used to beat me, but I had my friend Annie Ehrlich who always gave me courage. And at last came 14 April 1945 when we were liberated by the Americans.

1945: Saved by the Americans

Ilse survived two horrendous years in five different concentration camps. She was taken straight into hospital suffering from starvation and mental breakdown. She weighed only 80 pounds – before the war her weight had been 140 pounds. There a US military medical orderly cared for her and was shocked at her terrible condition. She did not even know her name and was unable to say anything except 'Peters London'. By sheer coincidence the orderly knew Ilse's brother, Walter, and knew that he was the son of the owner of C. F. Peters. He was able to contact Master Sergeant Walter Hinrichsen who was currently with his regiment marching on Leipzig from Thüringen. Walter then provided their brother Max's address in London and contact was made. After two weeks in hospital, she wanted to go home. But Ilse had no home any more and she had no family any more. She was taken by American army truck to Brunssum in Holland on 28 April where she was initially looked after in a convent. Then she went to live with a coal-mining family who cared for her with great kindness and sympathy. Starting what she called her 'second life' at the age of 41, she attended many courses and was determined to start work immediately in order not to be dependent upon others. She would not even let her remaining brothers and sisters help her. It took two years to restore her to physical health. But it took Ilse seven years of iron discipline trying to relearn everything she had forgotten before she felt psychologically able to cope with life. The inmates of the concentration camps had been driven into a psychological wilderness. Ilse's determined and strong character enabled her to adopt her father's motto: 'Put a line under it and start again.'

It was terribly difficult for her at first; this remarkable and well-educated lady, widow of a fine surgeon, worked as a dishwasher in a hotel, then in a raincoat factory, after which she worked at the conveyor belt in the Philips electrical factory. After seven years, she was promoted to forewoman. Ilse was happy to be able to be self-sufficient and capable of working. She was delighted to become naturalized as a Dutch citizen on 23 April 1952 – almost seven years to the day of her arrival from the concentration camps. Over the years, she worked her way up to hold a higher executive position at Philips than any other woman had ever held. As a woman, her retirement was due at the age of 55 but she begged to be allowed to stay working and exceptionally, because her work had become indispensable, she was allowed to remain until 29 January 1964 when she was 60. Her position then was as Secretary in the Technical Facilities Department.

But retirement was not something Ilse was interested in. At that time, the Brunssum council was looking for a suitable candidate to set up and manage art exhibitions as well as to run the local Tourist Information Office. She had no relevant experience and spoke very poor Dutch but she had boundless enthusiasm, her father's love of art and a way of persuading people to her way of thought. She made a huge success of the enterprise. She loved to collect people around her who needed her and she always managed to find people to work for others. She submerged her terrible experiences and the loss of her dear husband and children with an obsessive drive to prove to herself that her life was worthwhile; she was a powerhouse in her incessant activity and service to others. Ilse was known and loved throughout Brunssum where she was, in due course, awarded honorary citizenship.

This remarkable woman was omnipresent. Her private life and her work were completely merged and she was involved with all sorts of societies and sat on a variety of committees – like her father, before he had been persecuted and murdered by the Nazis. She was a born mediator and had many local connections which enabled her to be of service in a multitude of ways. Ilse found great fulfilment in being an unofficial foster mother to many youngsters and in promoting young artists. She felt that children's curiosity should be aroused and she helped them to love art. Ilse would celebrate her birthdays for three days, with many guests and plenty to eat and drink. The first day she would receive the mayor and leading citizens, the second, her friends and acquaintances, the third, her helpers and neighbours. But for her seventieth birthday, her tiny flat could not accommodate everybody so she persuaded the mayor to allow her to celebrate in her art gallery; at the same time, she tactfully pointed out to him that she could not possibly retire, as there was nobody to succeed her.

Ilse continued her work until the day after her eightieth birthday when she suffered a stroke. She died at the age of 83 in 1987. Her all-important motto, *Weiterleben* (to live on), will be remembered in Brunssum, the town where she lived her 'second life'. The Ilse Frankenthal Stichting (Foundation) was created in her memory in 1987 to support young artists. In 1997, a bronze head of her was erected in Brunssum. And in 1998 her biography was published: *Ludwig, ich lebe. Het tweede leven van Ilse Frankenthal-Hinrichsen 1904/1945–1987.* (Ludwig, I am alive. The Second Life of Ilse Frankenthal-Hinrichsen 1904/1945–1987.)

Chapter Sixteen

1937–1950: London – Enemy Aliens and Music Publishing

There had long been a Jewish community in Great Britain. By the 1880s, the Jewish population numbered around 60,000. It swelled to around 150,000 by 1905 as a result of those fleeing the repressive regimes, pogroms and persecution in Russia and Eastern Europe which were forcing the Jews into grinding poverty. Most of these immigrants were Ashkenazi, Yiddish-speaking tradespeople and middle-class Orthodox Jews, living in poorer areas. The British government was not altogether welcoming of these immigrants and began to impose strict immigration quotas as outlined in the Aliens Act of 1905 and subsequent Acts. In spite of restrictions, by the end of World War I in 1918 the Jewish population in Great Britain had doubled to around 300,000. This caused the government to instigate the Aliens Order of 1920, outlining the legislative framework which was subsequently to be used by the government to control the demands of Jews fleeing Hitler's regime from 1933 onwards.

An estimated 75,000 German Jews were amongst the 90,000 or so Jews who fled from the Nazis during the 1930s and found sanctuary in Great Britain. These were not economic migrants escaping poverty but refugees from political persecution. They were largely well educated and established in professions; many had been well off and were leaving substantial homes and careers behind. They were determined to settle in middle-class areas – even if they could only afford to rent a bedsit. The most popular areas were those around Hampstead, Finchley Road, Belsize Park and Swiss Cottage in London. The British government restricted the immigration of refugees from 1933 to 1938, giving preference to those who could bring some benefit to Britain. Those with creative skills, such as artists and musicians, or those in the scientific or technological field or creators of wealth in the world of business, were welcome and were granted entry visas. However, the many highly qualified doctors and lawyers who came were not welcomed by the British professional bodies who were afraid that the competition might be to their disadvantage. Refugees might also be turned back at the port of entry by the immigration officers who, up until 1938, decided to whom they would permit entry. It is estimated that no more than 10,000 refugees from Germany had entered Britain by 1938. The refugees' plight was aided by the Jewish Refugees Committee formed in 1933 which undertook to bear all the expenses of maintaining and accommodating the Jewish refugees, though not all British Jews welcomed the new immigrants, fearing an upsurge in anti-Semitism.

British government policy changed radically in 1938 to a more sympathetic attitude, following the Anschluss and *Kristallnacht* in November 1938. Between March 1938 and the outbreak of World War II eighteen months later in September 1939, British hospitality was overwhelmed by a further 60,000 refugees. But the gates were not opened easily; visas were difficult to obtain and thousands more whose lives could have been saved from the Holocaust were not admitted. By September 1939, it was proving unfeasible for the Jewish Refugee Council to support all these people and so the government took over the financial responsibility. Special provision was made for the rescue of children, with 10,000 being admitted on the *Kindertransport* – two of the fortunate ones were granddaughters of Henri and Martha Hinrichsen. Two entire schools were evacuated and there was a scheme to allow young men to work in Britain. Women could also acquire visas if they had a sponsor in the country who would employ them as domestic servants – work to which middle-class educated women fortunate enough to have connections in Great Britain were totally unsuited – but it saved their lives.

With the outbreak of war, all these refugees from persecution faced persecution in the land which had guardedly welcomed them such a short while before. They became 'enemy aliens' or, in popular parlance, 'bloody foreigners'. They were classified in different categories and accordingly sent to various internment camps, the best known being on the Isle of Man. Many were shipped to Canada and Australia. After some months, the government realized that no useful purpose was being served by imprisoning those with whom they shared a common enemy – Nazi Germany – and they were released. However, there were restrictions on the type of work they were permitted to undertake and there was a curfew for the refugees. There were also several strategic areas known as 'protected areas' in which the refugees were not permitted to live. The British were by and large mistrustful of these foreigners at a time of war and so these 'enemy aliens' generally kept a low profile. However, they contributed to the war effort in diverse ways – in factories, as land-girls, fire-watching, in civil defence units and so on. Young men were encouraged to join the armed forces, initially only the non-combatant Pioneer Corps but ultimately all branches. The Hinrichsen's youngest son, Robert, joined the British army. Their 17-year-old nephew, son of Martha Hinrichsen's brother and his wife who were murdered by the Nazis in Riga, arrived alone and also joined the British army.

1937: Max Hinrichsen arrives in England with his wife and baby

My parents Max and Marie-Luise Hinrichsen arrived in England from Leipzig in November 1937 with me. Applying for entry visas some time before the massive exodus following *Kristallnacht*, the regulations in Germany enabled them to bring their entire household with them – on payment of an exit tax equivalent to 100 per cent of the value. As they were not permitted to take any money out of Germany, they bought a certain amount of jewellery and other items with the intention of selling them. They left behind an elegant lifestyle in a lovely home, a vibrant social life and, more seriously, Max's father, Dr Henri Hinrichsen, owner of the music publishing company of C. F. Peters, Leipzig. He had been devastated that Max, his eldest son and business partner, had been persuaded by his non-Jewish wife Marie-Luise to leave Germany.

Hoping to continue to enjoy a similar standard of life, they purchased an elegant house, 30 Holycroft Avenue, in Hampstead. They brought with them their white Mercedes car and their dachshund called Bienchen (Little Bee) and they employed a refugee maid. In 1939, Marie-Luise saved the life of Marianne Peiser by inviting her to come and work as a nanny to look after me. She was a violinist who Henri Hinrichsen had spent happy hours accompanying at the piano.[1] The influx of refugees brought many relatives and friends of the Hinrichsens who arrived penniless. They were offered shelter in the spacious house in Hampstead and financial support. The result was that Max's financial resources were soon depleted. The Mercedes car was sold, the house was sold and sadly the dachshund was found a new home. We moved into a modest flat in Hampstead.

---

1 I didn't know this until some 60 years later. Out of the blue, I was contacted by Monica Lowenberg, Marianne's granddaughter, who had found my mother's letter of invitation amongst her deceased grandmother's papers, along with a photograph of my grandfather which he had dedicated to her.

Refugees were advised by the Refugee Council not to speak German in public but to speak English at all times; this posed no problem for Max who had spent a year in the USA during his apprenticeship. But for Marie-Luise, who had enjoyed a sheltered upbringing, it meant learning a new language from scratch – which pastime she chose to repeat only twelve years later.

1938: Hinrichsen Edition Ltd. is founded

The refugees were also not allowed to accept paid work that might deprive the indigenous population of a job. At the age of 37, Max Hinrichsen was not deterred by this regulation. As an experienced music publisher, he founded his own music publishing company, Hinrichsen Edition Ltd., in London on 10 March 1938. He set up his business with the assistance of a part-time secretary from a very small office in the offices of C. F. Peters' London agent, the music publisher Novello and Co. His two main objectives were: to issue updated editions of forgotten works of the past, especially those by British composers such as Arne, Blow, Boyce, Greene, Thomas Roseingrave, Stanley, Tallis and Wesley; and to issue new compositions by living composers. His first publications comprised a popular series of easy original compositions for piano by classical composers. H. E. numbers 1–7 covered respectively: Beethoven, Chopin, Haydn, Mozart, Schubert and Schumann. In publishing this series, he was acknowledging the pioneering achievements of his great-uncle, Dr Max Abraham, whose Edition Peters classics had been launched some 70 years earlier.

Max was a workaholic and man of boundless energy and great optimism for the future. It was this optimism and his belief in the pursuit of excellence which helped him succeed in the face of daunting problems. Tall, clean-shaven and with a prematurely bald head and brown eyes peering through spectacles which he had been obliged to wear since early childhood to counteract extreme short-sightedness, Max Hinrichsen was kind and generous, always eager to oblige and to help anybody in need. Like his father before him, he became actively involved in many musical organizations.

The outbreak of war in 1939 brought difficulties for publishing as paper was rationed. So Max published booklets and small-scale works. He became involved in entertainment for the troops. This probably accounted for his being one of the few 'enemy aliens' who were not interned. From 1942 to 1948, he was the Honorary Editor of a weekly newsletter, *On Leave in London*, issued for the troops by the London Regional Committee for Education among HM Forces. He also ran a successful concert agency, representing a number of musicians who were well known at the time.

Max Hinrichsen had become stateless with the issuance of the 'Eleventh Ordinance' regarding the Law of Reich Citizenship, promulgated on 25 November 1941, which deprived non-resident Jews of citizenship of the German Reich. He was granted all privileges of British citizens except the right of free travel but his naturalization was held up owing to the war, during which his official status was that of an 'enemy alien'.

Max's uncle Edmund Hinrichsen and his wife Lili arrived in England from Hamburg in 1939, just before the outbreak of war. They sat out the six war years in a flat in the Finchley Road, London. I have childhood memories of visiting them for Sunday teas during the war, when aunt Lili had miraculously managed to buy some 'extra' goodies 'under the counter' – a euphemism for buying on the black market for those who could afford it. She was a fussy woman, over-concerned with hygiene and purity at a time when we were all grateful for whatever food we could get. Edmund and Lili Hinrichsen returned to live in Hamburg after the war, around 1946, and were able to reclaim some of their confiscated fortune and to live in comfort. They were the only members of the Hinrichsen family to return from exile to live in Germany. Others were dispersed in far-off lands – in the USA, Canada, Argentina, Peru and South Africa as well as in Great Britain. Edmund died in 1952, leaving Lili a rich and cantankerous old widow who was receptive to any sort of flattery. She spent months every year gambling away part of her fortune in the casinos of Baden-Baden when she would stay at the Brenners Park Hotel. She used to upset all the staff so much with her complaints that the management finally asked her to stop coming when she was about 90. During her final years she formed a relationship with a young doctor to whom she left the bulk of her fortune when she died at the age of 92 in 1973.

The author's childhood

We were obliged to move home many times from 1940 onwards, partly because of the wartime restrictions imposed upon enemy aliens and partly for reasons of economy. So we inhabited fourteen different homes between 1937 and 1946, when we settled in our final flat in Belsize Park. One home lasted a bare two weeks before the address became designated a 'protected area'. Another one, in Amersham, comprised two rooms on opposite sides of the street. One room contained my father's desk, where he worked half the night, and his bed; my cot was behind a screen. The room on the other side of the street was my father's stock room for the sheet music which he had published; that was where my mother slept, between two armchairs.

In common with many London children, I was evacuated to the country. I lived for some time in Shropshire with my aunt and uncle, the ex-judge of the Prussian Court System from Berlin, Dr Otto Sobernheim and his wife Lotte, my father's sister. They had managed to flee to England just days before the outbreak of the war in September 1939. After having spent some time in domestic service, my aunt and uncle were provided with a ramshackle, condemned house – previously a poorhouse and aptly named 'The Haven' – which they ran as a hostel for refugees. Uncle Otto did the shopping, set the tables and swept the floors, whilst auntie Lotte managed to eke out the sparse wartime rations to provide nourishing meals for a house full of refugees. The local population welcomed them, though nobody could pronounce their name which they conflated to Soberime and even shortened to 'Soby'. There was no Jewish community there so they joined the Congregational Church. The church jumble sale was the source of all of our clothes. I still remember a green winter coat that was passed down to me after my two elder cousins had outgrown it; when it became too small for me, my mother sent it to Germany to my four younger cousins. My aunt and uncle's home became a home-from-home for me throughout my childhood; I spent most of my holidays from school there amidst the beautiful and peaceful Shropshire hills. It was there that we spent family Christmas holidays, celebrating Christmas in the German way, on Christmas Eve. Church Stretton in Shropshire provided the stability for me that was lacking in my parents' home. My father's youngest brother, my uncle Robert, would join us when he could get leave from the army. After the war when he lived in Birmingham and worked as a bookkeeper, he would always bring a goose which my aunt would roast for Christmas dinner; this was traditionally accompanied by delicious red cabbage – the succulent memory of which is still with me after some 60 years.

I was also evacuated to Dorking for a while but I attended boarding school most of the time. There were ten different schools all together – some of very short duration. One school was near an airfield in what became a 'protected area'. At the age of five, as an enemy alien I was considered to be a danger to the state and so I had to leave. When I was about seven years old, I went to Fortis Green School which was evacuated to Aspley Guise. My parents not having a proper home at the time, my mother worked and lived there as assistant matron with some other refugee women while my father lived in London. The staff had rooms in the attics, heated by coal fires. In order to save his wife from carrying buckets of coal up three flights of stairs, my father would carry the coal up for her when he came to visit at weekends. However, this upset the other female members of staff and so my father felt obliged to carry coal up for the other ladies too – a painful imposition for a desk-bound publisher who always suffered from severe back pain. After two years I was moved to a boarding school in Yorkshire for a further two years. I spent my final five years of schooling, from 1946 to 1951, at the school that was most influential in my life – a Quaker, independent, progressive, co-educational, vegetarian boarding school: St Christopher's School in Letchworth.

My father Max Hinrichsen, his wife Marie-Luise and I were granted British citizenship by naturalization on 1 May 1947.

1949: Divorce

Sadly, the years of deprivation and my father's long hours working to build his business took their toll on my parents' marriage. My father really appreciated my mother's excellent and imaginative cooking skills but otherwise they seemed to argue a lot. Perhaps my mother was frustrated at having little to do. Sadly, she was not interested in helping her husband with his business and his pride prevented him from allowing her to take a useful money-earning job. Possibly she considered herself to be somewhat redundant. She did not have to look after me, as I was hardly ever home and she had domestic help. A very attractive young woman with an elegant dress sense, she liked to go out and about and acquired a variety of escorts to take her to concerts and the theatre, as my father was generally too busy.

In 1947, Marie-Luise met and fell in love with a Hungarian pianist, Peter Solymos. The fraught courtship lasted two years – much of the time by mail – until my parents were divorced in 1949 and my mother went to live in Hungary, behind the Iron Curtain. She left on the eve of my fourteenth birthday during the Easter holidays and I was sent to my aunt in Shropshire. My mother and I were not to see each other again for almost eight years. Having endured the upheaval of moving from Germany to England, where she stayed for just twelve difficult years, learning a new language and enduring the war as an enemy alien, she left her new homeland just as she had become a British citizen and life was becoming easier. In Hungary and as a foreigner once again, she suffered great hardship under a terrible and repressive regime. She had to learn yet another new and extremely difficult language and managed to earn a little money by giving English lessons. Communist bureaucracy prevented her from obtaining a visa to visit the daughter she had left behind.

CHAPTER SEVENTEEN

1945–1950: Germany – The Aftermath – The US Army, Russian Occupation and the GDR

My family had been torn apart and many members murdered by the Nazi regime in Germany. Those still alive were dispersed in a world thrown into chaos by war. My father Max, the eldest son of Martha and Henri Hinrichsen, had fled to London in 1937 with his wife and myself as a baby. In 1938, he founded Hinrichsen Edition Ltd. Walter, the second son, was in the US army. Robert, the youngest son, was in England, in the British army. Charlotte Sobernheim and her husband, a former Berlin county court judge, were in England with their two daughters; their son was in the USA. Ilse Frankenthal was in Holland, coming to terms with life after her horrendous ordeal in the concentration camps where her husband and two sons had been killed. She was the only member of the Hinrichsen-Bendix families that entered concentration camps to have survived. The remaining brothers and sisters were desolate at the terrible loss of their parents and of their brothers Hans-Joachim and Paul, as well as of their brother-in-law, Ludwig Frankenthal, and of their two nephews, Günther and Wolfgang, and several aunts and uncles. In all, fourteen members of the immediate family had fallen victim to the 'Final Solution', dying in the most horrible circumstances.

The family music publishing company of C. F. Peters, Leipzig was intact. Its survival was due to its prestige as a publishing business of world stature and its ability to earn substantial sums of foreign currency for the German government. Throughout the war, the Nazi, Dr Johannes Petschull, managed the firm as his own business, acquired by Aryanization in 1939 when it had been confiscated from Henri Hinrichsen.

In order to safeguard all the necessary records and archives and a part of the Peters Music Library, Petschull had special metal boxes

constructed. One night in the summer of 1943, informing nobody of
his action, Dr Petschull and one colleague secretly buried these boxes
on farmland at Eisenhammer, about 40 kms from Leipzig. Had these
two men died, nobody would have been able to locate these valuable
documents.

There were major bombing raids on Leipzig in December 1943.
However, 10 Talstrasse, the premises of C. F. Peters, suffered little
damage. The last heavy bombing took place on 6 and 10 April, with
the final onslaught on 11 April 1945. The SS started systematically
murdering hundreds of Jews, slave workers and prisoners still in the
concentration camps and prisons around Leipzig. On 14 April, barri-
cades were put up in Leipzig in an effort to repel the advancing US
troops, but to no avail. American troops entered Leipzig on 18 April.
That day, Alfred Freyberg, the Nazi mayor since 1939, committed
suicide. The following day his predecessor as mayor during 1937–
1938, the Nazi Kurt Walther Dönicke, also killed himself. On 20 April,
after several days of fighting, the American army took full possession
of Leipzig and hoisted the Stars and Stripes on the flagpole of the New
Town Hall. Erwin Bumke, the president of the State High Court in
Leipzig, committed suicide, pre-empting Adolf Hitler's suicide on 30
April. When they took over the town hall, the American troops also
found the bodies of several other prominent Nazis who had taken
their own lives. Kurt Herrmann, Dr Petschull's partner and a staunch
supporter of Hitler who had profited enormously from his part in the
confiscation of Jewish assets, escaped to Liechtenstein to enjoy the
rich spoils of his dubious business dealings for many years to come. Dr
Petschull hid out in Eisenhammer.

The population of Leipzig welcomed their conquerors and 18 April
1945 became known as 'the day of freedom from the Nazis'. However,
with the division of Germany into allied zones, the American occupation would last only until the end of June. This division had been
agreed by the allied military powers as represented by Winston
Churchill, prime minister of Great Britain, US president Theodore
Roosevelt and Joseph Stalin, head of the Soviet Union at the Yalta
Conference of February 1945 and took effect in May. The Americans
would take control of the South, the French would take over the West
and the British would control the North, whilst the Russians took
control of the East – soon extending their control east to cover Poland
and the Baltic States. Many intellectuals took advantage of the inter-
vening three months to escape to the Western zones, taking valuable
documents and machinery with them.

1945: Walter Hinrichsen returns to Leipzig

Before the Russians took over, one member of the Hinrichsen family
was able to return to Leipzig. This was Walter Hinrichsen who had
joined the US army in 1942, becoming a US citizen in 1943. As a
master sergeant, he was with the Ninth Tank Division and the Second
and 69th Infantry Division as they advanced from Frankfurt/Main to
take over Leipzig on 18 and 19 April 1945. Walter was saddened to see
the bomb damage to his beautiful Leipzig but heartened that his
family home and business premises had been spared the devastation.
In order to prevent looting and to secure what assets there were left of
C. F. Peters, he persuaded the local commander to put the Hinrichsen
family home and business premises of C. F. Peters at 10 Talstrasse
under American protection. He saw to it that the Stars and Stripes flag
was in evidence at the door and that a US officer was installed in an
office to prevent any looting.

Walter's German background and experience in music publishing
qualified him to be appointed US Music Officer in the Allied Control
Commission and he was duly stationed in Berlin. The commission was
established by the allies to create democracy out of the chaos that was
Germany at the end of the war. It was in his role as music officer and
wearing his US army uniform that he returned to Leipzig late on the
evening of 26 April 1945.

A man of immense charm and the good looks of a film star, Walter
had the ability to attract friends with the genuine warmth of his personality. He was also very adept at circumventing tedious bureaucracy
which stood him in great stead, not only in his job with the American
military but also in his business negotiations, a talent which was ultimately perhaps to prove to his detriment.

His first aim was to retrieve the firm of C. F. Peters for the
Hinrichsen family. He wanted to replace Dr Petschull as general
manager. However, the only person suitable, the chief editor since
1929, had no desire to be business manager. Because Dr Petschull had
hidden many important documents where only he could locate them,
Walter, the unexpected and unwelcome returnee, was obliged to enter
into an agreement with him in order to attempt to reclaim what
belonged to the family. Some people might consider this to be black-
mail by the possessor of a valuable asset which had come into his so-
called 'ownership' in his capacity as the Nazi to whom it was assigned
six years earlier. The deal, which Dr Petschull negotiated for himself,
was that he would become an equal partner with Walter and Max
Hinrichsen as owners of C. F. Peters in Germany.

Walter was only able to stay in Leipzig for a few days and had to
return to his duties in Berlin on 3 May. Before leaving, however, he was

able to arrange the renaming of the Abrahamstrasse. Named after Dr Max Abraham in 1910, the Nazis had changed the name to Robert Naumann Strasse in 1935. It was officially renamed Abrahamstrasse on 19 May 1945. Walter returned to Leipzig at the beginning of June. On 7 June, the American military government officially sanctioned the continuation of publishing activity at C. F. Peters. During the short time he was able to spend in Leipzig, Walter also negotiated the return of a quantity of manuscripts and autographed letters which had belonged to his parents. Later he also recovered some of the paintings which his father had been forced to relinquish to the *Museum der bildenden Künste* (art gallery). This little triumph was achievable only after he agreed to donate three of the paintings and a considerable sum of money to the museum. It could be seen as an expedient bribe at a moment when time was short, the situation in Germany was chaotic and legal negotiations would have been too protracted.

On 21 June, shortly before the withdrawal of American troops from Leipzig, Dr Petschull transferred the ownership of C. F. Peters, Leipzig to Walter Hinrichsen at the Leipzig district court. In exchange, Petschull was granted power of attorney and a partnership and was to manage C. F. Peters, Leipzig. Before his departure, Walter also achieved the return of the family burial plot and paid for its upkeep until 2009 – which agreement was to be dishonoured some thirty years later by the government of the yet to be created Communist DDR (German Democratic Republic).

On 2 July, the Red Army moved in and Leipzig became part of the Russian zone. When the Russians took over, all bank accounts were confiscated so it was only with difficulty that business could be conducted. The centre of the town had been 60 per cent destroyed by allied bombing, the population was starving, there was a lack of medical care, most of the electrical and water installations were in ruins and refugees were streaming into town. In their three-month occupation, the Americans had not been able to make any substantial improvements so the Russians were confronted with a major task of rehabilitation. After the terrible treatment which the Germans had meted out to the Russians during the war, the population under Russian occupation was in fear of the retribution that they might receive at the hands of their occupiers.

In July 1945, Dr Petschull had to go through a de-Nazification process. Though he insisted at first that he had never joined the Nazi Party, on 16 July he allegedly signed a form saying that he had joined on 1 January 1939. However, there is evidence in the Berlin Document Centre that he had a Nazi Party membership card dated 6 July 1937 which would have been necessary to render-him eligible to take over C. F. Peters in the Aryanization process of 1939. Following his de-Nazification, on 22 August 1946 Dr Petschull was removed from his managerial position at C. F. Peters by the Soviet authorities and replaced with a 'custodian' approved by them. After considerable negotiation he was eventually reinstated. In January 1947, 'as an act of humane and legal duty', Walter Hinrichsen was once again recognized as the proprietor of C. F. Peters by the government of Saxony. Petschull received a licence to continue publishing from the Soviet military authority in Leipzig on 17 March 1947. But he and the Hinrichsen brothers knew that business under Soviet occupation would be unsatisfactory.

Secretly, Petschull negotiated the transfer of about 100 cases of the most valuable C. F. Peters documents to Switzerland and thence to Frankfurt in the American zone. At the end of 1948, the Russians once again confiscated C. F. Peters, Leipzig from the Hinrichsen family. The fact that the Hinrichsen family was hence unjustly robbed of its ownership of C. F. Peters for the second time was conveniently veiled by a legal manoeuvre which stated that 'the transfer of the business to Walter Hinrichsen was declared as unlawful and therefore annulled'. Thus Herrmann and Petschull were once again the legal owners but, as one-time members of the Nazi Party, the business was then confiscated from them. In November 1948, Petschull was arrested and imprisoned in Dresden. Another custodian was installed at C. F. Peters.[1]

Through the intervention of Walter Hinrichsen, Dr Petschull was released from prison after 14 months and went to Frankfurt in the spring of 1950. On 28 August 1950, C. F. Peters, Leipzig was officially taken over by the newly formed DDR and recognized as a *Volks Eigener Betrieb* (state-owned business) under the control of the government. The company was renamed VEB C. F. Peters, Leipzig. Neither Walter nor Max Hinrichsen nor Dr Petschull was involved in its management or ownership any more; they had been dispossessed. All profits from the business henceforth devolved to the German Democratic Republic.

By that time Walter Hinrichsen had left Germany but not before being materially responsible for the regeneration of classical music in Germany in his position as theatre and music officer representing the United States in the Allied Control Commission. Walter was shocked at the sight which met him on first entering Berlin as a member of the liberating forces. He barely recognized the city which he had last seen nine years earlier when he had emigrated from Germany. The elegant buildings had been reduced to ruins and heavy dust polluted the air.

---

1 A detailed account is given in Molkenbur, Norbert, *C. F. Peters 1800–2000 Ausgewählte Stationen einer Verlagsgeschichte*, Leipzig, 2001.

Fig. 33 1945. Yehudi Menuhin and
Master Sargent Walter Hinrichsen in Berlin.

People lived in dank cellars. Women were shovelling rubble to clear the streets and to find the decomposing bodies, the putrid smell of which permeated the atmosphere. The damage caused by allied carpet bombing and Russian vindictiveness on the ground brought tears to Walter's eyes; he remembered the beautiful, thriving exciting Berlin of his youth when he had visited his aunts and uncles who, as yet unbeknown to him, had been murdered by the Nazis. He thought of his sister Lotte's home in the leafy suburb of Dahlem where he had spent his last night on German soil before embarking for the USA.

As a member of the Allied Control Commission, Walter and his colleagues were battling against a non-existent infrastructure; without any experience or precedent, they were thrown into improvising to recreate a city where nothing functioned. It was a logistic nightmare. There was no public transport, virtually no food, no coal, the telephones and water mains were not working electricity was sporadic and illness and starvation were everywhere; doctors and medical facilities were almost non-existent. Music was perhaps not the first priority in this chaos. But the provision of music was Walter's fiefdom; music offered food for the soul whilst the body suffered.

Amongst Walter's many achievements was Yehudi Menuhin's first concert tour of Germany after the war. The two men remained firm friends for life (Fig. 33). Walter was also responsible for the instatement of Leo Borchard on 4 July 1945 as conductor of the Berlin Philharmonic Orchestra. Borchard, as a member of the wartime resistance, had helped many Jews to survive. In May 1945, he managed quite remarkably, with the help of the Russian General Bersarin,[2] to bring together a group of musicians in the ruins of Berlin. The first concert was on 25 May; sadly he was only to conduct 21 more. He gave what turned out to be his last concert for the allied troops on 24 August. A British officer's car running the conductor home after curfew encountered an American patrol at the border between West and East Berlin that was under orders to fire without warning on any suspicious vehicle. Only Leo Borchard was killed. He was 45 years old – a tragic loss to the music world. The American Security Service expected Walter to investigate the cause of the accident and was irritated at his lack of success. But he felt that in his position as music officer such an investigation was not part of his job.

Walter worked in close conjunction with his British counterpart, John Dennison (1911–2006), who remembered the two young officers purloining a US military ambulance which they loaded with sheet music for eventual distribution. He also collaborated fraternally with his French and Russian counterparts. With his job and his connections went a universal pass that enabled him to enter the Soviet zone so he was able to return to Leipzig during the later part of 1945. Perhaps somewhat naively Walter became friends with some of the young Jewish Soviet officers, a situation that was anathema to the Soviet secret police who kept him under constant surveillance. The US military authority was equally disapproving of his friendships. Rather rashly, Walter threw a New Year's Eve party in his apartment in Berlin which was attended by Dr Petschull and some young Soviet officers, as well as by his glamorous neighbour, the German film star Hildegard Knef; this action was to discredit him with both authorities. Through Walter's friendship and connections, Knef was able to obtain a pass to

2 Nikolai Bersarin (1904–1945) responsible for reorganizing the Berlin city government and health care. Killed in a motorcycle accident on 16 June 1945. Achieved such success in the regeneration of Berlin in six weeks that he was awarded a posthumous honorary citizenship of Berlin in 1975.

travel from the Soviet zone to visit Switzerland but on her return she was questioned in depth by the Russians as to who had enabled her to acquire the pass. On one occasion when the Soviet authorities had organized a film evening to which they invited various cultural officers but specifically excluded Germans, they were incensed to see Walter accompanied by the lovely Hildegard Knef.

It was Walter Hinrichsen who oversaw the creation of the Inter-Allied Music Lending Library in the *Staatsbibliothek* (state library) in Berlin, which opened on 28 September 1946 in the presence of officials of the British, French, Russian and US authorities, magistrates and leading men of Berlin cultural life. The main objectives of the library were to bring into Germany the best and most representative works of allied composers and to bring contemporary German composers back from the artistic isolation into which they had been plunged by the Nazi regime.

Walter Hinrichsen had accomplished much for the regeneration of musical life in Germany. But, though his military contract was renewable and expected to run until 1949, his term of duty in Berlin finished abruptly at the end of November 1947. The ostensible reason was that, having married Evelyn Merrell on a trip to New York in 1946, he wanted to start a family. His new wife was now pregnant and they wanted their first child to be born in the USA. Also, he was eager to start his own C. F. Peters business in the USA. However, it seems likely that his friendships with Jewish Soviet officers, considered by many to be undesirable, precipitated his sudden return to the USA. Also, at the beginning of 1947 he had negotiated quite openly with the responsible Soviet officer when trying to obtain the return of C. F. Peters to the Hinrichsen family which upset both the Soviet and the US authorities. In fact, after his return to the USA, early in 1948 he was summoned by the Committee for Un-American Activities and closely questioned. He was very fortunate that the Committee did not take formal proceedings against him for having socialized with Communists.

Walter and Evelyn's abrupt departure from Berlin was regretted by many. An article in the West Berlin newspaper *Die Neue Zeitung* (The New Newspaper) of 15 November 1947 stated:

> With him German music loses a friend and sponsor who, way beyond the call of duty, had understanding of all needs and difficulties and knew how to help. . . . The Inter-allied Music Library is to a large extent his work . . . His house in the Fabeckstrasse was a magnet where German and American musicians could meet. Walter Hinrichsen and his wife Evelyn Hinrichsen, who was herself employed for many years in American music libraries, leave many

genuine friendships in Berlin. Their departure is sad for all German musicians who knew them.

Walter and Evelyn Hinrichsen's two children, whom they named Martha and Henry after Walter's parents, were born in the USA in 1948 and 1949. Walter Hinrichsen founded C. F. Peters Corporation in New York City on 1 September 1948. His cousin Walter Bendix (the son of one of his mother's brothers who had been shot by the Nazis) became the sales director. Walter Hinrichsen set about reprinting the main works in the Edition Peters and soon started publishing the works of contemporary American composers such as John Cage, George Crumb, Alan Hovhaness, Ned Rorem, Charles Wuorinen and others. His attitudes towards publishing reflected those of his father, Henri Hinrichsen.

In 1963, C. F. Peters Corporation, New York, received a citation from the National Association for American Composers and Conductors. The American Composers Alliance Laurel Leaf Award 1964 was given to Walter Hinrichsen 'for distinguished achievement in fostering and encouraging American music'. He was a member of the board of directors of the Music Publishers Association, a member of the Music Library Association and the American Musicological Society. He died on 21 July 1969, shortly before his 62nd birthday. His widow, Evelyn, took his place as president of C. F. Peters Corporation, New York. She established the Walter Hinrichsen Award for Composers in his memory in 1971. Evelyn Hinrichsen died at the age of 94 on 14 January 2005.

CHAPTER EIGHTEEN

1950–1991: London, New York and Frankfurt – C. F. Peters Rises from the Ashes

In 1950, Dr Johannes Petschull, Max Hinrichsen in London and Walter Hinrichsen (who had by then founded C. F. Peters Corporation in New York) established the parallel music publishing company of C. F. Peters GmbH Frankfurt/London/New York. Petschull had been the Nazi who had taken over C. F. Peters, Leipzig from Henri Hinrichsen after it had been confiscated from him in 1938. Despite the enormous difficulties of the post-war years and the fact that all the printing plates had remained in Leipzig, the first major catalogue of works published by the three companies appeared in 1953, comprising some 900 titles. The three partners complemented each other by publishing different works from the huge catalogue, the sooner to be able to supply the whole of the Western world with most of the music published in the Edition Peters. However, negotiations with Dr Petschull were always riven by conflict. He ignored contracts between himself and the two Hinrichsen brothers when it suited him. There were constant legal actions against him but he refused to abide by the outcome and ran his business as he wanted which frequently led to considerable financial losses for the brothers.

The legal declaration of the nullification of the Aryanization contract and the worldwide legal fight for recognition of the Hinrichsen family as owners of C. F. Peters took many years. The establishment of the new company, the continuation of C. F. Peters, Leipzig, as well as the lengthy negotiations, contracts, copyrights and legal arrangements between the four different C. F. Peters companies are beyond the scope of this book. Legal processes for the reclamation of much of the Hinrichsen property dragged on for over sixty years, way beyond the lifespan of any of the surviving five children of Henri and Martha Hinrichsen.

1950: Max Hinrichsen versus Novello & Co. copyright action

On his arrival in Great Britain, Max Hinrichsen had been working with Novello and Co. Ltd. as the personal representative of the Edition Peters. The cramped office space and clashes of personality made it necessary for Hinrichsen Edition Ltd. to move in 1946 to more spacious premises at 25 Museum Street, near the British Museum.

Max was frustrated at not being permitted to publish the music which was his birthright. So he eventually made the decision to publish the all-time C. F. Peters bestseller, Sinding's *Rustle of Spring*, and some other works. Thereupon Novello and Co., claiming that he had no right to do so, took legal action against Hinrichsen Edition Ltd. for infringement of their copyright. They argued that Max Hinrichsen was not the owner of the copyright because his father had lost it and that they, as licensees under the emergency legislation, were the sole persons entitled to publish the works in England.

Bridging the years 1950 and 1951, the case lasted 19 days before Justice Wynn Parry in the Chancery Division of the High Court. Max Hinrichsen won. In his summing up of the case on 21 February 1950, Mr Justice Wynn Parry made it clear that Nazi decrees did not make law in England. He stated that the English copyright was never lost by Henri Hinrichsen and that his son Max was now the true owner:

> The courts of this country will not give effect, so far as regards assets within their jurisdiction, to the law of a foreign country which is confiscatory in policy . . . Novello and Co. have no merits in this case. I would have been quite unwilling in the interests of justice to allow the plaintiffs to succeed in depriving the Hinrichsen family, who have already suffered enough, of their inheritance.

Novello appealed against the judgement. The appeal occupied four days in the Court of Appeal in June 1951 before the Master of the Rolls Sir Raymond Evershed, supported by Lord Justice Jenkins and Lord Justice Birkett; Sir Raymond and his colleagues were in agreement with Justice Wynn Parry's earlier judgement and dismissed the appeal, with costs. Leave to appeal to the House of Lords was rejected. Max Hinrichsen was vindicated. His confidence in his own actions had been fully justified. This was the most important copyright action ever to have been heard in the British High Court of Justice. The judgements are fully reprinted in the Chancery Division records.[1]

This was indeed a triumph for Max. He could not possibly have been able to afford the costs of losing the case and he had piled up massive debts to his printers and other suppliers, to say nothing of the enormous legal costs of defending the action, throughout the many months. The publication of Edition Peters music in England, by its rightful owners, could now go ahead, without further hindrance. Max Hinrichsen then founded Peters Edition, London to publish in parallel with his own Hinrichsen Edition Ltd. By 1955, with increased personnel and a growing stock, it was necessary to move to larger premises. The only affordable address was in Islington, far from the cultural sites of Bloomsbury, but the name of the street drew my father – Baches Street. So he named the warehouse building into which the firm moved Bach House – a Leipzig connection with the composer J. S. Bach.

A major, lasting achievement of Max Hinrichsen's was the series of *Hinrichsen's Musical Year Books* which first appeared in 1944. In the compilation of these books he was emulating the *Peters Music Library Year Books* which he had helped edit in Leipzig. They were meticulously compiled reference works listing many aspects of musical life and containing a wealth of information. Nine books were issued and the title was changed to *The Music Book* when they no longer appeared annually. Volume X, *Organ and Choral Aspects and Prospects*, comprised the papers read at the first International Organ Congress, held in London in 1957, and Volume XI, the Proceedings of the 1959 Congress of the Association of Music Libraries, was entitled *Music Libraries and Instruments*.

Hinrichsen Edition Ltd. published music by contemporary British composers such as Richard Arnell, Gerald Finzi, Elizabeth Maconchy, Thomas B. Pitfield, William S. Lloyd Webber and Peter Wishart, and foreign composers. Much organ music was published. The series entitled *From Tallis to Wesley* comprised several volumes of early English music and was welcomed by keyboard players everywhere. Max Hinrichsen also commissioned and published new works for brass bands. The firm also made available modern music, which was not initially published, through CELL (Composers' and Editors' Lending Library), a service to composers and ensembles, providing a substantial library of works, largely in manuscript.

---

1 *All England Law Reports* (1951, pp. 44–61 and pp. 770–2). *Law Report, Chancery Division* (1951, pp. 595–611 and 1026–38). Also, several legal, musical and literary journals in Great Britain and abroad, as well as British newspapers including *The Times* (22.2.1951), *The Evening Standard* (23.2.1951).

Involved in every aspect of music publishing, Max Hinrichsen took an active lead in various associations including the Mechanical Copyright Protection Societies, the Music Trades Association, the National Book League, the Performing Rights Society and the Music Publishers' Association. He belonged to the Incorporated Association of Organists and other organ societies. He was a member of the International Association of Music Libraries, the Royal Musical Association, the Dolmetsch Foundation, the Galpin Society, the Society of Authors, the American Musicological Society, the *Internationale Gesellschaft für Musikwissenschaft* and more. He was Vice President of Holy Trinity Choral Society and of the Viola da Gamba Society. He was a council member of the Arts Committee of the London Council of Social Service, Vice President of the National School Brass Band Association, Vice President of the British Copyright Protection Association, London and a Deputy Member of the *Conseil d'Administration du Bureau de l'Edition Mecanique, BIEM,* Paris. He really was following in his father's footsteps and he achieved it all as an alien in a new country.

1951: Irene Hinrichsen's apprentice years in post-war occupied Europe

According to tradition, my father expected that his eldest son would one day take over his business. He and his forebears had always had an enlightened attitude towards the education and employment of women. So, despite his only child being a daughter, it was always understood that I would fulfil this role, an assumption which as a child I never questioned. I had grown up in England, as a British child, with the knowledge that we had come from Leipzig, as émigrés from Nazi persecution. The fact of my half-Jewish background did not influence my thinking until well into adulthood. At the time I left school, I had no idea of the inherited responsibility I was expected to carry. Neither was I aware of the importance of the Edition Peters in the realm of music publishing; nor did I know of the life and terrible fate that had befallen so many members of my family. My parents and remaining aunts and uncles had chosen to spare me as a child from the knowledge of the horrors. Probably because the memories were too painful for them, they had not told me anything about the family life in Leipzig.

Before joining Hinrichsen Edition Ltd., I needed to embark upon a similar type of apprenticeship to the one that my father, my uncles and my grandfather had undertaken. My father wanted me to learn French and so, after I left St Christopher's School, I was sent to school in the west of France for six months to learn French and attend courses at the University of Poitiers. The school was in a dilapidated old chateau in the wine-growing village of St Julien L'Ars. The area was still under occupation by the US Army and, as I was the only pupil at my rather bizarre school and there were plenty of empty rooms, three military married couples were billeted in the chateau. Apart from the usual subjects of French language, literature, history and geography, my education also included a good insight into the lives of the local landed gentry. These were largely impoverished once-aristocratic families, living in two rooms of their derelict chateau, surrounded by neglected grounds. They bore once-important names and were still assiduous in their quest for equally aristocratic marriage partners for their offspring. Years later when I read Balzac, I was fascinated to realize that the same standards, intrigues and jealousies prevailed in the 1950s as had been maintained in the 1850s.

On my seventeenth birthday in April 1952, I went to Paris for three months to work in the largest retail music and book shop. Then I travelled to Prades in the foothills of the Pyrenees and spent a wonderful month working at the Pablo Casals Music Festival. I was involved in every aspect of the festival – which was run on a shoestring – apart from performing. The great cellist and pacifist Pablo Casals was a Spaniard who, in demonstration of his disapproval of the fascist dictator Franco who ruled Spain, refused to set foot in his homeland whilst Franco was in power. When there was no concert on, Pablo Casals would invite me to his modest home to play ludo[2] with him, his favourite evening pastime. The festival director advised me that the 76-year-old cellist laid great store by being the winner and so I contrived, with some difficulty and a denting of my pride, to lose the game – but it gained me 'le Maître's' friendship. Casals always started his day playing Bach for one hour. On one memorable evening he accorded me the great privilege of performing a Bach Solo Cello Suite for me alone.

From the French Pyrenees I went to the Austrian mountains where I spent a musically rich month working in the music shop in Salzburg and attended many festival events – as a programme seller. The memory of standing at the back of the auditorium, hearing Elisabeth Schwarzkopf as the Countess in my first *Marriage of Figaro*, has remained with me ever since. My father assumed that I could speak German which in fact I had never done throughout my childhood. To my surprise, I managed adequately as a result of having heard it spoken by my relatives. However, when they had spoken German to me I had always answered in English – even I didn't know whether I could speak German.

---

2 Ludo: a board game played with counters and a dice.

Strict currency control regulations were in force in Europe and, as I would be working in Germany, I needed Deutschmark which I could not acquire legally. A friendly Austrian policeman told me how I could contact black market currency dealers. I had to ride to a village at the end of the bus line and then walk half a mile down a country road with the money that I wished to exchange. There, I was accosted by two unsavoury looking men who demanded US dollars which I didn't have. However, an amicable exchange was effected with my British pounds sterling and to my relief I was not shot in the back as I returned down the lonely country road.

My apprenticeship continued in Germany in 1952. With the benefit of hindsight, I am amazed that my father sent me back to the country of the Nazi regime that had murdered his parents, his brothers and so many of his relatives just seven years earlier. The country was still under the military occupation of the four allied powers: Great Britain, the USA, the Soviet Union and France. Leipzig, by then in the Communist German Democratic Republic, was banned to me. One irony was that, whilst food was still rationed in Great Britain, West Germany though the loser in the war, had food in abundance which was not rationed.

I started at the principal music shop in Munich where I spent seven interesting months including one at a music printing works. Munich, still showing much bomb damage, was in the American zone and full of lonely GIs who traded nylons and cigarettes for favours with the local girls. My boss was also one of the mayors of Munich and he introduced me to some stimulating musical and social life. In the shop I had the best opportunity of learning what other music publishers were publishing.

My next apprenticeship was for three months at the principal music shop in Cologne. Cologne was in the British zone but the British soldiers kept a much lower profile than their American counterparts – probably because they earned much less. The manager of the music shop was openly antipathetic towards me and I had no idea why; at the time I didn't recognize his attitude as anti-Semitic because it just didn't occur to me. I was told some time later that the moment I walked into the shop he had said: 'Ha, typically Jewish'. That was the only time in almost two years that I spent in Germany that I experienced any anti-Semitism. From Cologne I went to Wolfenbüttel, near Brunswick, still in the British zone, to a music publisher where the chief editor took it upon himself to teach me a great deal about publishing and production.

Three musically stimulating summer holidays were spent working in the exciting atmosphere of the Bayreuth Wagner Festival. The post-war years in German music were tainted by the association of Wagner's music with Nazism and Winifred Wagner's close friendship with and admiration for Adolf Hitler. This English woman, widow of Richard Wagner's son Siegfried, idolized the German dictator. However, her sons, Wieland and Wolfgang Wagner, did not apparently share her sympathies and welcomed my help with their Wagner festivals.

My final apprenticeship months were spent in Frankfurt/Main, again in the American zone, working at C. F. Peters, which should have been the most rewarding and enlightening experience of all but which turned out to be a total waste of time. This was the company that Max and his brother Walter Hinrichsen were compelled to allow Dr Johannes Petschull to found in 1950. He took great care to exclude me from being allowed to learn anything about the running of the company or any aspect of his publishing or business activities. Neither Dr Petschull nor his wife showed any concern for my welfare whatsoever. It subsequently became obvious why I was not welcome; there was constant strife between my father and Dr Petschull who steadfastly refused to honour the territorial and other agreements that the three partners had signed.

After two years of apprenticeships, I completed a course in Germany for those employed in the music trade and gained the appropriate certificate. My training abroad was considered to be concluded and I returned to London to start working with my father in Hinrichsen Edition Ltd. and Peters Edition in 1954.

My father was always too busy to instil his music publishing secrets in me which meant that I was unable to share the publishing work with him. My niche was in the sales field and my father constantly praised me for my achievements but I found this aspect of publishing to be tedious and frustrating. Unfortunately, in the position in which I found myself, I proved not to be the ideal 'eldest son'. Max Hinrichsen's chosen long working hours were not to my liking as a young adult and I wanted to spend my evenings with my contemporaries. My father, assuming that I would never become the type of workaholic partner that he had been for his father, looked around for a replacement. In March 1956, seven years after his divorce from my mother, he married an American, Carla Eddy. My father's new wife took my place by his side. Twelve days after their marriage, we three attended a Congress of Music Librarians together; it was a business trip and happened to coincide with my 21st birthday which I was therefore obliged to celebrate among a few hundred total strangers.

1956: Marie-Luise's only visit to see her daughter

In the cruel manner in which totalitarian regimes aim to taunt human sensitivities, the Communist authorities in Hungary suddenly granted

Fig. 34 1950. Marie-Luise (b. von Siegroth und Slawikau, married to Max Hinrichsen, divorced) Solymos 1909–1957. The author's mother.

my mother (Fig. 34) a visa to visit England in April 1956, just as my father's remarriage had been publicly announced. Out of respect for his new wife, my father urged her to delay her visit until August 1956. My mother and I hadn't seen each other for almost eight years and she stayed with me, in my bed-sit, for six weeks. She was a victim of multiple sclerosis, possibly as a result of the 22 years of stress she had suffered. By the time she arrived, I had met the man I was to marry – Dr Derek Lawford, a scientist, not a music publisher as my father would have wished. The visit was not without its problems and my mother returned to Hungary just days before the Hungarian Uprising of October 1956. I heard nothing from her for many weeks until finally the letter came stating, 'Thank God we are still alive'. Many Hungarians took the opportunity of fleeing their country. Thinking back 20 years, when she had successfully persuaded her first husband to emigrate from Nazi Germany to England, she tried to persuade her second husband, the pianist Peter Solymos, to escape the harsh Communist regime of Hungary for an easier life in the West with her. However, he refused on the grounds that his work as professor at the Liszt Academy of Music and his life as a Hungarian meant more to him than some doubtful prospects in the West. The Communist authorities did not permit my mother another exit visa when I married in December 1956. Her illness and her life in Hungary having become unbearable to her, on 7 February 1957, Marie-Luise Solymos took her own life with the sleeping pills that she had long been saving for just this course of action.

I continued to work at Hinrichsen Edition Ltd. until I left to start a family in 1960. I saw little of my father after that; my stepmother contrived to keep us apart. In 1961, we moved out of London and from then onwards I saw him only about twice a year. My daughter Julie was born in 1960 and her brother Trevor in 1963.

1965: Death of Max Hinrichsen Hon. FTCL

Max Hinrichsen was elected an Honorary Fellow of Trinity College of Music, London (Hon. FTCL) in July 1965 (Fig. 35). He was the first music publisher to be so honoured in the 92 years that the awards had been made. The citation, read by Dr Greenhouse Allt, former Principal of Trinity College of Music and Past President of the Royal College of Organists, in terms similar to those used by the University of Leipzig in honouring his father in 1929, read:

> In recognition of his scholarship in music, especially distinguished in the field of Bach research, the Board seeks to honour Max Hinrichsen. He is an outstanding progressive publisher of music and books of worldwide fame, mainly through the great Hinrichsen and Peters editions. And he is an educationalist in the most practical sense of the word, through and by the provision of up-to-date training material, and other facilities, for the use of students of music.

That was his proudest moment; it marked the recognition of 27 years of achievement as a foreigner who had been accepted by the British musical establishment.

Five months later, Max Hinrichsen suffered a heart attack and died on 17 December 1965. He was 64. Tributes appeared in newspapers and journals worldwide and hundreds of letters of appreciation and sympathy poured in from all over the world. He never learned that he had been awarded the Gold Medal of the United Poets Laureate

Fig. 35 1965. Max Hinrichsen Hon. FTCL 1901–1965.
The author's father. [Photo: Mark Gerson]

Society on Christmas Day 1965 for his 'record of distinguished service as publisher of books and other vital documents for the promotion of the Arts'.

Whilst people around the world expressed their admiration for Max Hinrichsen, his widow, Carla, evinced no signs of grief and in fact showed an appalling lack of respect for the man she had been married to for ten years. Unmoved by his death, she expressed great interest in all the medical paraphernalia around his bed and gave permission for an unnecessary post mortem 'in the interests of science'. My

husband and I went to London the following morning to offer her our
sympathy and any help. But she already had everything organized and
was busily disposing of his clothes and possessions. She gave me a
brooch which had belonged to my mother and then said: 'Of course,
you know that there is nothing for you in your father's will. He has left
everything to me'. She wanted to sell my father's business immediately
if it were possible, which turned out not to be the case. She said that
otherwise the business would need a second director and she offered
me the position. When I expressed interest, she immediately withdrew
the offer and said she would rather promote the sales Manager. She
described the business as a 'goldmine'.

To someone whose father had been dead less than 24 hours, the
whole tenor of the interview seemed entirely without any human
feeling for either my father or me. She did not want anybody to attend
the funeral and in fact was positively rude to my relatives who phoned.
The reason she gave me was that if people came she would have to buy
a more expensive coffin. My father wanted his ashes interred in the
family grave in Hamburg. However, his cantankerous old aunt Lili
would not allow this, so Carla said: 'That doesn't really matter; we'll
just wait for her to die and do it anyway then.' She preferred to keep
the ashes at home until such time in order to avoid paying the funeral
directors two shillings per week storage fee. At some point, my father's
ashes were lost. There is no certainty as to whether the ashes which
were eventually interred in Hamburg were my father's or not. I was not
allowed to attend the reading of my father's will and in fact was not
allowed to see a copy until after probate had been granted. I considered taking legal advice but litigation would have been too costly. So,
for the next forty years, we endured a courteous relationship, in
memory of my father.

The direction of the company, which Max had founded, was taken
over by his widow, Carla. She took on a manager. I moved back to the
London area with my husband and two children in 1968. I had wanted
to rejoin my late father's business but my stepmother did not want me
to have any part in the company. This was a deep regret to me, as music
publishing – and especially the Edition Peters – was what I was born
into, had grown up with and what I was trained for and the only profession at which I was competent.

In 1975, the name of Hinrichsen Edition Ltd., the company whose
high reputation Max Hinrichsen worked so hard to establish over
the course of 27 years, was relegated to a minor position when the
company was renamed Peters Edition, Ltd., London. In 1976, Carla
Hinrichsen established the Hinrichsen Foundation, a charity devoted
to the promotion of music. The foundation derives its income from
being the sole beneficial shareholder of Peters Edition Ltd. This

totally cut me out of any rights or participation in my family's business. At some point the management decided that the business premises that my father had so proudly named Bach House should cease to have a name. I'm sure that these three decisions would have hurt him deeply.

1965–1991: the interim years

To celebrate the fiftieth anniversary of the founding of Hinrichsen Edition Ltd., a prestigious dinner was held in 1988. It was the only time in 30 years that I was included in any aspect of my late father's company. My exclusion continued until 1995 after a new manager had been taken on, though by then too much time had passed for me to want to become productively involved. The music publishing industry had embraced new technologies and my knowledge and experience were long since obsolete.

Whilst I was out of the world of music publishing, I could not turn my back on music, however obliquely. In keeping with Henriques–Hinrichsen family tradition, I created something new. In 1969, I became co-founder and eventually president of the Philatelic Music Circle, an international society for collectors of all aspects of music philately. I became editor of the society's magazine *The Baton*, took a course in journalism and wrote articles on music and philately for a number of magazines. As a keen correspondent, I acquired friends the world over and was invited to participate in exhibitions in many countries, for which my knowledge of languages, which by then also included Italian, served me well. Music philately, whilst important, did not dominate my life. I followed several courses and then took an arts degree with the Open University, graduating with a BA (Hons) in 1985. By this time my husband had been suffering from a severe lung disease for several years; sadly he died in 1988, aged just 60.

My children had grown up and left home and I was ready to embrace a new direction in my life. Politics again decreed my fate: in November 1989, the Quiet Revolution which started in Leipzig culminated in the demise of the German Democratic Republic and the reunification of Germany a year later. This momentous event was to presage the course of my life for the next few years. I decided that I would return to the city of my birth to discover my roots. What I didn't realize was that I would not only be going back but that I would also be going forward and involving myself in new developments, acquiring skills and creating something lasting.

CHAPTER NINETEEN

1991: Leipzig – The Author Returns to the City of her Birth

When World War II ended in 1945, Germany was divided into four zones. The Western zones were controlled by the military powers of the USA, the United Kingdom and France, whilst the Soviet Union controlled the Eastern zone which became the DDR – German Democratic Republic – in October 1949, governed by a Communist dictatorship and controlled by the Red Army. The Berlin Wall – separating East and West Berlin which formed an island within the DDR – was constructed in 1962 and the Communists erected electrified wiring and lookout posts manned by armed guards along the entire length between the two halves of Germany. The inhabitants of the DDR were effectively imprisoned in their own state and spied upon by the secret police, the Stasi. Those who were too outspoken in their negative opinions about the state found themselves tortured as political prisoners. The people's freedoms were strictly limited, consumer goods were scarce, buildings fell into disrepair and the economy was badly mismanaged. After forty years the population finally rebelled against the repression.

1989 was the end of an era in European politics. The peoples of the Communist-ruled countries rebelled and demanded their freedom. The phenomenon, which hailed the end of the Cold War, can be said to have started in January when Poland's Communist party voted to legalize Solidarity; this resulted in Solidarity's victory in June in the first partly free parliamentary elections in post-war Poland which led in August to the first non-Communist being elected as prime minister in 42 years. In March, the first free elections for the Soviet parliament went against the Communist party. Hungary dismantled its 150 miles of barbed wire fencing, opening its borders to Western Europe in May, removed all border restrictions with Austria in August and opened its western border to admit refugees from the DDR in September; in October the Hungarian Republic, replacing the Hungarian People's Republic, was officially declared. In August, the people of Latvia, Lithuania and Estonia formed a human chain to demand freedom from the occupying Soviet Union which they ultimately achieved.

There had been rumblings of discontent for some time in Eastern Germany and on 10 September the formation of a political group calling itself *Neues Forum Leipzig* (New Forum) was announced. It was immediately declared illegal by the Communist authorities. On 25 September, the first silent protest procession took place in Leipzig, when 6,000–8,000 brave souls defied their government with a candlelit procession. Similar processions were held weekly on Monday nights with ever increasing numbers taking part. Soon other cities followed suit. These protests, demanding legalization of opposition groups in the DDR, which started in Leipzig led directly to the resignation of Erich Honecker as Communist leader on 18 October and the resignation of the Communist government of East Germany on 7 November. Two days later, East Germany opened checkpoints in the Berlin Wall, allowing its citizens to travel freely to West Germany for the first time in more than 40 years. The next day Germans began to tear down the hated wall. A year later, the two Germanys were reunified.

Fired on by the success of other Communist-controlled countries in overturning their political systems, in November, after 45 years of Communist rule in Bulgaria, the party leader was replaced and the name changed to the Bulgarian Socialist Party. Also in November, the Velvet Revolution began in Czechoslovakia, which succeeded in overthrowing the Communist Party in December when Vaclav Havel was elected president. Mongolia's Democratic Movement was announced in December, peacefully changing the Communist country into a democratic society. All these successful revolutions encouraged the terribly repressed Romanians towards their uprising in Timisoara in December which toppled the Communist regime there and resulted in the execution of the leader, Nicolae Ceausescu, and his wife.

Suddenly, within the space of one year, the Cold War, which had prevailed for over forty years (since the end of World War II), was over. Before 1989, uprisings of the peoples of Communist-ruled Eastern Europe had been crushed by Russian military intervention; but now President Gorbachev of the Soviet Union accepted that this was not the best way forward. By not supporting the despised regimes nor sending tanks to suppress the uprisings, he made it possible for these peoples to achieve the right to choose, so long denied them, which the peoples of Western Europe enjoyed.

In every ending lies a new beginning and these events presaged not only a new beginning for European politics, but also a new beginning for me personally.

When the phenomenon of the Quiet Revolution started in the DDR in autumn 1989, I watched the television with great excitement, avidly following the progress of the Monday Silent Demonstrations and candlelit processions which started in Leipzig. For the first time in my life, I saw what Leipzig looked like and I saw Leipzigers and I was deeply moved by their actions. I had often thought about going to Leipzig which I was determined to do 'when the wall comes down'; there was no doubt in my mind that this would inevitably happen. I wondered how I should go to Leipzig, as I knew nobody there and certainly had no family there. However, fate took a hand. In the spring of 1991, Peters Edition, London forwarded me a letter which they had received from the director of the *Fachschule für Sozialpädagogik Henriette Goldschmidt Leipzig* (Technical College for Social Education Henriette Goldschmidt), called the Henriette Goldschmidt Schule. This college, celebrating its Eightieth Jubilee in November of that year, was trying to locate any possible descendants of Geheimrat Dr Henri Hinrichsen who had been the original founding benefactor. I had never come across any reference to this college before. In order to find out what my grandfather's connection with it had been, I decided to read Henri Hinrichsen's *Chronik des Hauses C. F. Peters* which he had written in 1933 and which had been languishing in my cupboard since my father's death in 1965.

1991: Irene Lawford-Hinrichsen returns to Leipzig

I replied to the letter, telling the director that I was Henri Hinrichsen's granddaughter. She was thrilled and replied that it was through the diligence of one of the teachers, Frau Annerose Kemp, that I had been 'discovered'. The name of Henri Hinrichsen had been completely expunged from all records of the college after the Nazis had come to power in 1933. The institution had gone through several metamorphoses and survived the 40 years of the DDR. By the time that Germany was reunified in 1990, all trace of the history of the college before World War II had vanished. My grandfather had had the college built in 1911 on land that he had bought just around the corner from his home and the business premises of C. F. Peters at 10 Talstrasse. What had, up to 1938, been my grandparents' garden, in which my father had played as a child with his six brothers and sisters, had become the communal car park for the teachers at the Henriette Goldschmidt Schule and the staff of C. F. Peters. This is where Annerose Kemp had met Norbert Molkenbur, the director of the state-owned C. F. Peters Leipzig, from whom she had obtained the address of Peters Edition, London.

I was invited to be the guest of honour at the Eightieth Jubilee celebrations of the Henriette Goldschmidt Schule in Leipzig. I like to say that I was reborn in Leipzig in November 1991. I arrived, not dangling from the beak of the proverbial stork, but nonetheless on wings – metallic, not feathery. Three people greeted me – the large form of Norbert Molkenbur, the ebullient Annerose Kemp and her husband Horst – and they bore offerings of brightly coloured flowers, as was customary in the former DDR. This was their first sight of the 'reborn' and in fact their first sight of any British person. I was somewhat nervous of these strangers who, for the past forty years, had inhabited the forbidden world enclosed by the Iron Curtain. But they turned out to be kindness and helpfulness personified and they have become dear friends. My presence in Leipzig aroused a flurry of interest with press and radio interviews and I unexpectedly found myself in the position of a minor celebrity.

It was 54 years, almost to the day, since I had left Leipzig as a baby when I returned on 17 November 1991. I found a disappointingly grimy, polluted, crumbling relic of what I imagined had once been a beautiful city. The streets were potholed and the thick smoke from the factory chimneys created a foul-smelling haze over the entire city. The elegant family house and business premises at 10 Talstrasse itself was in a shamefully dilapidated condition, the DDR authorities never having granted permission for repairs and renovations. The people though, as compensation for the uniform drabness, went out of their way to be friendly. Those I met welcomed me and made it clear that, far from not knowing who my grandfather Henri Hinrichsen had been, they were most interested in reviving the fact of his existence and in acknowledging what he had done for Leipzig. The involvement that I forged with various Leipzig institutions led to my returning to the city of my birth many times over the course of the next fifteen years. Giant cranes and massive building works took over the streets and, as I watched the city blossoming and being restored to its former architectural glory, I was also very much aware of the profound, and often sad, social changes taking place as a result of political reunification.

There was a tremendous resurgence of life which manifested itself in an attempt to put the clock back by 60 years – to a time before the DDR and before the National Socialists. I found a desire in people to reinstate and to reinvigorate all that had been suppressed and destroyed during those years. This was particularly apparent in aspects that concerned the Jewish contribution to life in Leipzig. The 15,000 pre-war Jewish population of Leipzig that had been totally annihilated or dispersed and whose memory had been obliterated was to be accorded a historical status. This process had in fact started towards the end of the DDR when, in November 1988, an exhibition of photographs and documents of Leipzig Jews had been mounted in commemoration of the fiftieth anniversary of *Kristallnacht*, 9–10 November 1938. Organized by the University of Leipzig – then called the Karl Marx University – from 5 November to 17 December 1988, surviving Jews were invited from Israel and Erich Honneker, the president of the DDR, presided. A large catalogue was issued[1] a year after the exhibition was staged. It included a photograph of Henri Hinrichsen with a copy of the document of 1928 drawn up by the professors of the University of Leipzig, proposing that he be awarded an honorary doctorate.

Apart from the exhibition, a journalist, Bernd-Lutz Lange, had been researching the history of the Jews in Leipzig for some years. He had been trying to achieve some posthumous recognition for Henri Hinrichsen and had suggested to the Culture Department of Leipzig that a street should be renamed after him and that a commemorative plaque should be applied to 10 Talstrasse. So I was not arriving in a vacuum. My visit was a personal and private visit and I was in no way representing either my family or any one of the C. F. Peters firms in London, New York or Frankfurt, with which my connection was negligible. Inevitably, though, I was regarded as representing the Hinrichsen family; I was the only member of the family to show an interest in Leipzig after half a century and, as the 'eldest son' of the eldest son, I found myself held in some esteem.

The women's college founded by Henri Hinrichsen

The Henriette Goldschmidt Schule, after 80 years and in spite of many changes in purpose, depending upon the political climate of the times, was still a thriving establishment of further education, catering for 800 students and supported by 80 teachers. In their desire to commemorate the past, the college wanted a portrait of the founding benefactor to replace the portrait commissioned by the town council in 1929, removed by the Nazis in 1933 and subsequently destroyed. As a mark of gratitude for my invitation to Leipzig, I was delighted to be able to present framed, photographic enlargements of portraits of both Henri and Martha Hinrichsen, which were hung in a prominent

---

1 *Juden in Leipzig. Eine Dokumentation*, edited by Manfred Unger (Director of the State Archive of Saxony in Leipzig) and Hubert Lang (a solicitor specializing in Jewish restitution claims). Published by *Rat des Bezirkes Leipzig, Abteilung Kultur* (Cultural Department of the Council of the Leipzig Region), 1989.

position in the college, where they have remained. There were many problems to be faced by the college post-reunification. The director who had replaced the last Communist director was dismissed after 18 months to be replaced by an interim 'management', before a new, dynamic young director, Dr Eberhard Ulm, was appointed about a year later. A historian, his great interest is in the twentieth-century history of the Jews. To add a personal dimension to his teaching of the subject, he asked me to lecture on many of my subsequent visits to Leipzig on Henri Hinrichsen, his social concerns in Leipzig and his treatment by the Nazis.

Ghostly reminiscences of the past abounded. On my first visit to the college, one of the students told her grandmother about me and I was invited to tea with the old lady. She told me that as a five-year-old, in the 1920s, my grandparents had welcomed her as a playmate for their youngest son, Robert, then three. The two had remained friends until 1939 when Robert emigrated. They corresponded until she was married, then her husband forbade her to continue to correspond with a Jew. I met another old lady who told me about the large cupboard which my grandparents had given her mother when they left Germany. It is still in her family and now in use in her son's home.

Reading my grandfather's *Chronik* before my first visit, I realized that of the several trusts which Henri Hinrichsen had founded and supported, the main ones apart from the Henriette Goldschmidt Schule were the Peters Music Library and the Music Instruments Museum of the University of Leipzig. So these were amongst my goals on my first visit. I decided to use my week there, not only to see Leipzig but also to see whether the name of Henri Hinrichsen still had any relevance in any of the institutions with which he had been so closely associated until almost 60 years earlier.

The Music Instruments Museum

The then director of the Music Instruments Museum, Dr Schrammek, was delighted to welcome me and proudly showed me around the museum, still in its original generous premises. I wanted to see the Henri Hinrichsen Hall. When he showed me the room, which in the past had housed the prize pieces of the collection, I asked why there was no sign indicating the name of the room. He assured me that it was planned to remedy this. He wanted me to return to Leipzig in three weeks' time when the museum would be inaugurating a *Freundes-und Förderkreis des Musikinstrumenten Museums* (Society of 'Friends of the Music Instruments Museum'). He asked me to give a talk on Henri Hinrichsen, his publishing, his social involvements and benefactions in Leipzig and what had happened to the family in the

Holocaust. I had never given a talk in German before; in fact I had never given a talk on the subject before but I felt that this was something I had to do. If people wanted to know what their fathers and grandfathers had done to others, who happened to be Jews, 50 years earlier, then I felt morally bound to speak up for those who had been murdered and persecuted.

The University of Leipzig is responsible for the museum and the chancellor attended the event in December 1991. In my talk I also mentioned the stand that the university had made against the Nazis when asked to withdraw Henri Hinrichsen's honorary doctorate which he had been awarded in 1929. My talk made such an impact on the audience that the University of Leipzig had it reprinted as a booklet.[2] This has since formed a source document on Henri Hinrichsen, quoted in many subsequent publications. It was also the first of many talks I gave in Leipzig. Afterwards I was interviewed by the *MDR* (*Mitteldeutscher Rundfunk*), the radio station for the region. This interview was to have repercussions.

During that second visit, Dr Schrammek took me to the cellar of the Music Instruments Museum and showed me the remains of the original notice proclaiming the 'Henri Hinrichsen Saal' which had been found on a heap of rubbish after almost 60 years. It was comprised of large brass letters and was being restored by one of the finest musical instrument restorers. By the time of my next visit to Leipzig, it was hanging above my grandfather's portrait at the entrance to the Henri Hinrichsen Hall. I maintained cordial relations with the Music Instruments Museum, the direction of which, after Dr Schrammek's retirement, was taken over by Dr Eszter Fontana. My grandfather would have been delighted to learn that it underwent complete refurbishment between 2004 and 2008.

The International Mendelssohn Foundation

I had heard in London that the *Internationale Mendelssohn Stiftung* (International Mendelssohn Foundation) had been formed by the Gewandhaus with the intention of purchasing the 'Mendelssohn House' – the house in which Felix Mendelssohn-Bartholdy had spent the last years of his life at 12 Goldschmidtstrasse. The project was being organized by Bernd Pachnike, a past director of C. F. Peters, Leipzig, who in 1991 was artistic director of the Gewandhaus, whilst

---

2   *Festliche Gründungsveranstaltung am 14. Dezember 1991* (Celebratory Founding on 14 December 1991). *Freundes- und Förderkreis Musikinstrumenten Museum der Universität Leipzig e.V. 1992.*

Kurt Masur was Gewandhaus *Kapellmeister* (Principal Conductor of the Gewandhaus Orchestra). Like me, Herr Pachnike had a strong interest in the history and tradition of C. F. Peters. When the Mendelssohn House idea had originally been mooted in DDR times, it had been intended to incorporate a memorial to Henri Hinrichsen in the house. Mendelssohn had inhabited an apartment on the first floor and later Dr Max Abraham had taken this over for C. F. Peters until the house at 10 Talstrasse had been built. Hence I was interested in becoming a part of this project.

Pachnike attended my talk at the Music Instruments Museum when my visit coincided with a Press conference for the Mendelssohn House under the chairmanship of Kurt Masur. I was included in this and, along with Masur and a great-niece of Mendelssohn's, the pianist Frau Winand-Mendelssohn, we all viewed the dilapidated condition of the Mendelssohn House. I became associated with this project through to its completion in time for the festival to mark the 150th anniversary of Mendelssohn's death in November 1997 when I attended the opening ceremony. My interest in this project continues to this day.

Paintings, Aryanization and archive come alive for me

I wanted to see the paintings in my grandfather's collection which the Nazis had confiscated, three of which, in 1945, Walter Hinrichsen had allowed the *Museum der bildenden Künste* (art gallery) of Leipzig to keep. Since its own premises had been bombed during the war, the gallery had been housed in the old *Reichsgericht* (High Court of Justice).[3] I was intrigued to note, when I saw the paintings, that my grandfather had expressed a very gentle taste in his choice of pictures. His collection comprised largely German paintings of the nineteenth century. My visit there led to an invitation to give a talk on a subsequent visit. Like my previous talks, this one also had repercussions. Afterwards, an unknown man thrust a sheaf of papers into my hand and disappeared. Herr Prieberg had just handed me the results of his research into the Aryanization of C. F. Peters, details that I might otherwise have been unable to assemble for myself. His notes formed an important part in the book I subsequently wrote.[4] At that time, I had not yet even formulated the idea of writing a book.

A side entrance of the *Reichsgericht* led to the temporary (already some fifty years) accommodation of the *Sächsische Staatsarchiv Leipzig*

---

3 A new purpose-built art gallery was opened in 2004.
4 *Music Publishing and Patronage – C. F. Peters: 1800 to the Holocaust.* Edition Press, 2000.

(the State Archive of the City of Leipzig)[5] where most of the archive of C. F. Peters, going back to 1800, was housed. The director, Dr Manfred Unger, showed me hundreds of boxes of correspondence. I saw some of the poignant and desperate letters which my uncle Dr Hans-Joachim Hinrichsen had written to Dr Petschull in 1939 when he was trying to secure his and his parents' departure from Leipzig. I was shown the entries in the jail records when he and my grandfather had been imprisoned 'for political reasons'. And I saw the entry for my birth in the official birth register designating me as *Mischling ersten Grades* (first-degree mixed race). It was a shock to realize that the Nazis had accepted neither my father's baptism nor my own.

Leipzig commemorates the memory of its pre-war Jewish population

Concurrent with my first visit to Leipzig in 1991, a trust was founded, the *Ephraim Carlebach Stiftung*, named after the founder of the Jewish School in Leipzig which the Nazis forcibly closed. It is dedicated to commemorating the lives and achievements of Leipzig Jews. Dr Manfred Unger and Dr Renate Drucker, whose father was a solicitor who had known my grandfather professionally, started the Stiftung. The president was the late Fred Grubel, an ex-Leipzig Jew and vice president of the Leo Baeck Institute in New York. The *Ephraim Carlebach Stiftung* has published several books, to one of which, *Judaica Lipsiensia*, I contributed a lengthy article on Henri Hinrichsen. Since 1995, it has also organized a biannual *Jüdische Kultur Woche* (Jewish Cultural Week) when elderly ex-Leipzig Jews are invited to revisit the town of their birth, a poignant first visit for many since their long-vanished childhood. It is also an occasion for talks and exhibitions directed at the Leipzig population. I am a regular speaker at these events. In 1998, I was appointed to the *Kuratorium* (board) of the *Ephraim Carlebach Stiftung Leipzig.*

My new life had begun and it was to gather momentum and lead me in entirely unexpected directions over the next fifteen years when I became involved in so much that was new to me and in which my grandfather, Henri Hinrichsen, had played such a prominent role.

---

5 A new state-of-the-art archive was subsequently built.

CHAPTER TWENTY

1992–2008: Leipzig – Reconciliation and Commemoration in the Shadow of the Swastika

1992: The Hinrichsen Memorial Stone and memorial concerts

The past was rearing itself in uncanny ways and demanding to be revitalized. Early in 1992, the director of the Südfriedhof (South Cemetery) in Leipzig contacted Norbert Molkenbur, manager of C. F. Peters, Leipzig. The cemetery records showed that the burial plot which commemorated Fallen Heroes of the Revolution actually belonged to the Hinrichsen family. This was the plot which Henri Hinrichsen had purchased in 1909 and in which Martha Hinrichsen's parents, Waldemar and Bertha Bendix, had been buried in the 1920s when Dr Max Abraham's remains had been re-interred. In 1947, Walter Hinrichsen had paid for the upkeep of this prominent plot until the year 2009. Ignoring this agreement, the DDR authorities had, in 1974, flattened the site and created their own memorial.

The existence of the graves was as unknown to me as it was to all my living relatives. Now the Hinrichsen plot was offered back to the family. We decided to commission a commemorative memorial stone. It was to name not only those who had originally been buried there, but also those who had no grave. The tall squared sandstone memorial carries inscriptions on three sides: to my great-grandparents Waldemar and Bertha Bendix; to my uncles who had been killed in the concentration camps, Dr Hans-Joachim and Paul Hinrichsen; and to Dr Max Abraham, Dr Henri and Martha Hinrichsen. The Edition Peters logo is engraved on the fourth side (Fig. 36). The unveiling, which I was to carry out, was to take place on 17 September 1992; this marked the fiftieth anniversary of Henri Hinrichsen's murder in Auschwitz concentration camp.

The event was planned as a grand civic event with the participation of top Leipzig dignitaries. But it almost turned into a fiasco when the swastika cast its ugly shadow. Shortly before the due date, Herr Molkenbur wrote to me that a boycott had been planned as a result of action taken by C. F. Peters, Frankfurt. The company had taken over the VEB (DDR state-owned) C. F. Peters, Leipzig on the reunification of Germany. Dr Petschull, at the age of 90 still director of C. F. Peters, Frankfurt, had announced the closure of the Leipzig company and the dismissal of all remaining employees, having already recently dismissed 45 of the 60 employees. He was planning to liquidate the Leipzig mother-house completely and in due course he dismissed all the remaining employees except Norbert Molkenbur.

This caused a great deal of bitterness in Leipzig, especially amongst the dismissed employees. C. F. Peters had always been considered one of the great institutions of Leipzig and throughout the DDR years as a state-owned company had produced many worthwhile publications. The Leipzig authorities, eager to maintain the prestige of Leipzig as a centre of music publishing, were angry. I found myself in the middle of an embarrassing political situation which I somehow had to find a way of deflecting from myself. Having been made welcome in Leipzig, I did not now expect to be reviled for actions carried out in the name of my family by the ex-Nazi Dr Petschull, the person who had already caused the Hinrichsens so much distress. The positive value of all that I was achieving was in danger of being destroyed. In order to mitigate the damage and rescue my nascent reputation, I sent carefully worded faxes to the mayor and everybody in Leipzig in an official position who, I felt, might be concerned in the boycott. I pointed out that what was happening now in C. F. Peters was not my responsibility and was certainly not the fault of Henri Hinrichsen. I wrote that whatever the people of Leipzig felt about the current situation, this should not detract from the commemoration of all that my grandfather had done for the city in the past. I saved the situation.

The unveiling of the Hinrichsen memorial stone was attended by the president of the city of Leipzig and the mayor, who both made speeches, as did I. The event was enhanced by musical contributions from the brass players of the Gewandhaus Orchestra. Wreaths and flowers were contributed by many Leipzig institutions. There were press interviews and photographers; reporters and television cameras ensured that the event was shown on the evening news bulletins. Lilo Bendix-Stern, one of Martha and Henri Hinrichsen's Berlin nieces, came from New York, paying her first visit to Leipzig since her youth in

DR. MAX
ABRAHAM
3.6.1831 — 8.12.1900
DR. HENRI
HINRICHSEN   WALDEMAR
5.2.1868 — 17.9.1942   BENDIX
KZ AUSCHWITZ   15.9.1849 — 31.7.1924

MARTHA   BERTHA
HINRICHSEN   BENDIX
2.3.1879 — 7.10.1941   9.11.1855 — 3.3.1920

Fig. 36 Memorial stone for the Hinrichsen family. Unveiled
17 September 1992.

the 1930s; apart from me, she was the only member of the family to
come. No representative from C. F. Peters, Frankfurt dared put in an
appearance in Leipzig. My stepmother ignored the event and no representative came from the company that she had inherited from
my father, Peters Edition London. Nobody came from C. F. Peters
Corporation, New York. This disregard for what, to Leipzig, was an
early act of reconciliation for the iniquities of the past shocked me
deeply.

The Nazi ethos of more than 50 years ago was still very much in evidence – or perhaps the next episode could be put down to senility. Dr
Petschull had told Herr Molkenbur that the wording on the stone
should be changed and that Henri Hinrichsen's name should not
appear as he had nothing to do with C. F. Peters, and that he was not
Dr Max Abraham's nephew. I felt compelled to stop such a ridiculous
rumour in its tracks. Dr Petschull also wanted the Edition Peters logo

removed from the stone. As this had been Molkenbur's idea in the first place, he resisted that instruction too.

The memorial stone was not to be the only commemoration of the fiftieth anniversary of Henri Hinrichsen's murder in Auschwitz. Bernd Pachnike was highly enthusiastic about my idea that the Gewandhaus might consider staging a memorial concert. He suggested dedicating the concert on Remembrance Sunday, 22 November 1992, to Henri Hinrichsen and he asked me to write about my grandfather's life and fate for the programme. This event, too, was in danger of being boycotted but successfully took place as a result of my faxes. The Gewandhaus Quartet gave a beautiful and moving concert.

The Music Instruments Museum also organized a memorial concert on the morning of the same Sunday. Amongst works performed by the Leipzig Chamber Choir were some songs from the *Volksliederbuch für die Jugend* (Folk Song Book for the Young). This was the book published by C. F. Peters in 1930, for which modern arrangements had been commissioned, some of which were by Jewish composers. The Nazis had banned the book and ordered all copies to be destroyed; but a copy was located that had lain undetected in a library for 60 years.

Whilst Norbert Molkenbur, director of the almost defunct C. F. Peters, Leipzig supported the concerts, no representative from either C. F. Peters in Frankfurt or Peters Edition in London attended to offer their respects. However, I was delighted that two of my cousins, Henry and Martha – Walter Hinrichsen's son and daughter – travelled from New York to be present and that my own children – Julie and Trevor, two of Henri Hinrichsen's great-grandchildren – came with me from London. They were all visiting Leipzig for the first time.

The 'lost' Hinrichsen trusts

Not everything had a positive or just conclusion. In 1992, the town council showed an interest in reviving the evaporated Henri Hinrichsen Stiftung, the trust fund set up by my grandfather to finance the Henriette Goldschmidt Schule and other institutions. I was asked to participate on the board and that interested me but nobody was available who could unravel the financial arrangements of 60 years ago or who could devote the time to tracing unknown bank account details so the project was eventually abandoned.

One of the houses in the Henri Hinrichsen Trust was called the Henriette Goldschmidt House. My grandfather had given it in trust to Henriette Goldschmidt for her educational activities and as living quarters for some of her students. It had become a study centre and kindergarten and had served as headquarters for a number of local feminist organizations before and during the DDR years. It should have continued to be used for such purposes, as stipulated by Henri Hinrichsen, but it fell into disrepair, was abandoned and boarded up. The Leipzig authorities sold the house, quickly, shortly after reunification, to a member of the town hall staff for a paltry sum without establishing who owned it. She immediately sold it at a huge profit. When the new feminist organizations found out what had happened, a great deal of publicity was generated and demands were made to nullify the sale. The mayor of Leipzig was adamant that the sale was legitimate. The new owner did not develop the property which by that time was half derelict and it was subsequently earmarked for demolition as part of a road-widening scheme. In spite of renewed efforts to rescue it, and though the road-widening scheme was abandoned, the house was demolished in 2000.

Another of Henri Hinrichsen's houses in trust was a kindergarten in the Spittastrasse for the children of working-class mothers. This functioned throughout the DDR years but in 1994 the town council wanted to sell the house and its grounds to a developer who planned building a hotel on the site. The feminist groups, discovering the origins of the house, mobilized the parents of the children at the school to protest. A stay of execution was obtained but, failing any legal intervention, due to a lack of funds, in 1997 the town council successfully circumvented any ties that might have been imposed under the terms of the trust and put the house on the market.

1993: Dr Petschull directs threats against me

There was a great deal of bitterness in Leipzig for some considerable time over the liquidation of C. F. Peters, Leipzig. Several of the dismissed employees obtained jobs in the media as journalists and broadcasters and some of them researched old state archives of the Nazi era, finding that Dr Petschull had carried two Nazi party membership cards. Some vitriolic articles and broadcasts against him resulted. On the advice of his solicitor, he sued the MDR for damages about a broadcast in March 1993.

Whilst I did not collaborate in any way with these activities, I was nonetheless used as a pawn. The radio interview that I had given in December 1991 had been broadcast then in its entirety, as part of a music programme. In the offending broadcast of 1993, short extracts from this interview had been used without my permission to suggest other than what I had said. Further, I had been commissioned to write an article for the prestigious magazine *Leipziger Blätter* which was published in the spring 1993 issue. This was editorially intertwined with a factually accurate but bitter article by Tom Fugmann which made it look as though I had collaborated on his article.

Being quite determined not to take sides on the issue and wanting to avoid litigation at all costs, I had been very careful in all my talks, interviews and articles not say anything damaging about anybody. I refused to voice any opinion about the liquidation of C. F. Peters, Leipzig as I was not in possession of all the facts and I personally had no formal connection with C. F. Peters. I had no intention of falling victim to any court action against myself. My decision to exercise reticence was endorsed when I received a letter dated 20 October 1993 from J. Bergemann, solicitor for Dr Petschull. In this he warned me: 'I can only ask you with insistence, not only in the interests of C. F. Peters but also in your own interest, to consider carefully with whom you take up contact and which information you impart. A letter from Dr Petschull, dated 19 October 1993, reinforced this threatening advice.

Dr Petschull won the court case against the MDR and a considerable sum in damages. He offered his compensation as a donation to the new Jewish community of Leipzig but they refused to accept the gift. In a letter sent by their solicitor, Hubert Lang, to the *Landgericht Leipzig, Zivilkammer* (Leipzig District Court, Civil Division), dated 16 March 1994, they let it be known that they were not party to this process and did not wish to benefit from it in any way. They had the highest respect for the Hinrichsen family who had done so much for Leipzig and, in spite of the fact that they were not practising Jews and did not belong to the Jewish community, had been persecuted in the most terrible manner by the Nazi government. The letter added that the Jewish community had absolutely no intention of taking advantage, either directly or indirectly, by commemorating National Socialism in the name of the Hinrichsen family and its extraordinary generosity towards Leipzig. This was a remarkably altruistic gesture from a community of mostly Russian immigrants who had no connections with Leipzig's pre-war Jewish community.

1993: Return of the stolen books in Bremen

Another strange resurrection of the past occurred in the autumn of 1993 when I received a surprising letter from a Frau Elfriede Bannas, a retired high school head in Bremen. She informed me that she was in a position to return some books to me which had been stolen from my grandparents over 50 years earlier. A patron of the *Staats- und Universitätsbibliothek Bremen* (State and University Library of Bremen) had noticed that several of the books in the library were marked with the letters 'J. A.', followed by a Roman numeral pencilled inside the front cover. After investigation, Frau Bannas had ascertained that this marking referred to 'Juden Auktion' (Jewish Auction) number so-and-so; this led her to the *Staatsarchiv Bremen* (the Bremen Archive) where she uncovered the background. In 1942, the Gestapo had confiscated all the packing cases belonging to Jewish émigrés that were still in the dockside warehouses in Bremen awaiting shipment abroad. Amongst these were all the worldly possessions of Martha and Henri Hinrichsen which they had despatched from Leipzig in 1940 to be sent to the USA where they were hoping to be able to emigrate. The contents were all auctioned off for the benefit of the state. The Bremen University library acquired many of the books. The Bremen Archive also held a file of correspondence between Walter Hinrichsen and the Bremen authorities during the 1950s and 1960s regarding compensation claims which were eventually abandoned.

Frau Bannas found a total of 1,500 books marked 'J. A.' in the Library. She managed to identify 47 names establishing the ownership of just 300 of the books. She could positively attribute 30 of these as belonging to Martha and Henri Hinrichsen. Any clues as to addresses were over 50 years old so she wrote to the journalist in Leipzig, Bernd-Lutz Lange, who was able to give her my address. On 30 November 1993, I went to Bremen and, as a representative of the first 'book family' to be 'discovered', was presented with the 30 books that had belonged to my grandparents. The event aroused a great deal of publicity, with broadcasts, television and press interviews. Though the university library had acquired the books under the laws of the Third Reich, it was now trying to rectify the injustices perpetrated by a previous generation. Elfriede Bannas's researches made history in the library world and many articles appeared about her work in the press when my participation and the Hinrichsen story were also often included. A film was made for a German language cultural channel, 3SAT Television, in 1997 in which I appeared. This gave me the opportunity to pay tribute to Elfriede Bannas and Henri Hinrichsen, as well as displaying some of the books themselves. I was pleased to be invited to Bremen in 2005, first, when I participated in an exhibition of some of the books and again, when Elfriede Bannas was awarded the *Bundesverdienstkreuz* (equivalent to a CBE) for her work – she was then in her eightieth year. Some other German libraries are now trying to return 'stolen' books.

1994: The centenary of the Peters Music Library

During the DDR years, the Peters Music Library had become the foundation of the Music Library of the city of Leipzig, which also incorporated other smaller collections. It is now housed in the splendid new premises of the Leipzig city library. Whilst no longer called the Peters Music Library, all the original books, manuscripts and pictures are still marked as being a part of the Peters Music Library. The marble bust of Dr Max Abraham, the founder and original donor, which Henri

Hinrichsen had commissioned from the sculptor Carl Seffner, was hidden during the Nazi years and is now prominently displayed in the Library.

The Peters Music Library had originally occupied the ground floor of 26 Goldschmidtstrasse (then Königstrasse) in the same block as the Henriette Goldschmidt Schule and 10 Talstrasse. It was the house that Dr Max Abraham had bought to accommodate the *Frauengewerbeverein*, his educational establishment for working-class women, which had been on the upper floors. The library was moved to safer premises during the war and the house sheltered institutions that had been bombed out. It was then taken into state ownership in the DDR. From 1947 to 1992, it was home to the *Deutsche Buchhändler Lehranstalt* (German College for the Book Trades) another of the bodies to which my grandfather had given generous sponsorship. The house then became home to the *Wissenschaftszentrum Leipzig*, a historical research centre for Leipzig. In 1994, this organization put on an exhibition to celebrate the centenary of the foundation of the Peters Music Library in that building. The director, Wieland Zumpe, asked me to open the exhibition and to give a talk about my family. The event was recorded on film as part of a documentary to publicize the work of the *Wissenschaftszentrum*.

In my talk, I mentioned my grandfather's sponsorship of the College for the Book Trades. Someone from the college was present and this led to the Assistant Director, Frau Dr Waschkies, inviting me to give a talk to the students, in the new premises of the college in the Gutenbergplatz. This also became a regular obligation once or twice a year on my subsequent visits to Leipzig, each group of students wanting to hear about the history of C. F. Peters and the family who had owned it.

1995 and 1997: Publication of the Max Reger and Edvard Grieg correspondence

In his *Chronic* of 1933, my grandfather had expressed the hope that it would one day be possible to publish the massive correspondence between himself and the composer Max Reger to whom he had given so much encouragement and support between 1900 and the composer's early death in 1916. It took almost 80 years for his dream to be realized. This comprehensive correspondence of huge interest to musicologists was finally edited and published in 1995 under the auspices of the Max Reger Institute, Bonn.[1] I was invited to write an intro-

---

1 *Max Reger – Briefwechsel mit dem Verlag C. F. Peters*. Ed. Susanne Popp and Susanne Shigihara. Dümmler Verlag, Bonn 1995.

duction on Henri Hinrichsen and to speak at the launch of the book in Leipzig. The book is a lasting tribute to an extraordinarily generous and supportive publisher for a composer whose music never achieved the recognition for which both parties had striven so hard.

As with the Reger correspondence, it had always been Henri Hinrichsen's wish to publish the complete correspondence of the 400 letters from Edvard Grieg to Max Abraham and Henri Hinrichsen with their replies. Finally, 90 years after the death of the composer, this was accomplished when the Leipzig musicologist and Grieg researcher, Prof. Dr Hella Brock co-edited the book published by C. F. Peters, Frankfurt.[2] Her excellent biography of Edvard Grieg, written during the DDR years, had first appeared in 1990.[3]

1997: Restitution of the family and business property

In 1939, the Nazis had confiscated 10 Talstrasse, 26 Goldschmidtstrasse and other property from the Hinrichsen family. After the war, the properties had shared the same fate as most in the DDR and had become state-owned. For almost 60 years, there had been no hope of retrieving them for the family. With the reunification of Germany, a claim was made for restitution of property. The case was long, complicated and costly and involved four sets of solicitors. There were also counter-claims, one being from the daughter of Kurt Herrmann, the Nazi friend of Goering who had 'bought' C. F. Peters with Dr Petschull in the Aryanization process in 1939. The processes of law went back and forth for six years, before being finally settled in 1997. The properties had been allowed to fall into such a dilapidated state by the DDR and were so hemmed about by preservation orders that a sale was difficult to effect and the price eventually achieved fell well short of what should have been the market value. Subsequently, 10 Talstrasse fell into even greater disrepair and was shamefully van-dalized on several occasions before any restoration was foreseen. Other claims for what had once belonged to Henri Hinrichsen were even more protracted and complicated and the lawyers appeared to become the principal beneficiaries.

Whilst the Peters Edition premises had been allowed to fall into ter-rible decay by the DDR authorities, the house was still in parts habit-able, even though not yet restored by its new owner. That all changed in December 1999 when, as an echo of the destruction caused on

2 *Edvard Grieg – Briefwechsel mit dem Musikverlag C. F. Peters.* C. F. Peters, Frankfurt. 1997

3 Hella Brock. *Edvard Grieg.* Reclam-Verlag-Leipzig. 1990. 2nd revised edition. Atlantis Musikbuch-Verlags, 1998.

Kristallnacht 1938, vandals broke in on three occasions and tried to wreck what was left and steal what they could. The stockroom was flooded and thousands of volumes of sheet music were ruined when they pulled the water pipes from the walls; the cellar was set on fire. Artworks, which had belonged to my grandfather, were stolen, including portraits of Felix Mendelssohn and Johann Sebastian Bach and a bust of Bach as well as a nineteenth-century clock. They tried to remove the wood panelling in the music salon as well as an enormous cast iron stove. The vandals were never caught and nothing was recovered.

On a happier note, the festive event in 1999 to celebrate the Seventieth Jubilee of the opening in 1929 of the Music Instruments Museum recognized that, without Henri Hinrichsen's contribution, there would have been no such museum in Leipzig. I was proud to be invited to give the keynote speech; there were more speeches about the history and the future aspirations of the museum, as well as suitable musical interludes.

2000: Three books celebrate the bicentenary of C. F. Peters

My growing interest in my family's past and in C. F. Peters and my involvement with Leipzig led to my researching the subject thoroughly. The result was my first book, published in London in February 2000 in anticipation of the 200th anniversary of C. F. Peters in December 2000. *Music Publishing and Patronage – C. F. Peters: 1800 to the Holocaust* received excellent reviews in the musical press and in the Jewish press. The book should have appeared in a German translation but I was badly let down by two Leipzig publishers and thus withdrew from the projects.

Concurrently with my writing my book, two others were working on the same theme, in German. We each treated the subject in an entirely different way and were happy to able to help each other with information from our own researches. Norbert Molkenbur wrote a dedicated history of C. F. Peters, with emphasis on the DDR years. Erika Bucholtz wrote an immensely well-researched PhD thesis on the subject of Henri Hinrichsen.[4] None of the books were published by Peters Edition.

The bicentenary of the company was celebrated in grand style with a concert and banquet in Frankfurt in December 2000 by the three sister firms: Peters Edition Ltd., London with Hinrichsen Edition Ltd.,

---

4 Bucholtz, Erika. *Henri Hinrichsen und der Musikverlag C. F. Peters.* Leo Baeck Institute, London, 2001. Molkenbur, Norbert. *C. F. Peters 1800–2000: Ausgewählte Stationen einer Verlagsgeschichte.* Sachsenbuch, Leipzig, 2001.

C. F. Peters Corporation, New York and C. F. Peters, Frankfurt/Main. Walter Hinrichsen's son and daughter, Martha and Henry, and Henry's son Christian, as well as our mutual second cousin Lilo Bendix Stern, came from New York.

We, the family, then went on to Leipzig, where the bicentenary was celebrated with an exhibition at the Bach House entitled: *Bach war schon immer unser Nummer 1* (Bach has always been our Number 1). It was not only a celebration of C. F. Peters but also a tribute to Henri Hinrichsen and I was asked to speak about him by way of introduction to the concert of music published by the company. Martha Hinrichsen had recently assumed the Presidency of C.F. Peters New York and as Nicholas Riddle, the Managing Director of Peters Edition London and Karl Rarichs, the Manager of C.F. Peters Frankfurt were also present, this marked the first occasion when the heads of all the Peters publishing houses were in Leipzig together. Nicholas Riddle's involvement with Leipzig went back to 1994, when he had eagerly accepted an invitation onto the Board of the International Mendelssohn Foundation.

There was also an exhibition to commemorate the Jews of Leipzig organized by Dr Andrea Lorz, in which I participated, in the Leipzig City Museum.

The following year, after public pressure led by the journalist Bernd Lutz-Lange over the course of almost 15 years, a street was renamed in honour of Geheimrat Dr. hc. Henri Hinrichsen. In renaming a prominent street the Hinrichsenstrasse, the council of the city of Leipzig gave public recognition to the man who had done so much for the city in which he had chosen to make his home and his career. I was delighted to be invited to unveil the street-sign and to open an exhibition in my grandfather's honour at the local residents' association.

Commemorations and celebrations

17 September 2002 saw the sixtieth anniversary of Henri Hinrichsen's murder in Auschwitz. The Henriette Goldschmidt Schule organized a day to commemorate the founding benefactor. There were events in the college throughout the day and a visit to the cemetery to hold a ceremony at the memorial stone. Other events took place over the course of three months.

Two years later, there was a further commemoration at the college when a new bust of Henriette Goldschmidt was installed in 2004. Henri Hinrichsen had commissioned the well-known sculptor Carl Seffner to create a marble sculpture bust to commemorate her but the Nazis had destroyed this memorial to a Jewish woman. However, a plaster copy was located which had been in hiding for almost 70 years.

When this was rediscovered, a pre-war ex-student now living in the USA commissioned a replica to be placed on the original heavy pedestal which the Nazis had not destroyed. The unveiling of the new bust was attended by the grandson of Carl Seffner and myself – there are no direct descendants of Henriette Goldschmidt who could have attended. The Nazis had also removed the commemorative plaque which my grandfather had commissioned for the opening of the college. By tapping the walls, a member of staff had been able to identify where the original niche had been before the Nazis had plastered it over seventy years earlier. A new plaque was commissioned which echoed the original style. It was placed in the original spot on the 180th anniversary of Henriette Goldschmidt's birth in 2005.

My uncle, the surgeon Dr Ludwig Frankenthal, and his two young sons, had been murdered in Auschwitz. The historian Dr Andrea Lorz had been researching his life for some time, preparatory to writing a book about some of the Jewish doctors of Leipzig murdered by the Nazis. I was able to supply her with a great deal of documentation which I compiled into an album for her. I presented this to her in 2004 when I gave a talk about my uncle and aunt Ilse to a packed auditorium. The documentation enabled her to write an in-depth account of his life and his very important work. The book was published the following year.[5]

From time to time, centenaries of organizations with which my grandfather was involved occur. One such was the LBA (the Leipzig Bibliophiles Association) of which he was a founder member in February 1904. I was pleased to be invited to its centenary celebration in February 2004 as one of only two known grandchildren of a founder member.

Commemorations take many different forms; one unusual one concerns bookplates. My grandfather had commissioned the creation of two Hinrichsen bookplates around the 1920s. Having discovered these in the books that had been returned to me from the Bremen University Library, I was commissioned to write an article about them for an American bookplate journal; this was seen by the president of the German Bookplate Association who asked for permission to print a translation in his very prestigious yearbook, which in 2004 concentrated on Jewish culture and ex-libris art.[6]

---

5 Andrea Lorz. *Die Erinnerung soll zum Guten gereichen*. Passage Verlag, Leipzig, 2005.
6 Irene Lawford-Hinrichsen. *Zwei Leipziger Bücherzeichen*. DEG Jahrbuch, Frankfurt, 2004.

Edvard Grieg celebrations

Edvard Grieg had been the most important composer for C. F. Peters; this remarkable relationship between composer and publisher had spanned more than 40 years. In 1933, at the start of his persecution, Henri Hinrichsen wrote in his *Chronic*: 'Whenever [Edvard] Grieg was in Leipzig Dr Abraham ensured for him his "workroom guarded by Cerberus" . . . to restore those rooms as a memorial to him, with documents from the Peters' archive and souvenirs remains an undertaking for forthcoming generations.' It was to take 72 years before my grandfather's wish could be realized.

On studying the *Chronic*, Norbert Molkenbur, the Peters' historian, took this idea to heart and, together with the Grieg scholar and biographer Professor Dr Hella Brock, formed the *Edvard Grieg Gedenk-und Begegnungsstätte Leipzig e.V* (Edvard Grieg Commemoration and Meeting Centre) in 1998. However, it was to be a further seven years before the meeting centre could be opened. In the meantime, other events were held in Leipzig to commemorate the composer. In 2004 the Fifth German Edvard Grieg Congress took place in Leipzig. This two-day event, in which I took part, was another occasion for the commemoration of Max Abraham and Henri Hinrichsen.

In 2005, Norway celebrated the centenary of its independence from Sweden. This was another occasion which the Grieg Society of Leipzig in conjunction with Peters Edition was able to celebrate with a gala event. All involved were delighted that I could participate in the events.

Later in 2005, after seven years, during which time the house 10 Talstrasse was finally restored, the Grieg Society was able to inaugurate its designated centre. The main salon in the house where my grandfather had held his musical soirées, with the original wood panelling beautifully restored and replica wallpaper applied, is the splendid room dedicated to Edvard Grieg. Sadly and inevitably, grandfather's Steinway grand piano is gone, stolen by the Gestapo more than 60 years ago. However, an upright piano of the time of Grieg was made available on loan from the Music Instruments Museum – a collaboration that would have pleased my grandfather. By 2006, enough money had been raised through sponsorship to purchase a grand piano of the right vintage.

For some years, several Leipzig citizens had been lobbying the Cultural Department of the city of Leipzig to name the area around Talstrasse and Goldschmidtstrasse, the Henri Hinrichsen Caré (locality) but this did not happen. Instead, the Department said it would sponsor a plaque in his memory to be affixed to 10 Talstrasse after the restoration of the house by the end of 2005. At that point, the city of

Leipzig said that it was short of cash and could not afford the nominal sum needed. Instead, Norbert Molkenbur took it upon himself personally to sponsor the plaque, which also commemorates Dr Max Abraham. I was privileged to be invited to unveil this in November 2005 in the presence of the Minister for Culture and many others, including the local press. The event marked the completion of the restoration of the building and the opening of the new home of the Edvard Grieg Centre of Leipzig. Molkenbur also sponsored the plaque for the Grieg Centre, which he unveiled.

2006: *Stolpersteine* (Stumbling Stones)

A way of commemorating Jews who were murdered by the Nazis has been devised by the sculptor, Gunter Demnig. Local residents and relatives of those murdered sponsor bronze cobblestone-sized *Stolpersteine*, engraved with the name and details of the deceased, which are embedded in the pavement in front of the house in which they once lived. This idea has been gathering momentum and by 2006 Demnig had laid more than 10,000 plaques in 202 German cities and towns. The project has been described as the largest artwork in Europe. Demnig recognizes that 'six million is an incomprehensible figure' (referring to those Jews murdered by the Nazis). 'But carving the name of a single person on a single marker says: "Look, this individual lived right here. This was someone just like you or me, not just an anonymous victim of history".'

Dr Ulm, director of the Henriette Goldschmidt Schule, and a group of supporters sponsored such stones for Martha, Henri, Hans-Joachim and Paul Hinrichsen to be embedded at the entrance to 10 Talstrasse and a further stone for Henri Hinrichsen in front of the College (Fig. 37). They also sponsored stones for his son-in-law, Dr Ludwig Frankenthal, together with his two sons, Günther and Wolfgang, to be placed in front of the house in which they had lived in Leipzig.

2007: Exhibitions and commemorations

A major exhibition about the Aryanization of Jewish businesses by the Nazis took place during Jewish Week in July 2007. Henri Hinrichsen and Peters Edition were central to this, as they were to the excellent book accompanying it.[7] I gave a talk about the effects of Aryanization on my family to a packed audience.

---

7 *Arisierung in Leipzig.* Ed. Monika Gibas. Leipziger Universitätsverlag, Leipzig 2007.

On 17 September, there was a ceremony at the memorial stone to commemorate the 65th anniversary of Henri Hinrichsen's murder. This was organized jointly by C. F. Peters and the Henriette Gold-schmidt Schule.

An eager journalist, discovering that my grandfather was born on 5 February 1868, wrote a long article in the local paper in honour of the 140th anniversary of his birth. Rediscovered, Leipzig is determined to keep promoting the memory of one of its greatest benefactors who was treated so shamefully by an earlier generation.

Fig. 37 2006. *Stolperstein* for Henri Hinrichsen.

The Hinrichsen family marginalized at C. F. Peters

C. F. Peters, Frankfurt's majority shareholder, Dr Johannes Petschull, died in January 2001 – three months short of his hundredth birthday. A contemporary of my father Max Hinrichsen and of his brother Walter, this one-time Nazi, who had contrived to deprive them of their birthright, outlived them by almost 40 years. The company was subsequently owned jointly by Max's widow Carla Hinrichsen, Walter's widow, Evelyn Hinrichsen, and the heirs of Dr Petschull. With the deaths of Evelyn Hinrichsen in 2004 and of Carla Hinrichsen in 2005, Nicholas Riddle, the managing director of Peters Edition, London as chief executive, currently runs the New York and London companies. After 143 years, there is no longer a member of the Hinrichsen family at the helm of this world renowned music publishing company. Peters Edition, London, which my father founded as Hinrichsen Edition Ltd., was bequeathed by my stepmother Carla Hinrichsen to the charitable foundation that she established, the Hinrichsen Foundation. She also bequeathed all her rights in the Frankfurt company, together with my father's entire share of the Hinrichsen family assets in Leipzig deriving from my grandfather Henri Hinrichsen, to the foundation. I was thus totally disinherited of my family's heritage in Peters Edition and of the Hinrichsen family assets by a woman whose motives, be they altruistic or jealous, displayed no feeling for family tradition or loyalty.

As we go to press the opening of a new company, Edition Hinrichsen GmbH, in the original Peters Edition premises and home of the Hinrichsen family, 10 Talstrasse, in Leipzig is announced for September 2008. This event though not, unfortunately, to be witnessed by those who suffered so terribly, is a small vindication for past evils.

Conclusion

This book has been a historical voyage through fourteen generations of my family, a span of five hundred years of persecution, business, turmoil and murder. Starting in Catholic Spain, from whence the Jews were forced to flee in 1492, when my ancestors settled in Portugal and were again forced to flee in 1610, it proceeds to Hamburg and thence to Glückstadt, where after some years of achievement they were once again obliged to move on. The next few generations made their home successfully as Court Financiers in Schwerin from 1688 to 1869, with a younger son settling once again in Hamburg in 1830 to enjoy the cut and thrust of business life in a big city. From there, my grandfather moved to Leipzig in 1887 and was murdered in Auschwitz concentration camp in 1942. His eldest son, my father, emigrated to England in 1937 and his second son, Walter, emigrated to the USA in 1936. Another son and daughter just managed to escape to England and one daughter survived five concentration camps, though two other sons were murdered. Now the remaining family is fragmented throughout the world.

Because my ancestors and their brethren generally had substantial families there are, in spite of the Nazi attempt to annihilate all the Jews, still many Hinrichsens around the world. Our ancestor, poor old Henrique de Milão, who himself had nine children some 450 years ago and was burnt at the stake for his beliefs, would have been proud that his dynasty has survived the persecutions and privations of the years to thrive in the twenty-first century.

I like to say that I was reborn in Leipzig on 17 November 1991. On that date I went back to the city of my birth, after 54 years, and embarked on a new direction in my life, very much motivated by a desire to explore the historical events surrounding my family's past. My involvement with the city of my birth and my family's past, with all its political connotations, continues.

Bibliography

Bacon, Gershon (ed.). *Danzig Jewry: A Short History*. Wayne State UP, 1980.

Baddiel, David. *The Secret Purposes*. Abacus, London, 2005.

Baedekers Leipzig. Karl Baedeker, Freiburg, 1973.

Bajor, Frank. *Aryanization in Hamburg*. Berghahn Books, New York and Oxford, 2002. Originally published as *Arisierung in Hamburg. Die Verdrängung der Jüdischen Unternehmer 1933–45*. Hans Christians Verlag, Hamburg, 1997.

Barkai, Avram. *From Boycott to Annihilation. The Economic Struggle of German Jews 1933–1943*. Trans. William Templer. Published for Brandeis University Press by University Press of New England, USA, 1989.

Benestad, Finn and Brock, Hella (eds). *Edvard Grieg, Briefwechsel mit dem Verlag C. F. Peters 1863–1907*. C. F. Peters, Frankfurt, 1997.

Blumenthal, W. Michael. *The Invisible Wall; Germans and Jews: A Personal Exploration*. Counterpoint. Washington DC, 1998.

Brith, Joseph Ben. *Die Odyssee der Henrique-Familie*. Peter Lang, Frankfurt/Main, 2001.

Bucholtz, Erika. *Henri Hinrichsen und der Musikverlag C. F. Peters*. Leo Baeck Institute, London, 2001.

Cambridge Encyclopedia, The. Ed. David Crystal. CUP, Cambridge, 1990.

Childs, David. *Germany in the Twentieth Century*. Icon, London, 1991.

Crankshaw, Edward. *Bismark*. Macmillan, London, 1981.

Crutsen, Christine and Pasing, Theo (eds). *Ludwig, ich lebe! Het tweede leven van Ilse Frankenthal-Hinrichsen 1904/1945–1987*. Stichting Ilse Frankenthal, Brunssum, 1998.

Diamant, Adolf. *Chronik der Juden in Leipzig. Aufstieg, Vernichtung und Neuanfang*. Verlag Heimatland Sachsen, 1993.

Eban, Abba. *Heritage – Civilization and the Jews*. Weidenfeld & Nicholson, London, 1984.

Elon, Amos. *The Pity of it All*. Penguin, London, 2002.

Evans, Richard J. *Death in Hamburg*. Penguin, New York, 2005.

Fabre-Vasa, Claudine. *The Singular Beast – Jews, Christians and the Pig*. Trans. Carol Volk. Columbia University Press, New York, 1997.

Festliche Gründungsveranstaltung am 14. Dezember 1991. Freundes- und Förderkreis Musikinstrumenten Museum der Universität Leipzig e.V, 1992.

Finkelstein, Norman G. *The Holocaust Industry.* Verso, London and New York, 2000.

Frank, Ben G. (ed.). *A Travel Guide to Jewish Europe.* 2nd edn. Pelican, Gretna, USA, 1996.

Frankenthal-Hinrichsen, Ilse. See Crutsen, and Pasing 1998.

Frankenthal-Hinrichsen. *Documentation.* Original documents. Unpublished. Author's archive.

Frauengewebeverein. From Leipzig newspapers 1902, 1907, 1909, 1910, 1911, 1913.

Freimark, Peter and Herzig, Arno (eds). *Die Hamburger Juden in der Emanziptionsphase 1780–1870.* Hans Christian Verlag, Hamburg, 1989.

Gilbert, Martin. *The Holocaust – The Jewish Tragedy.* (Collins 1986) Fontana Press, London, 1987.

Grünberger, Richard. *A Social History of the Third Reich,* (Weidenfeld & Nicholson 1971), Penguin, London, 1991.

Henri Hinrichsen. Ein Gedenkblatt zu seinem 60. Geburtstag. Gewidmet von den Angestellten der Firma C. F. Peters. Leipzig, 1928.

Hinrichsen, Henri. *Chronik des Hauses C. F. Peters – 'Geschichte des Verlagshauses C. F. PETERS von seiner Gründung am 1. Dezember 1800 an bis zum 1. Oktober 1933'.* Unpublished, 1933. [Referred to as *Chronik*].

Herzig, Arno and Rohde, Saskia (eds). *Die Juden in Hamburg 1590 bis 1990.* Dölling & Galitz Verlag, 1991.

Herzog, Andreas (ed.). *Das Literarische Leipzig.* Edition Leipzig, 1995.

Hinrichsen, Max (ed.). *Music Book Volume VII.* Hinrichsen Edition, London, 1952.

Hinrichsen, Max (ed.). *Music Book Volume VIII (2nd edn.).* Hinrichsen Edition, London, 1966.

Hinrichsen, Max. *Peters Edition and Max Hinrichsen.* Hinrichsen Edition, London, 1955.

Hinrichsen, Walter. A Tribute. C. F. Peters Corporation, New York, 1969.

Johnson, Paul. *A History of the Jews.* Weidenfeld & Nicolson, London, 1987.

Kapp, Yvonne and Mynatt, Margaret. *British Policy and the Refugees 1933–1941.* Frank Cass, London, 1997.

Karg, Wolf, Schmied, Hartmut and Münch, Ernst. *Die Geschichte Mecklenburgs.* Hinstorff, Rostock, 1993.

Kellenbenz, Hermann. *Sephardim an der Unteren Elbe.* Steiner, Wiesbaden, 1958.

Kemp, Annerose. *Henriette Goldschmidt – Vom Frauenrecht zur Kindererziehung.* Private print, Horst Kemp, Leipzig, 1993.

Kemp, Annerose and Nimschowski, Ilse. *Henriette-Goldschmidt-Schule 1911–1991.* Fachschule für Sozialpädagogik Henriette-Goldschmidt-Schule Leipzig, 1991.

Kluger, Ruth. *Landscapes of Memory.* Feminist Press, New York, 2001.

Krause, Peter. *Die Musikbibliothek Peters in Leipzig. Zur Erinnerung an ihre Eröffnung vor einhundert Jahren.* Reprint from *Forum Musikbibliothek,* 2/1994.

Krause, Peter. *Die musikalische Bibliothek in Leipziger Amts-Blatt,* 7 February 1994.

Krause, Peter and Roeser, Ellen. *Die Musikbibliothek der Stadt Leipzig.* Reprint from *Jahrbuch zur Geschichte der Stadt Leipzig,* 1979.

Kruse, S. and Englemann, B. (eds). *Mein Vater war portugiesischer Jude.* Steidl, Göttingen, 1992.

Lawford-Hinrichsen, Irene. *Music Publishing and Patronage – C. F. Peters: 1800 to the Holocaust.* Edition Press, London, 2000.

Lehrer, Natasha (ed.). *The Golden Chain.* Valentine Mitchel, London, 2003.

Leipziger Neunundneunzig, Die. Leipziger Bibliophilen Abend, Leipzig, 1929.

Leipzig Stadt der Musik. VEB Edition Peters, Leipzig, 1990.

Leipzig – The Little Blue-Yellow City Guide. Fackelträger-Verlag GmbH, Hanover, 1990.

Leipziger Historischer Kalender 2005. Lehmstedt, Leipzig, 2004.

Levi, Erik. *Music and National Socialism: The Politicisation of Criticism, Composition and Performance.* In *The Nazification of Art.* Ed. Brandon Taylor and Wilfred van der Will. The Winchester Press, 1990.

Lexikon Leipziger Strassennamen. Ed. Stadtarchiv Leipzig. Verlag im Wissenschaftszentrum, Leipzig, 1995.

Lindlar, Heinrich. *C. F. Peters Musikverlag. Zeittafeln zur Verlagsgeschichte 1800 – 1867 – 1967.* C. F. Peters Frankfurt, 1967.

Lorz, Andrea. *Suchet der Stadt Bestes.* Pro Leipzig, Leipzig, 1996.

Lorz, Andrea. *Die Erinnerung soll zum Guten gereichen.* Passage, Leipzig, 2005.

Loschek, Ingrid. *Reclams Mode und Kostüm Lexikon.* Reclam, Germany, 1987.

Lyth, Peter J. *Inflation and the Merchant Economy – The Hamburg Mittelstand, 1914–1924.* Berg Publishers Inc. Providence, RI, USA and Oxford, England, 1990.

Meetenheim, Amelis von. *Felix Meyer (1875–1950).* P. Lang, Frankfurt/Main, 1998.

Molkenbur, Norbert. *C. F. Peters 1800–2000: Ausgewählte Stationen einer Verlagsgeschichte.* Sachsenbuch, Leipzig, 2001.

Musikinstrumenten-Museum. Sonderdruck. Auszug aus *Kunstschätze der Karl-Marx-Universität-Leipzig,* herausgegeben im Auftrag des Rektors. E. A. Seemann Verlag, Leipzig, 1981.

Neues Forum Leipzig. Jetzt oder nie – Demokratie! Leipziger Herbst '89. Forum Verlag, Leipzig, 1989.

Noakes, J. and Pridham, G. (eds). *Nazism 1919–1945, Volume 2: State, Economy and Society 1933–39.* University of Exeter Press, 1984.

Ollendorff Paul. *Max Abraham. Jahrbuch der Musikbibliothek Peters für 1931.* C. F. Peters, 1932. (Reprint of the obituary written in 1902.)

Pachnicke, Bernd (ed.). *1800–1975 Edition Peters. Erschienen anlässlich des 175 jährigen Bestehens des Musikverlages Peters am 1 Dezember 1975.* C. F. Peters, Leipzig.

Prieberg, Fred K. *Historisches Gutachten, MDR Leipzig, 1994.* (Unpublished, for inclusion in *Deutsche Musiker 1933–1945* in preparation.)

Pulzer, Peter. *Emancipation and its Discontents.* Sussex University, 1997.

Rektorwechsel an der Universität Leipzig am 31 Oktober 1929. Leipzig, 1929.

Reston, James Jr. *Dogs of God.* Faber & Faber, New York, 2005.

Rotrund, Ries and Battenberg, J. Friedrich (eds). *Hofjuden Ökonomie und Interculturalität. Die Jüdische Wirtschaft im 18. Jahrhundert.* Christiansverlag, Hamburg, 2002.

Schinköth, Thomas (ed.). *Musikstadt Leipzig im NS-Staat. Beiträge zu einem verdrängten Thema.* Verlag Klaus-Jürgen Kamprad, 1997.

Schnee, Heinrich. *Die Hoffinanz und der moderne Staat.* Dunber & Humboldt, Berlin, 1954.

Schultz, Helmut (ed.). *Führer durch das Musikwissenschaftliche Instrumenten Museum der Universität Leipzig.* Breitkopf & Härtel, Leipzig, 1929.

Sereny, Gitta. *The Healing Wound.* Norton, New York, 2001.

Sohl, Klaus (ed.). *Neues Leipzigisches Geschicht-Buch.* Commissioned by the Council of the City of Leipzig. Fachbuchverlag, Leipzig, 1990.

Sohl, Klaus (ed.). *Das Völkerschlacht-Denkmal.* Sachsenbuch Verlagsgesellschaft, Leipzig, 1993.

Studemund-Halévy, Michael. *Zerstört die Erinnerung Nicht.* Dölling & Galitz, Hamburg, 2002.

Tatsachen über Deutschland. Societäts Verlag, Frankfurt/Main, 2000.

Tent, James. F. *In the Shadow of the Holocaust.* University Press, Kansas, 2003.

Unger, Manfred. *Die Juden in Leipzig unter der Herrschaft des Nationalsozialismus* in *Verdrängung und Vernichtung der Juden unter dem Nationalsozialismus.* Hans Christian Verlag, Hamburg, 1992.

Unger, Manfred (ed.). *Judaica Lipsiensia. Zur Geschichte der Juden in Leipzig.* Ephraim Carlebach Stiftung, Leipzig, 1994.

Unger, Manfred and Lang, Hubert (eds). *Juden in Leipzig. Eine Dokumentation.* Rat des Bezirkes Leipzig, Abteilung Kultur, 1989.

Walk, J. (ed.). *Das Sonderrecht für die Juden im NS-Staat: Eine Sammlung der gesetzlichen Massnahmen und Richtlinien – Inhalt und Bedeutung.* Karlsruhe, 1981.

Warburg, G. *Six Years of Hitler: the Jews under the Nazi Regime.* George Allen & Unwin, London, 1939.

Wilke, Martina and Winter, Albrecht (eds). *Dokumente, Programe, Biografien Zur Arbeit des Jüdischen Kulturbundes Leipzig e.V.* Ephraim Carlebach Stiftung, Leipzig, 1994.

Zimler, Richard. *The Last Kabbalist of Lisbon.* Arcadia Books, London, 1998.

MUSIC PUBLISHING AND PATRONAGE

C F Peters: 1800 to the Holocaust

Irene Lawford-Hinrichsen
With a Foreword by Yehudi Menuhin OM KBE

'. . . this book will provide enlightening reading not only to all people associated with music, but also to the general reader who wants to know how destiny and history impinge on the human being.'

'Irene Lawford-Hinrichsen's account of her family's firm, the relationships between C F Peters and many great composers and a hundred and one other matters of fascinating importance to the music lover, has here produced a volume which many will find difficult to put down. Over and above the rich tapestry of musical, social and commercial history which this book chronicles, runs the family history. History made more astonishingly gripping in its conclusion by the horrendous fate meted out to the great Henri Hinrichsen in Auschwitz at the age of 74 by the Nazis.'

Robert Matthew-Walker. 'International Record Review'

'. . .This powerful story . . . reveals many characters in the music world, including Max Reger, Edvard Grieg, Gustav Mahler, Arnold Schönberg, Sigfrid Karg-Elert and Karl Straube . . . It tells a story that is much more than just music publishing, more even than music generally. It tells of the growth of a family business into a world leader, and how such a firm was all but toppled in the most savage of periods in the last millennium.'

Simon Fitzgerald. 'The Organ'

'. . . an excellent history of the publishing house and its two Jewish proprietors, who dedicated their lives to the publication of great music and to endowing musical institutions for the citizens of Leipzig.'

Carole Rosen. 'Jewish Chronicle'

'. . . What lifts the book on to an entirely different plane is the enormous amount of autograph correspondence and other documentary material which [the author] has had at her disposal.'

Beresford King-Smith. 'The Baton'

'. . . *Music Publishing and Patronage* is well written, clearly organised and is remarkably and all the more tellingly cool in its later pages, when a horrific story is quietly, even bleakly recorded . . . The book is excellent value for its price. . . and will have three immediately preceding generations of [the author's] distinguished family . . . applauding her from the Elysian fields.'

Dr Lionel Carley. 'The Delius Society Journal'

'. . . The book rather reminds me of *Budenbrooks*'

D W Krummel. 'Notes – Journal of the Music Libraries Association'

If you love music; if you yearn to get under the skin of some of the most influential composers of their time; if the history of Germany and the Holocaust fascinates you; or if the lives of generous, dedicated, passionate people of culture inspire you, then this book is for you. Within its pages you will find a wealth of real life stories, which bring history, culture and remarkable personalities alive.

**MUSIC PUBLISHING AND PATRONAGE –
C F Peters: 1800 to the Holocaust**
Edition Press, London 2000. 350pp. Hardback. 32 ills.
ISBN 0-9536112-0-5

**Payment with order in favour of I. Lawford:
£25.00 with free p&p (€40.00)($50.00 bills)**

Irene Lawford, 22 Bouverie Gardens,
Kenton, Middx. HA3 ORQ
Tel: 020 8907 2790. E-: *Irene.Lawford@btinternet.com*
Web: *www.btinternet.com/~irene.lawford*